Charleston Jazz

ON THE COVER: No other band is as representative of the Charleston jazz tradition than William Louis Gilliard and the Royal Sultans. It performed for decades and included many of the fine musicians that came out of Charleston. The band's heyday was in the 1950s. It performed in nightclubs, dance halls and all other manner of venues and was known for its excellent musicianship and professionalism. (Avery Research Center.)

Charleston Jazz

Jack McCray

ARCADIA
PUBLISHING

ISBN 0-7385-4350-0

Published by Arcadia Publishing
Charleston SC, Chicago IL, Portsmouth NH, San Francisco CA

Printed in the United States of America

Library of Congress Catalog Card Number: 2006930542

For all general information contact Arcadia Publishing at:
Telephone 843-853-2070
Fax 843-853-0044
E-mail sales@arcadiapublishing.com
For customer service and orders:
Toll-Free 1-888-313-2665

Visit us on the Internet at www.arcadiapublishing.com

Contents

ACKNOWLEDGMENTS

This book would not have been possible without the support and assistance of many people. They include Adam Ferrell, Dr. Karen A. Chandler, Herb Frazier, the late Ellis McCray, Katherine E. McCray, the *Post and Courier*, George Kenny, Lonnie Hamilton, the Charleston Jazz Initiative, Tony Bell, Sherman Pyatt, Dr. Marvin Dulaney, Jeffrey Green, Raymond Rhett, the late George Payton, Fletcher Linton, the late Harriet Mack, Melvin Hodges, Rachel Dowling, the late Lida Anderson, Joyce Coakley, and many, many others.

I give a special thanks to all the unknown and unsung heroes of the Charleston jazz tradition who, through their art and labor, have contributed mightily to American and world culture. Artists are the truth tellers of society. Jazz artists in particular, because they tell of themselves through their art, deserve special recognition. Those who nurture them, produce them, record them, represent them, broadcast them, and write about them have also contributed greatly.

Those who came before us paved the way by paying dues and making supreme sacrifices. In the case of African Americans, these accomplishments were made against all the odds. Artifacts of beauty, such as jazz music, were wrought from horrific living conditions. Dreams were fashioned out of nightmares.

I hope this work will inspire those continuing the struggle as they search for beauty, especially as it is found in jazz music.

INTRODUCTION

As the band made its way through the song, my trumpet felt more and more like an extension of my hand, the left one. Only the heel of my right hand rested against the horn, but too gently to meld. It had to be positioned lightly so the middle three fingers could strike the valves.

The warmth of the Charleston night and the heat of the intense anticipation of my impending task made the instrument feel attached. I wasn't scared, though. I had worked hard. I felt up to it. We were at the end of our pre-game show, rendering a spirited but respectful rendition of the national anthem on the College Park football field. We had a big sound of which we were very proud.

Then, the time came. It was the end of the song's penultimate phrase, the one made up of ascending notes. "O'er the land of the free" are the words. Then, it descends as it ends: "And the home of the brave." As the band held the note for "free," one full beat later, I would hit a high C, above the staff, hopefully stirring soaring emotions in the listeners and galvanizing the band while signaling the end of our task in spectacular style. It was quite a challenge. At the same time that I was among my many bandmates, I was alone. It was exhilarating. The whole band was on hold while I exposed myself for all to see and hear. When I nailed it—and I always did, thank God—the applause and screams cascading from the stands swelled into a vibrating envelope of appreciation.

The whole idea of doing this came out of the camaraderie of our trumpet section. It was the Burke High School Band, 1961. I was only a freshman but had known and played with the guys before. In the previous school year, trumpeters William Foster, John Brooks, and I auditioned for and made the concert band, a feat that still ranks for me as one of my most special accomplishments. As far as we knew, no one from a junior high school, in our case Simonton, had ever made the legendary Burke High School Band. We had joined Joe "Big Ten" Brown, who soon after became fierce on the baritone horn, and Gabriel Mack, to whose house on Pitt Street we would go to mimic Miles Davis records.

So we were a tight section. We worked on things, pushed each other, and always looked for new ways to do things. We had been wood shedding hitting the high C in practice, as we did many things not in our regular regimen. Often we would try to cut each other, each one trying to outdo the other.

Melvin "Fess" Hodges not only liked the idea of putting the high C into our program, he reveled in it. He was as competitive as we were, always looking for an edge, a leg up on other school bands. He chose me. He knew I was anxious when I accepted the challenge. All week leading up to the first game in which we used the high C, he encouraged me and showed he had faith in me. I felt reinforced. After all, Fess was the one who picked Foster, Brooks, and me for the band the previous concert season when we were in junior high.

I was in my sixth year as a school band trumpeter. Making that high C was a watershed occasion for me. I started playing in the third grade at Buist Elementary School under the direction of Fletcher Linton, who was also school principal. I was seven years old, 52 years ago. Linton was a master trumpeter and teacher. He was from Cheraw, South Carolina, where he was a boyhood pal of the great Dizzy Gillespie. He took whatever talent he saw in me and made me into a first-chair player, a position I would hold through my time at C. A. Brown High School, where I went after Burke. In those six years, I played in bands at Buist, Columbus Street Elementary (now Wilmot Frasier Elementary), East Bay Street Elementary (now Sanders-Clyde), and Burke. Simonton did not have a band.

Over those same years, we would hang out and talk about music, practice all the time, and play along with records. Some of my early favorites were *2075*, *Cherry Pink and Apple Blossom White*, and *Amen*. Then I heard Miles. It was quite unlike anything I heard before, and I had been around music all my life—at home, church, and school. We had an old upright piano at our home on Alexander Street, just a few blocks from where I went to church and school. Charleston was a music town. It was everywhere. Just about everybody sang or played an instrument. There were even street-corner musicians, sacred and secular. I had heard Louis Armstrong and loved his sound and his showmanship, but Miles was so modern—cool, detached, and intricate. For me, the trumpet won out over the piano, which I now regret. I wish I had kept learning the piano.

I heard Miles, Dizzy, Thelonious Monk, Coleman Hawkins, Art Blakey, Sarah Vaughan, Ella Fitzgerald, and many, many others as a kid. I was in awe. My father, Ellis McCray, and my uncle, Alvin Capers, who lived on Amherst Street, belonged to the early record clubs in the mid-1950s and I would listen as much as I could, sometimes clandestinely. I was hooked.

Ever since, I loved jazz music and the people who played it.

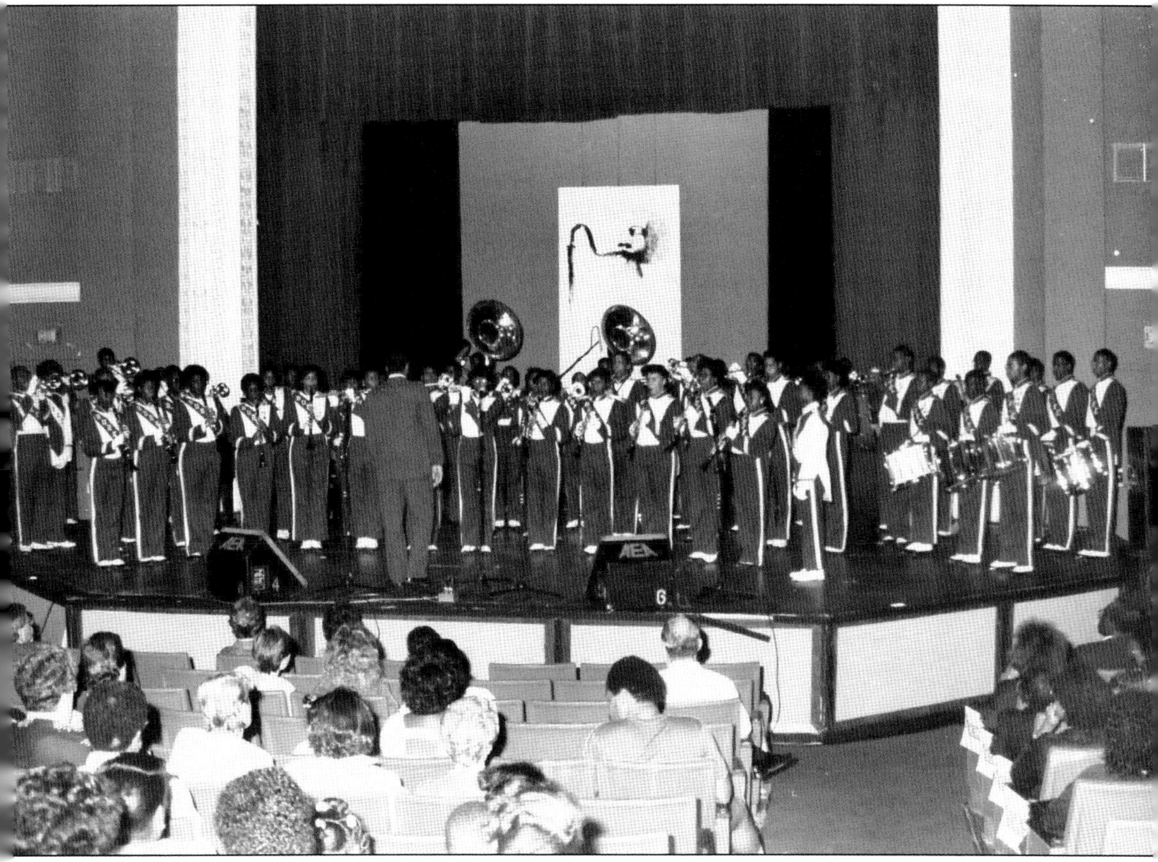

The Burke High School Marching Band performed at the Moja Arts Festival at the Garden Theater in 1987. The large ensemble completely filled the stage and made quite a spectacle. For the last half-century or so, the band has been one of the biggest attractions in Charleston. In the middle of the 20th century, it often shared instructors and leaders with the Jenkins Orphanage, a Charleston cradle of music, including jazz. In a sense, the Burke High School Marching Band's history is a kind of metaphor for the evolution of jazz music in Charleston. For one thing, many of the jazz musicians went to school there. For a long time, it was the only public high school for blacks in the Charleston area. Its students performed at a very high level in many areas of discipline, and they stood out as they dispersed around the country and around the world. Its bands and choirs were always among the best, and the arts have always been taken seriously. Given its origins, it provided a way up and out for many people who found themselves in the throes of impoverishment and racial segregation. Pride and dignity were hallmarks of a Burke education, and they served its graduates well as they embarked on careers—crafts, trades, and academics—or higher education. Like the Avery Normal Institute, a private school across town, Burke also had a big hand in preparing educators to come back to Charleston to teach others. It also worked hand in hand with other institutions such as the Jenkins Orphanage, especially in music. Like jazz from Charleston, Burke High School and its graduates have made major contributions but in some circles it is largely unknown and unheralded. (Wendell Johnson.)

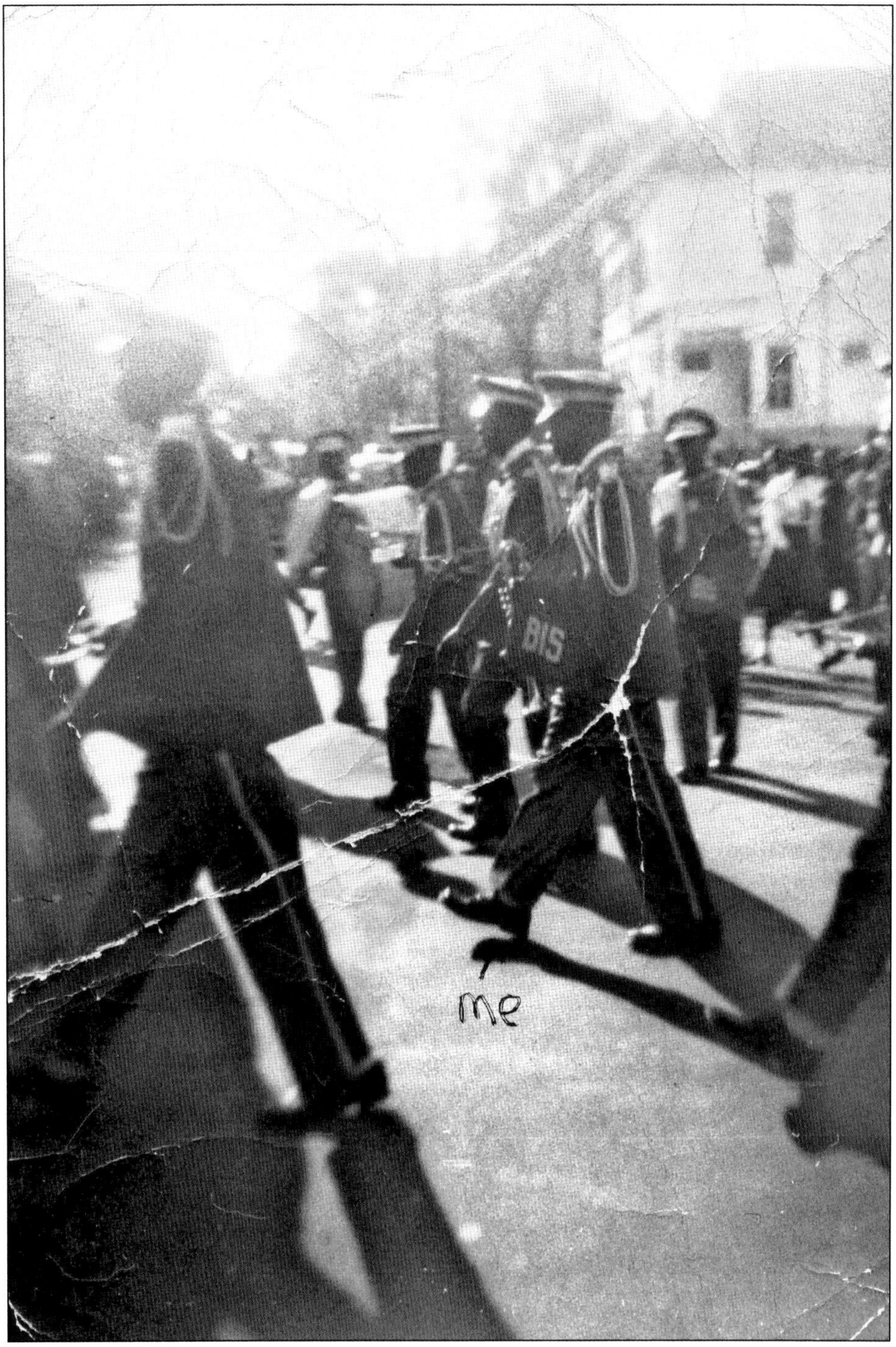

George Kenny marched in the Burke High School Marching Band in the 1950s. The school and its band produced many fine musicians and instructors and continue to do so today. For instance, the band is one of the main feeder programs for the famed Florida A&M University's marching and concert bands. The Tallahassee, Florida, school's music program is one of the highest-regarded programs in the country. (George Kenny.)

One

What Is Jazz?

Among of the biggest concerns in the history of jazz music is when and where it began. The conventional wisdom is that it got started in New Orleans, that famous Creole city atop the Gulf of Mexico, in the early 20th century. It's as good a theory as any other, but based on what we now know about other places with a jazz history, what we know about social and cultural evolution, and what we know about plain old common sense, something tells us that what happened in Charleston, South Carolina, at the same time (and before) has to be taken into account when we consider this art form that was created by, but not limited to, African Americans.

In fact, it might boil down to the simple notion that we know more about New Orleans' jazz origination and that those beginnings have been trumpeted more loudly than those of any other of the many birthplaces of American improvisational music.

Charleston is one of those cradles—a very important one.

Its jazz history and legacy is so strong, a case can be made for its importance in development of what many believe to be America's most important art form without a comparison to New Orleans, or any other city for that matter.

The Crescent City is the standard, but it's not the only urban center to swing the country into the 20th century. Consider the famous composer and performer Eubie Blake's take on artistic development. "Eubie Blake once told me that any place you had a group of Black people, you had hot [improvisational] music," said Larry Ridley, a highly regarded bassist, educator, and jazz artist in residence at the New York Public Library's Schomburg Center for Research in Black Culture. Ridley is also an advisor to the Charleston Jazz Initiative, a multi-year research project exploring Charleston's jazz experience for the past three years and making exciting discoveries. He shared his thoughts in Charleston in 2004 at the initiative's first annual conference, Return to the Source, held at the College of Charleston's Avery Research Center for African American History and Culture.

Blake (1887–1983) was an eyewitness to the growth of American swing and was very familiar with the pulse of Carolina. He collaborated with Noble Sissle in 1921 on the Broadway musical *Shuffle Along*, the first Broadway show written and directed by African Americans. That show included a popular tune called "Charleston Rag." In the 1923 Broadway show *Runnin Wild*, pianist-composer James P. Johnson debuted the Charleston, one of the most popular American dances ever.

Ragtime, a composed musical form that is highly syncopated and a kind of blend of European and African American music, is considered a precursor to jazz, prominent from the 1890s to the 1920s. It came out of, among other forms, the minstrel tradition, another important forerunner to jazz.

Chris Smith (1879–1949), a composer and performer born in Charleston who became a minstrel in a medicine show, ended up in New York City writing rags and show tunes for the likes of Bert Williams, Fanny Brice, and Jimmy Durante. He had taught himself to play the piano and guitar. He published his first piano solo, "Monkey Rag," in 1911. In 1913, he had his career hit song, "Ballin' the Jack," with lyrics by Jim Burris. The resulting dance was the big craze in the country before the Charleston.

Charleston's role in the development of American popular music, including jazz, is indisputable. The rub seems to be the definition of jazz. As a result, the discussions, debates, and arguments about when, where, and by whom jazz was "discovered" seem to be semantic ones.

For the purposes of this book, jazz is an American music invented by African Americans that is blues-based; is improvisational, solo, and group; employs the bending of notes (blue notes); features call and response; and has swing, an implied propulsive groove.

Improvisation is the most important singular feature of jazz. There have been all kinds of forms of this great music, but they all include some or all of the above-mentioned traits.

They have come out of many geographic incubators, Charleston as notable as any of them.

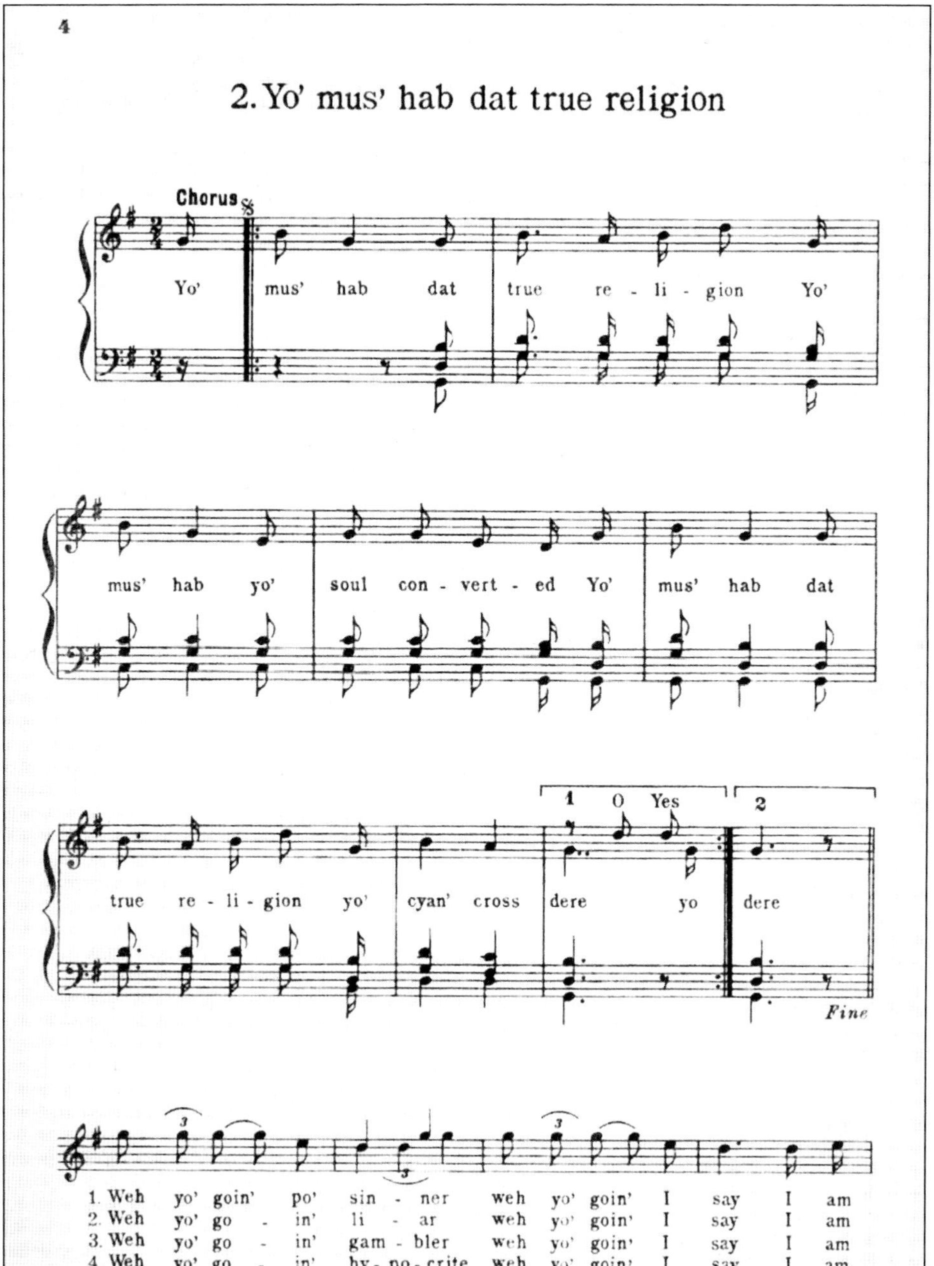

This is an arrangement of a traditional spiritual at Avery Normal Institute. The body of work known as Negro spirituals is fundamental to black American music and, by extension, American music in general. Spirituals, traditional sacred Christian music, were first heard in South Carolina, although they were sung by enslaved Africans and freemen all over the South. The state of South Carolina has named the spiritual the official music of the Palmetto State. (Avery Research Center.)

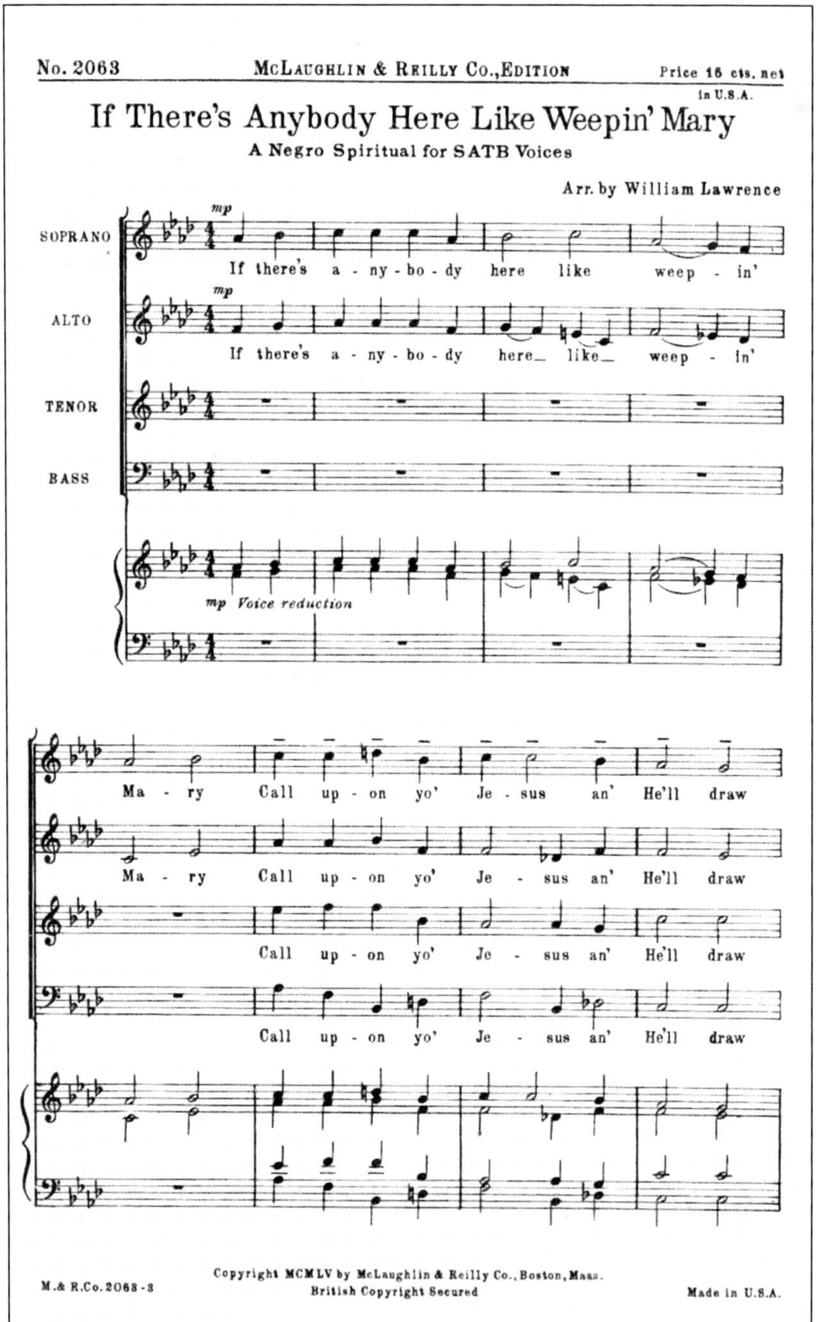

This is an arrangement of a Negro spiritual by William Lawrence, a highly regarded musician at the Avery Normal Institute early in the 20th century. Lawrence was known around the world as a very fine musician and accompanist. Lawrence was active in what can be described as a salon scene in Charleston during his time. Entertainments would be put on in various venues, even homes, for mostly small, invited groups, featuring vocals or instrumentals or both. These were very serious but by most accounts enjoyable events that were very popular. They also dispelled the myth that blacks possessed no "culture." (Avery Research Center.)

Two

CHARLESTON JAZZ ROOTS

The beginnings of jazz music on the southeastern coast of the United States was centered in Charleston, South Carolina, one of only a handful of places in the Western Hemisphere where Africa interacted with Europe in a seminal way to produce New World culture. Europeans settled Carolina more than 300 years ago. Its capital, Charleston, was the crown jewel of the British Empire before the American Revolution, and it was the North American cradle of the African slave trade, similar to other incubators on this side of the Atlantic Ocean, such as Havana, Cuba, and Salvador, Brazil.

Gradually, enslaved Africans infused the culture of their captors with African style and substance, creating the underpinnings for what has emerged over nearly two centuries as American culture. This infusion—not hybridization, as is commonly held—took place in architecture, language, textiles, cuisine, and music.

As happened in many other places, black music on the southeastern coast manifested itself through the spirituals—first heard and recorded in St. Helena, South Carolina, down the coast from Charleston—field hollers, chants, work songs, and the blues.

Twentieth-century modernity brought ragtime and jazz, which is still thought of by many today as the highest form of American art.

From enslaved African drummers, to black drummers attached to white militias, to military bands, to community brass bands, has come Charleston jazz.

Africans and their descendants in the New World are master improvisers. Based on an individual and collective real-time, organic worldview, African Americans approached music, like everything else, viscerally as well as intellectually, trying to make their sounds better as they played them, not writing them down and then playing, as is the European way. It's unfortunate that the best description of improvisation we've come up with so far is to define it as "making it up as you go along." Root words for improvise are "provide" and "improve." The Latin root word *improvisus* means unforeseen. Yes, jazz musicians "make it up," but their flights are based on a rooted structure and common language. And they flew like crazy in Charleston.

The whole point is to make the result better and to make it their own. Historians and anthropologists, most notably William S. Pollitzer, believe that Africans brought to this country improvised individual African lifestyles to maintain their existence, not just to entertain themselves and others.

The democratic principles of African culture are found in jazz. Everybody has a chance to say something, to solo, to play by themselves while everyone else listens as they await their turn. Jazz is diverse and inclusive. It's an experiment, just like American democracy. There's never been anything like it before. It will always be a work in progress.

No wonder Charleston musicians excelled at jazz. This port city is often referred to as the Ellis Island for African Americans. Estimates say upward of 40 percent of Africans imported into North America came through Charleston.

For Charleston, jazz is just like the distinctive taste of okra soup, the plaintive cries of the early-20th-century street vendors, and the meticulous artistry of sweetgrass baskets.

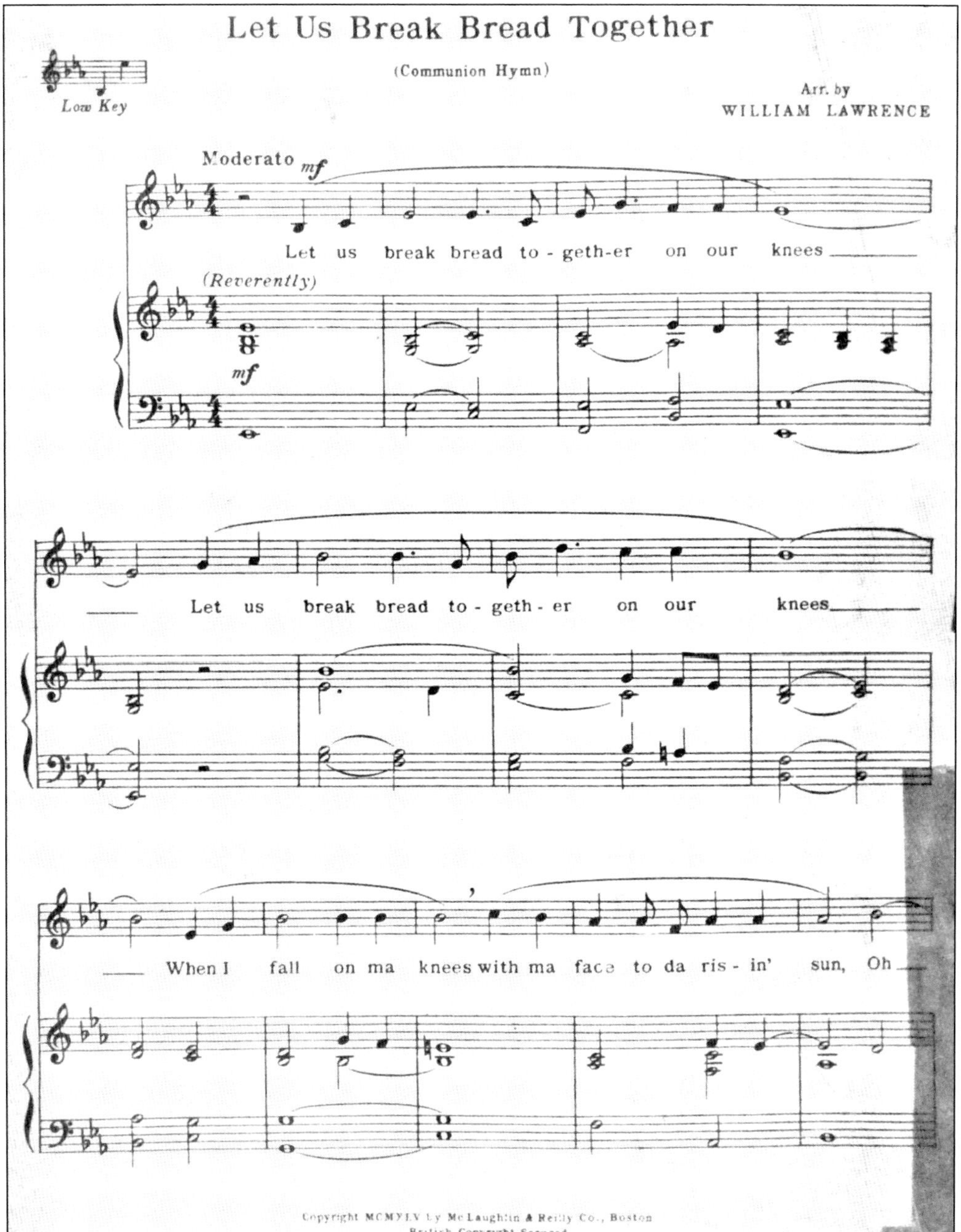

This is William Lawrence's arrangement of the famous hymn "Let Us Break Bread Together." To African Americans, hymns are a very important genre of music that was often "jazzed" by popular music performers. Church life was important to black people in Charleston, and music was central. There were ongoing discussions about what kind of music to use in black churches, but hymns were always there. The Methodist Church was a big influence on churches blacks started, including Methodist hymns. Early on in Charleston, the largest Afrocentric church, the African Methodist Episcopal Church, retained much of Methodism. Hymns were much loved and remain so today. (Avery Research Center.)

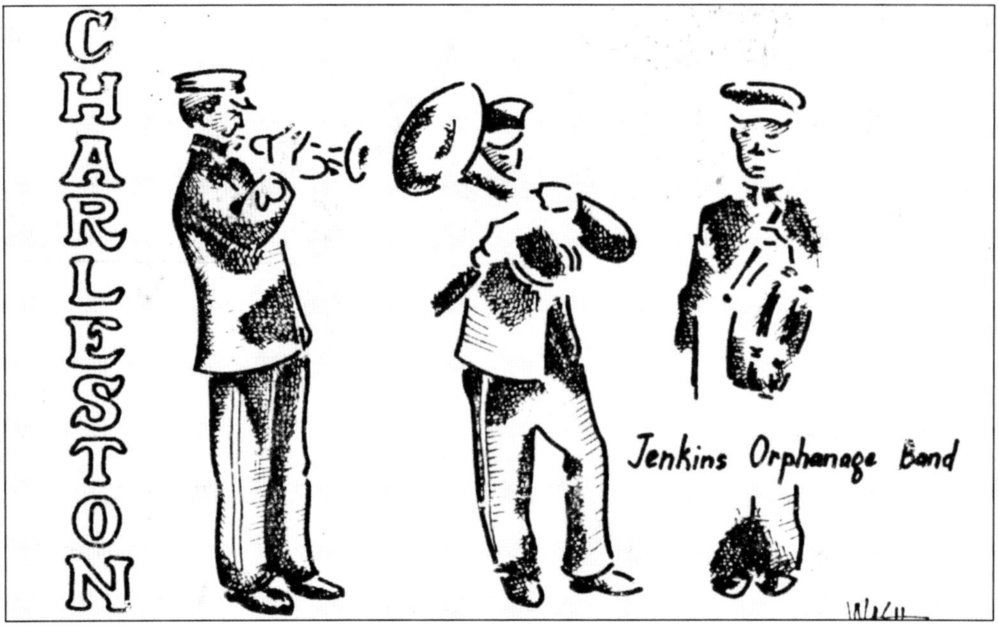

This note card was produced in 1983 by Charleston artist Robert Washington commemorating the old Jenkins Orphanage band. The band and its story have provided material for artists for more than 100 years. Lowcountry artist John Carroll Doyle, famous around the world for his Charleston scenes and people, has recently created two large acrylics drawn from Jenkins band members as he perceives them. (Jack McCray.)

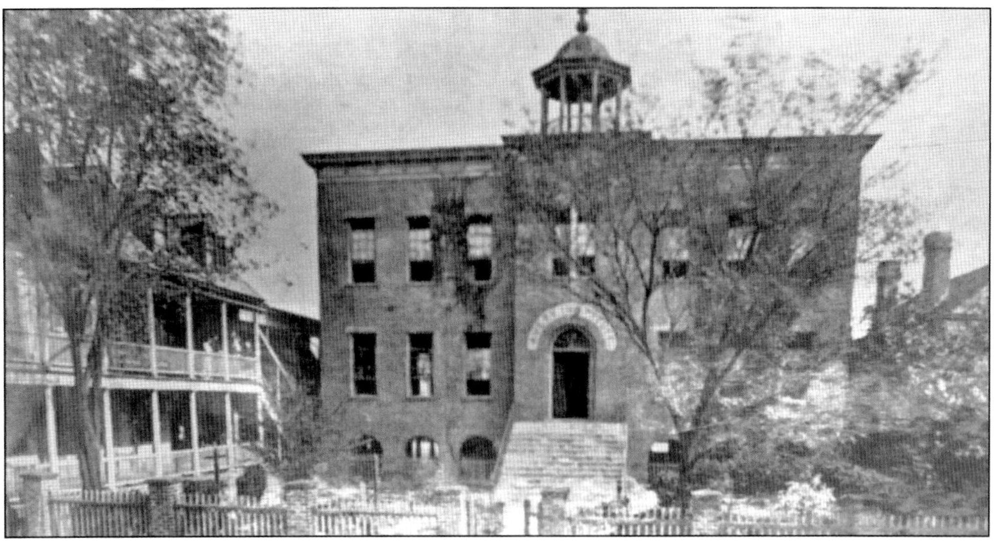

Completed in 1868, the Avery Normal Institute at 125 Bull Street was paid for by principal Francis Cardoza with $10,000 from the estate of Rev. Charles Avery from Pittsburgh. The American Missionary Association, the founding organization of the school for freed blacks, solicited the funds. Students and graduates have contributed to social, economic, and cultural progress in Charleston since the Civil War, and for much of its history, the school's mission was to train teachers in many areas, including music. As a school, Avery closed in 1954. The Avery Research Center for African American History and Culture at the College of Charleston began in 1978 and is housed in the building.

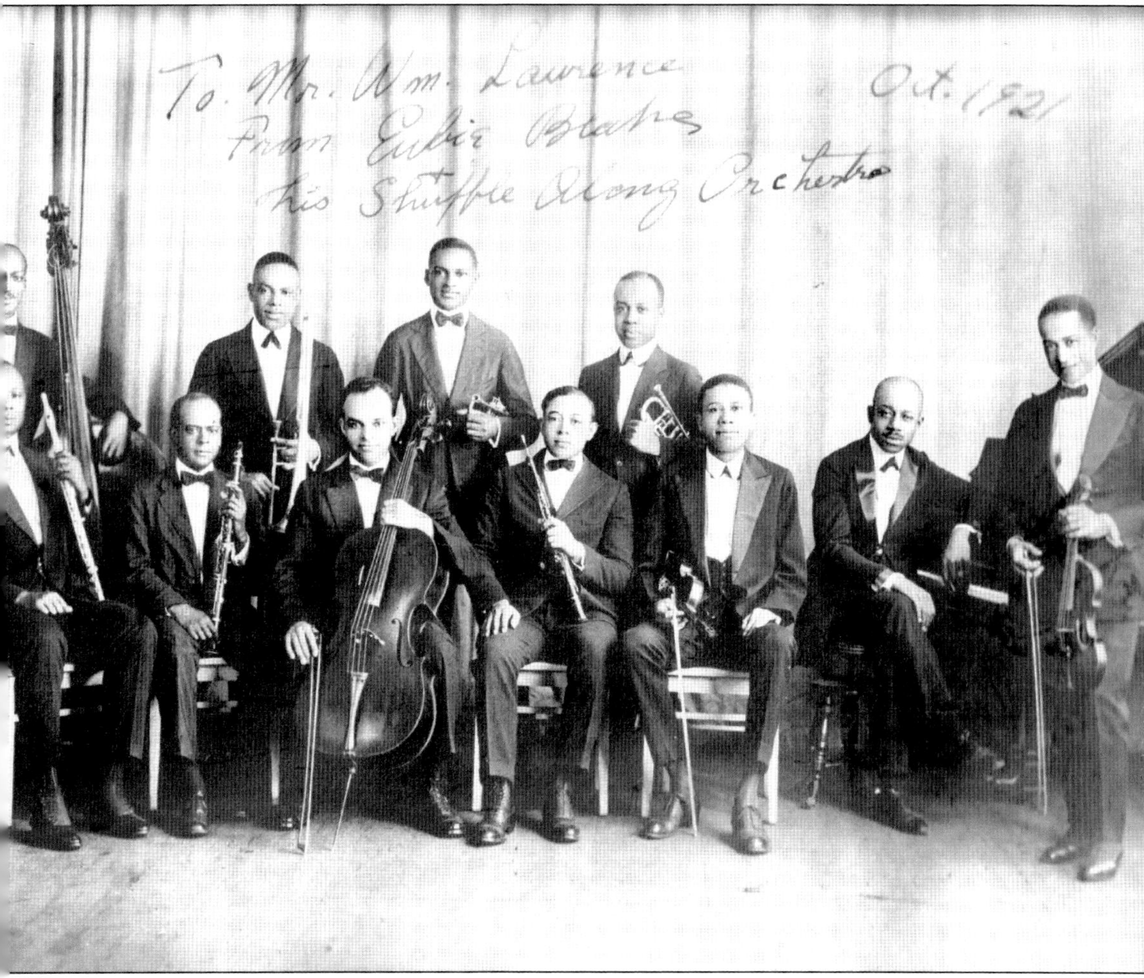

This picture of Eubie Blake (at the piano) and his Shuffle Along Orchestra was given to Avery Normal Institute's William Lawrence in 1921. *Shuffle Along* was the Broadway play that debuted the dance, the Charleston. Blake worked with Charleston musicians in New York City when Broadway was black, in the so-called Jazz Age of the 1920s. Charleston jazz musicians stocked the pit bands and orchestras on Broadway and all around New York City. They were also well represented in house bands in nightclubs and speakeasies such as Smalls Paradise in Harlem. Charlie Johnson's Paradise 10, the house band at Smalls, included the likes of Claddys "Jabbo" Smith, who played the trumpet in the wildly popular ensemble. Smith learned music at the Jenkins Orphanage. Owner Edwin Smalls was also a Charlestonian. Smalls Paradise was the longest-running nightspot in Harlem. (Charleston Jazz Initiative.)

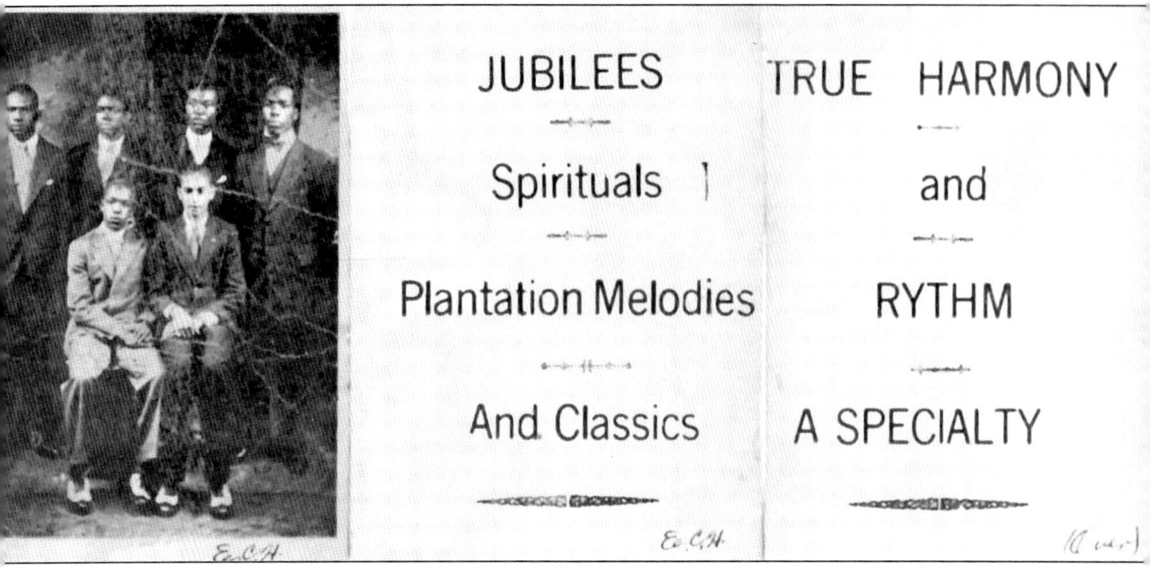

The Avery Sextet traveled the East Coast in 1933 to raise money for the Jenkins Orphanage. Traveling music bands was a serious tradition for black institutions, first made famous by the Fisk Jubilee Singers from Tennessee. The Jenkins Orphanage bands took full advantage of that tradition, traveling the East Coast and Midwest of the United States, as well as other parts of the world, to raise money to run the institution. (Avery Research Center.)

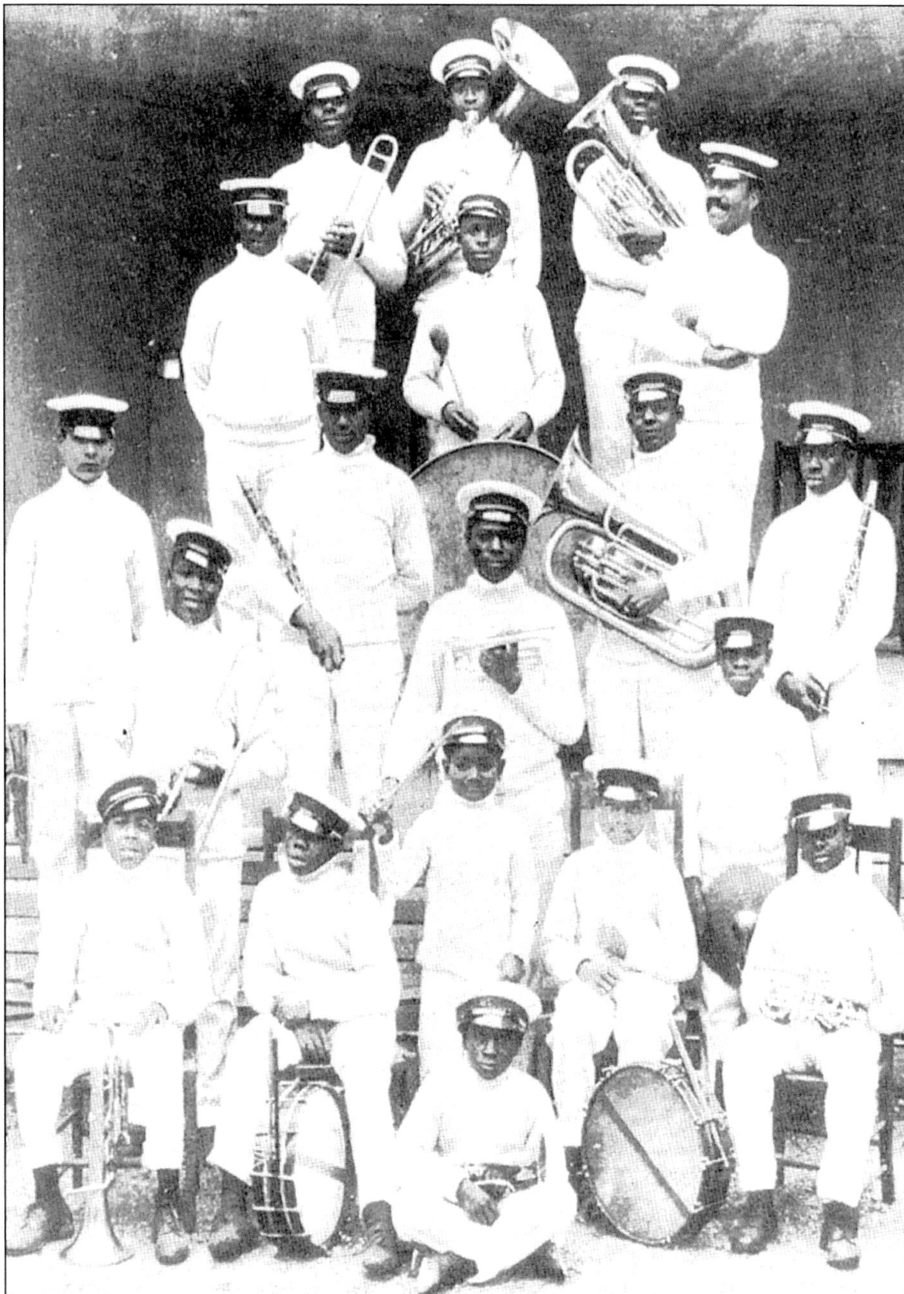

The Jenkins Orphanage Band traveled to London, England, in 1914 to perform at the Anglo American Exposition, a world's fair. World War I broke out while it was there. The band was known in Europe at that time as the Pickaninny Band, a term used to describe children that was not as denigrating as it is now seen to be. The band was big hit and raised a lot of money to support the orphanage. This was the band trip that exposed Edmund Thornton Jenkins, seventh son of Jenkins orphanage founder the Reverend Daniel Joseph Jenkins, to officials from the Royal Academy of Music in London. Edmund Jenkins, a clarinetist, joined the band on the trip at the behest of his father. (Charleston Jazz Initiative.)

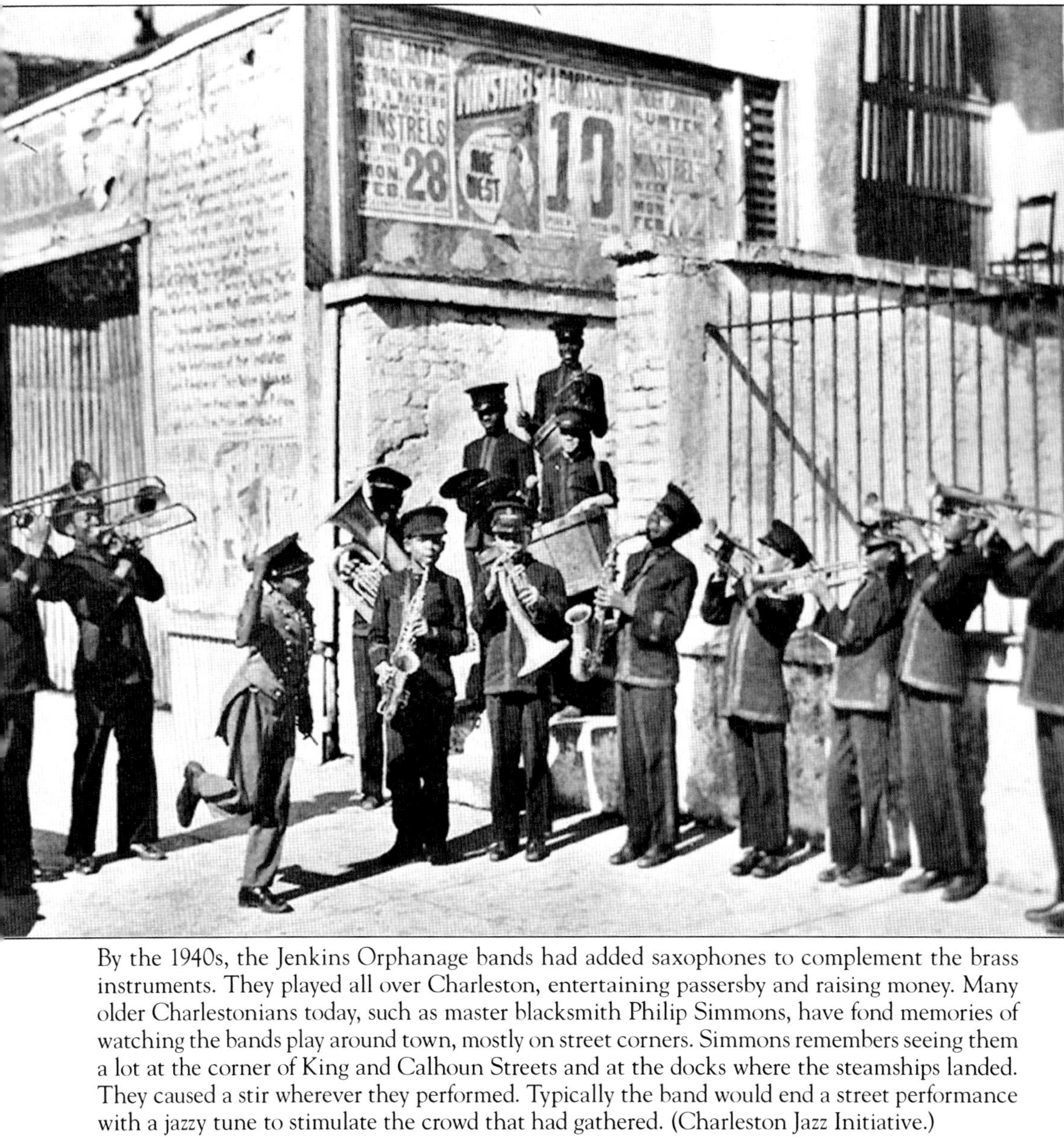

By the 1940s, the Jenkins Orphanage bands had added saxophones to complement the brass instruments. They played all over Charleston, entertaining passersby and raising money. Many older Charlestonians today, such as master blacksmith Philip Simmons, have fond memories of watching the bands play around town, mostly on street corners. Simmons remembers seeing them a lot at the corner of King and Calhoun Streets and at the docks where the steamships landed. They caused a stir wherever they performed. Typically the band would end a street performance with a jazzy tune to stimulate the crowd that had gathered. (Charleston Jazz Initiative.)

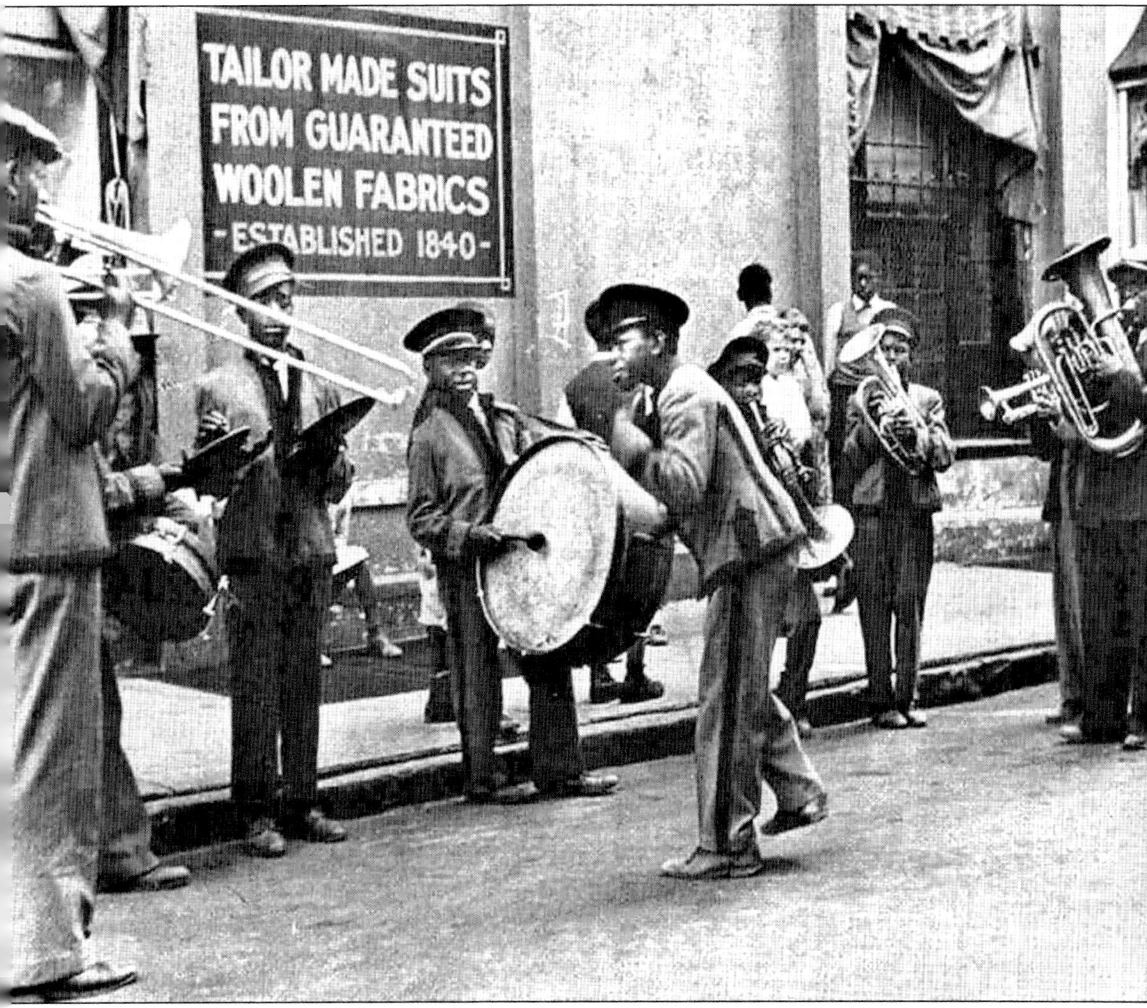

The Jenkins Orphanage bands sometimes wore castoff uniforms from the Citadel, the military college of South Carolina. The college also donated instruments. At right is William Leroy Blake (1886–1956) who led the bands from 1920 until his death. Like the rest of the orphanage, the bands depended largely on contributions of money, furnishings, and other supplies from the general public. Donations came in from around the world. The Reverend Daniel Joseph Jenkins and his key staff and agents were master fund-raisers. (Charleston Jazz Initiative.)

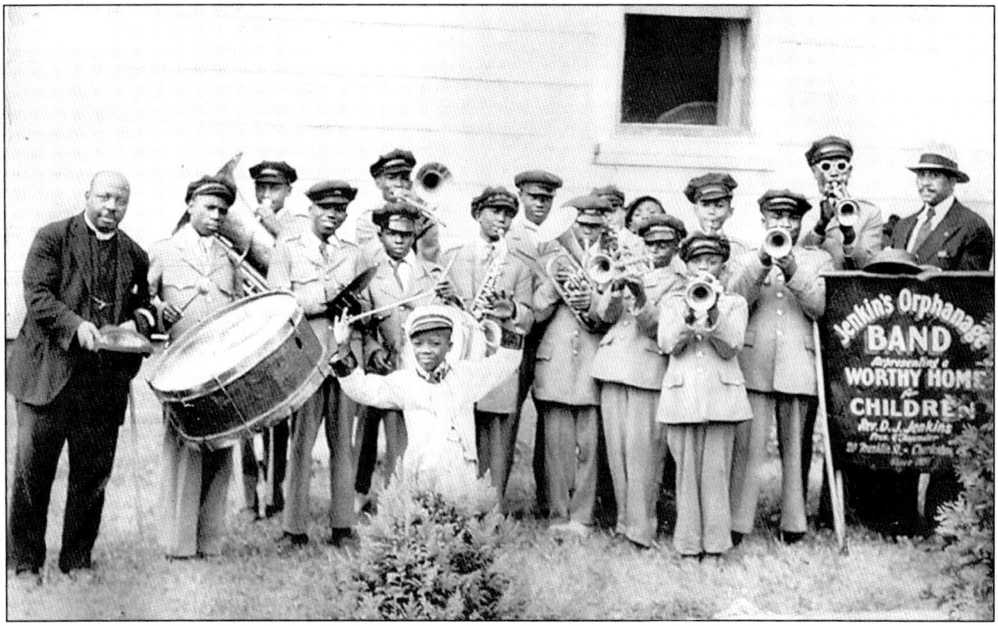

This Jenkins Orphanage band was in Schenectady, New York, some time in the 1930s on a fund-raising trip. As shown here, the bands almost always featured a smaller member out front conducting and sometimes dancing, illustrating the band's showmanship. The trumpet player on crutches, Wilbur Carter, returned to Schenectady when he left the orphanage. (Charleston Jazz Initiative.)

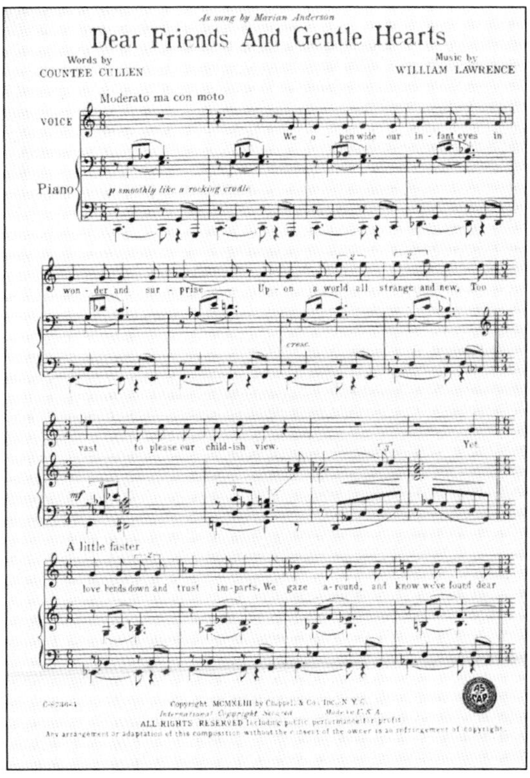

Avery Normal Institute's William Lawrence collaborated with famous Harlem Renaissance poet Countee Cullen on a song sung by Marian Anderson. Anderson was a famous African American opera singer to whose aid Eleanor Roosevelt came when she was denied an opportunity to perform at Constitution Hall in Washington, D.C., by the Daughters of the American Revolution in 1939. Lawrence's work was considered by many to be as fine as any that came out of the Harlem Renaissance, which he preceded. (Avery Research Center.)

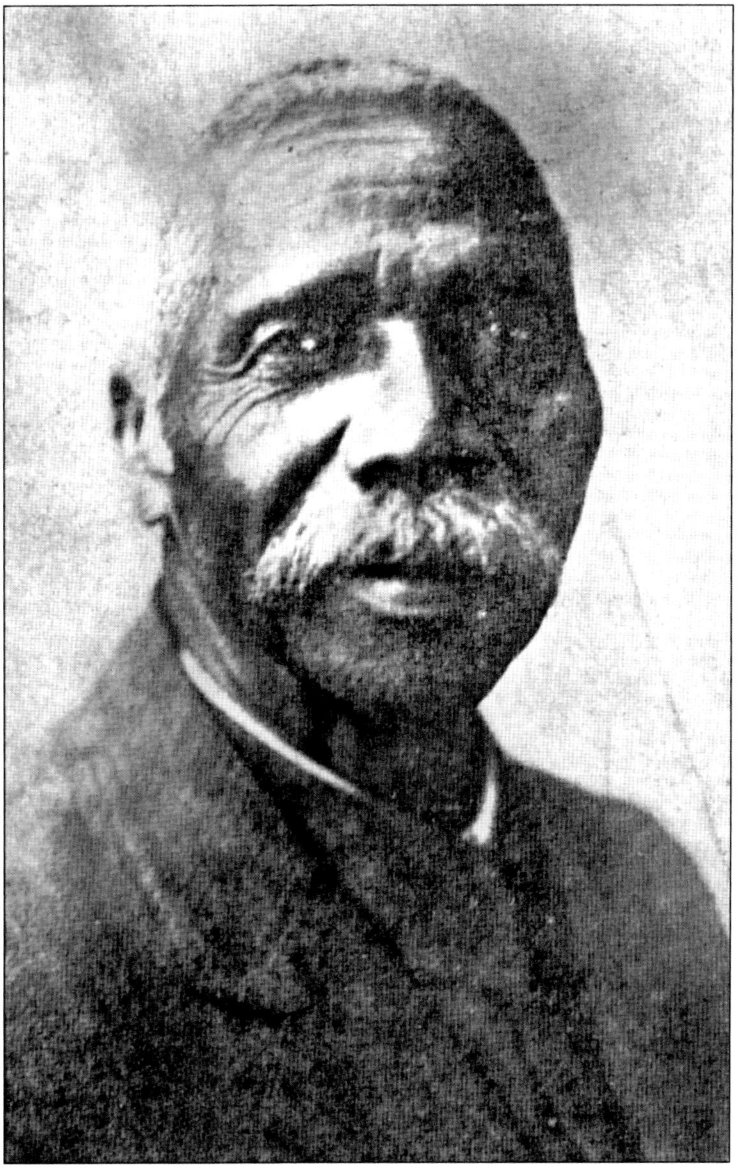

The Reverend Daniel Joseph Jenkins was born in 1867 in Barnwell County, South Carolina. He migrated to Charleston, probably in the 1880s, and emerged as an entrepreneur and preacher. He owned a lumber business, and after coming across a small group of young destitute children in Charleston, he started the famous Jenkins Orphanage, now known as the Jenkins Institute for Children, in 1891. He started on upper Meeting Street then took over the old Marine Hospital building at 20 Franklin Street, the first official home of the orphanage. The building currently houses the City of Charleston Housing Authority and is marked as the first home of the orphanage. Reverend Jenkins founded the Palmetto Street Baptist Church, whose congregation moved to a new building on Charlotte and Elizabeth Streets, becoming New Tabernacle Fourth Baptist Church. Reverend Jenkins was known around the world for his work with the orphanage, even being written about in publications such as *Time* magazine. He was one of South Carolina's most prominent blacks during his lifetime and was highly regarded among other clergymen, philanthropists, and politicians. (Avery Research Center.)

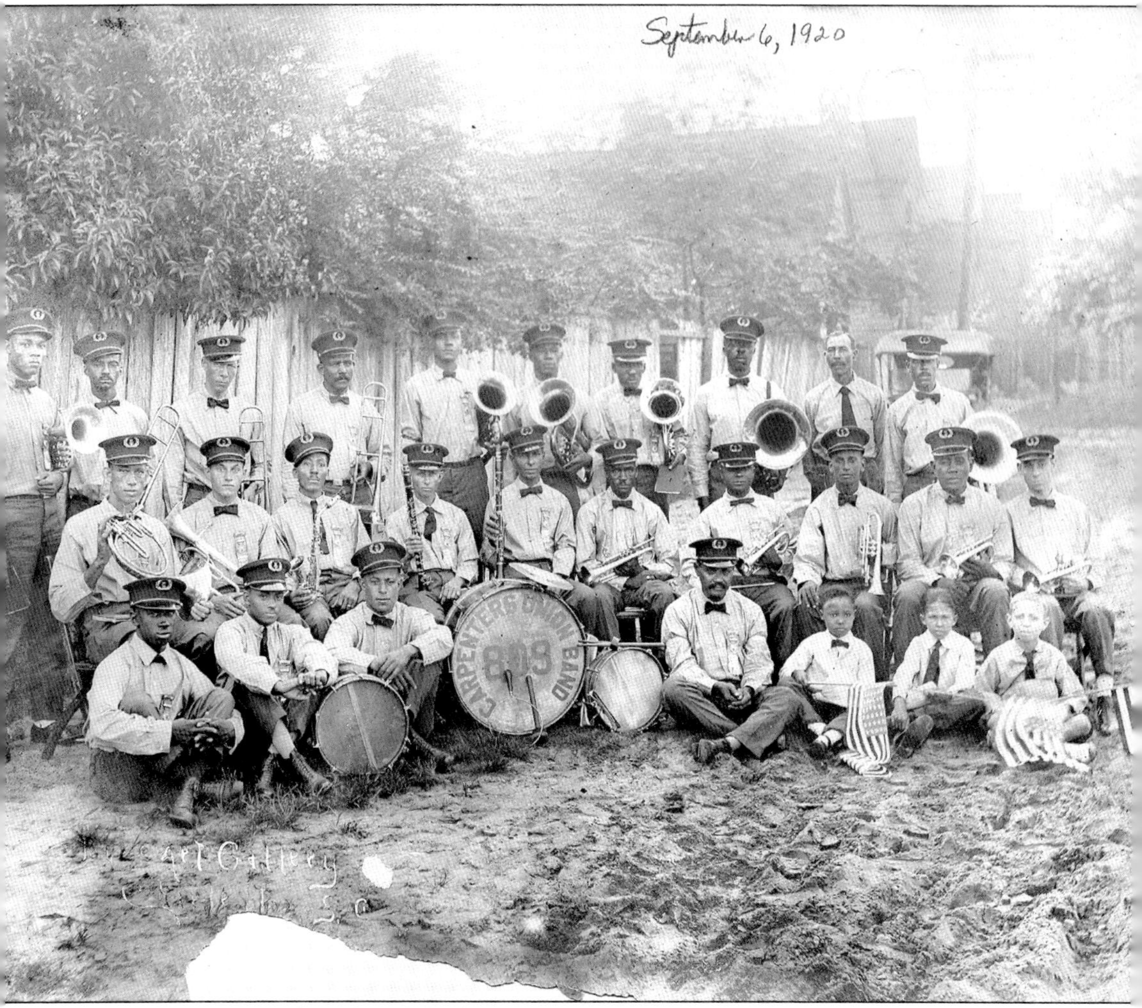

Brass bands were the order of the day in Charleston in the late 19th century and into the 20th century. They were affiliated with all sorts of organizations, including labor unions. Shown here is a band drawn from Chapter 809 of the local carpenters' union. Trades of all sorts had a large presence over the course of Charleston history, and many of them had bands. (Avery Research Center.)

Three

The Jenkins-Avery Tradition

Two institutions in Charleston have played a particularly significant role in the development of jazz music in the South Carolina Lowcountry. Seminally important was the Jenkins Orphanage (Orphan Aid Society), founded in 1891 and now known as the Jenkins Institute for Children. The other was the Avery Normal Institute, a school founded in 1867 by the American Missionary Association for freed blacks.

Given the way things have worked out, a very good case could be made for an Avery-Jenkins tradition, an approach to life and history with its own standards and practices with the pursuit of excellence at its base.

While started separately for completely different purposes, the two venerable education agencies came together around the arts, music especially. The Avery-Jenkins tradition is a way of life that has created an education strategy that uplifted its students utilizing principles and methods from established canon and their own take on what was needed in the Charleston area at any given time—their own improvisations.

For the past 110 years, participants in the Avery-Jenkins tradition have taught succeeding generations, creating a lineage and legacy that's alive and well today. It continues with contemporary local musicians and with musicians everywhere.

Avery mostly produced teachers, catering to children of people of some means in post–Civil War Charleston. Jenkins worked mostly with destitute children, though in later years, after its music program developed into one of the finest in the country, children from other classes studied there. In the 1890s, the two schools began to slowly come together around music. The Reverend Daniel Joseph Jenkins, a Baptist minister who founded the orphanage, recruited P. M. Logan, an Avery graduate, to teach his waifs music. Others followed. Another Avery graduate, Francis Eugene Mikell, led the Jenkins bands in the early 20th century, inculcating the program with excellence and achievement that have made American music history.

In 1894, the Jenkins Orphanage bands were established to train orphans to read and play all kinds of music. At Jenkins, printed scores were used, and bandmasters taught musical literacy. Residents weren't taught jazz, but oral history accounts, such as interviews conducted by the Charleston Jazz Initiative research project, indicate music students "swung" on their own time, especially at night in the dormitories.

From 1895, Jenkins bands toured extensively until the middle of the century, and their popularity grew. They performed at the Buffalo Exposition, the St. Louis Fair and Exposition, on visits to England in 1904 (and possibly again in 1906), at the inauguration of President Taft in 1909, and frequently in the northeast region of the United States between 1907 and 1912. The bands created a world craze that became the symbol of the Jazz Age, the Charleston. The popular 1923 song "The Charleston," composed by James P. Johnson, was inspired by observing Charlestonians and Jenkins musicians dancing movements called geechee, a colloquial term applied to South Carolina Gullahs.

Great musicians connected to Jenkins include trumpeter William "Cat" Anderson, who played first chair with the Duke Ellington Orchestra; trumpeter Claddys "Jabbo" Smith, Louis Armstrong's most serious rival; Freddie Green, rhythm guitarist for the Count Basie Orchestra for 50 years; drummers Tommy Benford and Rufus "Speedy" Jones; clarinetist Emerson "Geechie" Harper; Leo Shepherd, high-note trumpet player for Lionel Hampton's band; and brass player Gus Aitken, who played for Armstrong.

Avery's music program and the musicians taught there really began to flower in the 1920s. Its players and teachers were at the core of a thriving music salon scene in Charleston that offered mostly European classical music. They provided music for all sorts of social events around town

The institute hosted African American literary and musical celebrities such as poet and writer Langston Hughes and world-renowned vocalist Roland Hayes. In later years (Avery closed in 1954), the Bull Street school hosted jazz bands as well, such as the Erskine Hawkins Orchestra.

A prominent player in the Hawkins band was Avery graduate St. Julian Bennett Dash, a tenor saxophonist held in very high regard by other musicians and the general public. The band started at Alabama State College and went to New York City in the mid-1930s, eventually becoming one of the house bands at the famed Harlem dance parlor the Savoy Ballroom. Dash cowrote "Tuxedo Junction," a hugely popular tune that put the famous Glenn Miller Orchestra on the map.

Willie Smith, another Avery graduate, is one of the most heralded big-band players of all time. For years, he played first alto saxophone chair in the Duke Ellington Orchestra. He also worked for Harry James and Jimmy Lunceford. He was a great soloist as well as ensemble player.

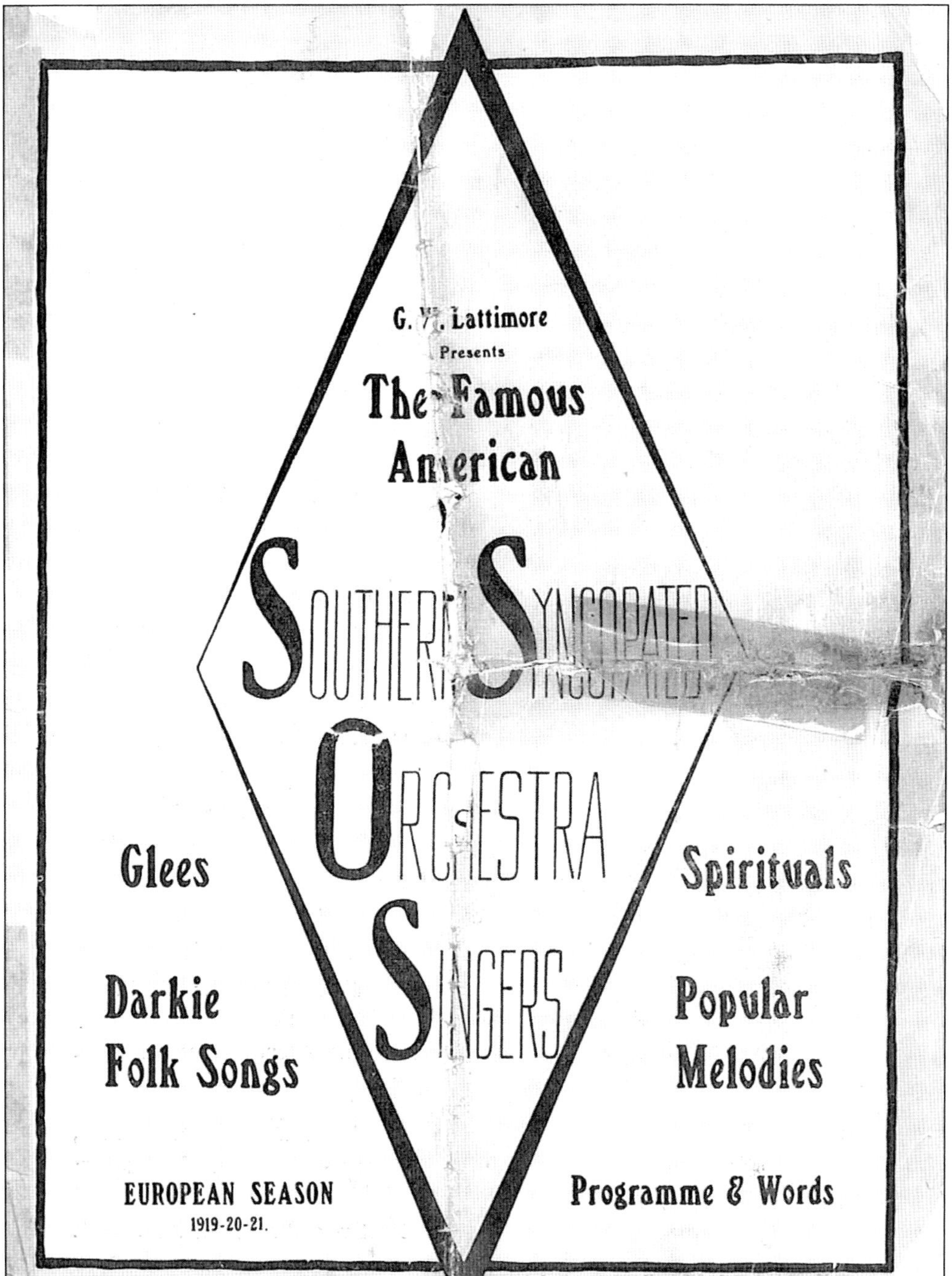

This is a flier for the Southern Syncopated Orchestra, one of the earliest bands to play improvised music and credited with helping to bring jazz to Europe. Many great jazz players performed with this band, including clarinetist Sidney Bechet. It was led by Will Marion Cook, who had ties to Charleston musicians. (Charleston Jazz Initiative.)

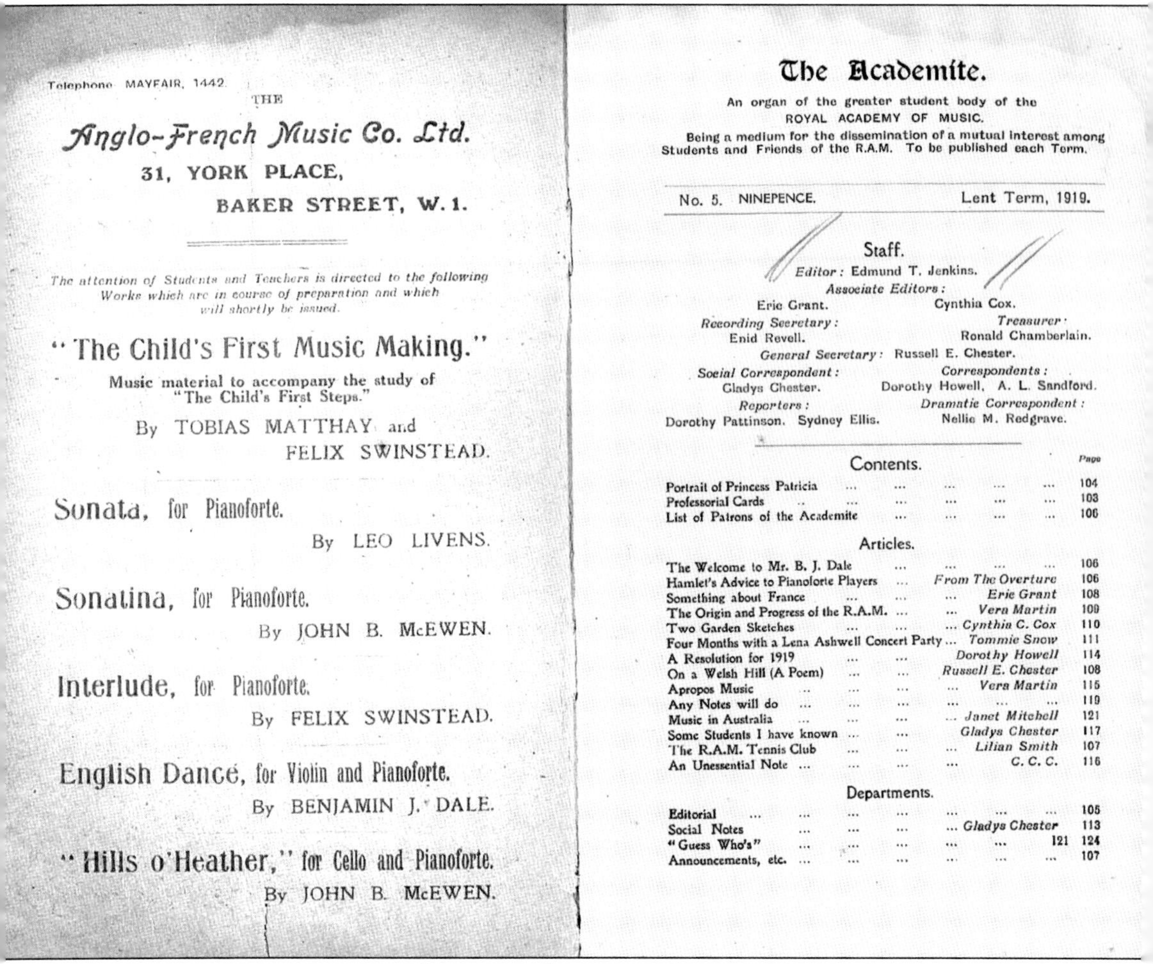

Telephone MAYFAIR, 1442.

THE

Anglo-French Music Co. Ltd.

31, YORK PLACE,

BAKER STREET, W. 1.

The attention of Students and Teachers is directed to the following Works which are in course of preparation and which will shortly be issued.

"The Child's First Music Making."

Music material to accompany the study of "The Child's First Steps."

By TOBIAS MATTHAY and FELIX SWINSTEAD.

Sonata, for Pianoforte.

By LEO LIVENS.

Sonatina, for Pianoforte.

By JOHN B. McEWEN.

Interlude, for Pianoforte.

By FELIX SWINSTEAD.

English Dance, for Violin and Pianoforte.

By BENJAMIN J. DALE.

"Hills o'Heather," for Cello and Pianoforte.

By JOHN B. McEWEN.

The Academite.

An organ of the greater student body of the ROYAL ACADEMY OF MUSIC.

Being a medium for the dissemination of a mutual interest among Students and Friends of the R.A.M. To be published each Term.

No. 5. NINEPENCE. Lent Term, 1919.

Staff.

Editor: Edmund T. Jenkins.

Associate Editors: Eric Grant. Cynthia Cox.

Recording Secretary: Enid Revell.

Treasurer: Ronald Chamberlain.

General Secretary: Russell E. Chester.

Social Correspondent: Gladys Chester.

Correspondents: Dorothy Howell, A. L. Sandford.

Reporters: Dorothy Pattinson. Sydney Ellis.

Dramatic Correspondent: Nellie M. Redgrave.

Contents.

Articles.

Departments.

This is the cover and program of a 1919 *Academite*, a publication of the Royal Academy of Music in London edited by Charleston's Edmund Thornton Jenkins, a student and teacher there and son of the Reverend Daniel Joseph Jenkins, Jenkins Orphanage founder. (Charleston Jazz Initiative.)

Edmund Thornton Jenkins's skills in writing, editing, and publishing probably didn't match his skills in musical composition and performance, but they were formidable. He evidently had a way of organizing his thoughts and ideas in such a way that he could convey them legibly and understandably to readers. (Charleston Jazz Initiative.)

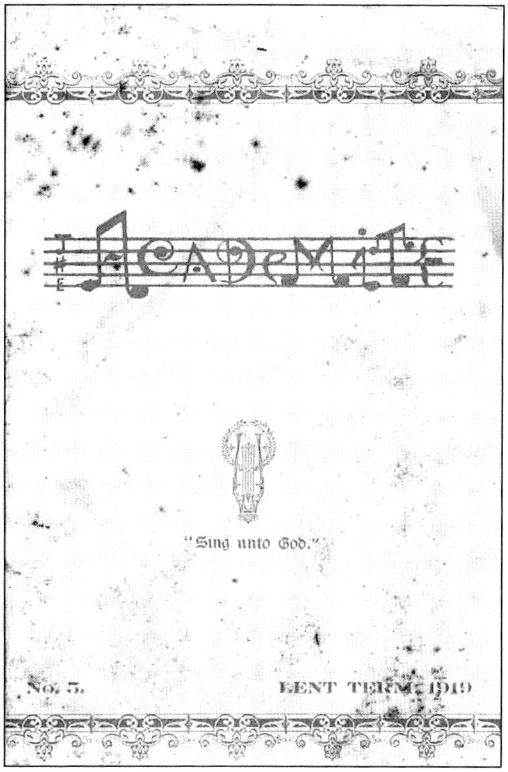

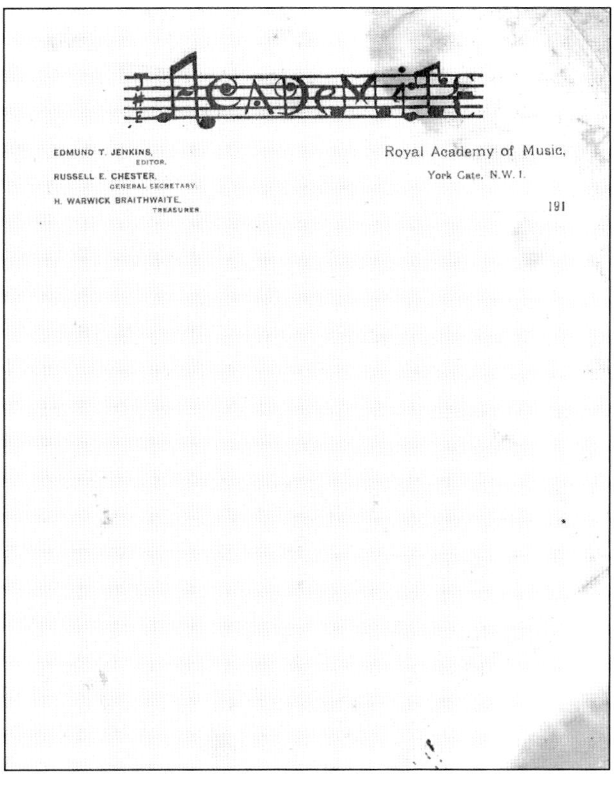
ACADEMITE

EDMUND T. JENKINS, EDITOR.
RUSSELL E. CHESTER, GENERAL SECRETARY.
H. WARWICK BRAITHWAITE, TREASURER.

Royal Academy of Music,
York Gate, N.W. 1.

191

With Edmund Thornton Jenkins at the helm, those who worked on the *Academite* reported on matters important to them and to those who they thought could benefit from their reportage and editing. There were many issues of great import at play while Jenkins was in England. The magazine was a major outlet. (Charleston Jazz Initiative.)

Mr. GEORGE WILLIA

PRESENTS

The American Southern Syncop

LIEUT. E. E. THOMPSON,
JOHN C. PAYNE, Cho

PART I.

			Words
I.	"Go down, Moses" - - *Arr. by E. Aldama Jackson*	page 4	No. 1
	ORGAN, CHORUS and ORCHESTRA. BRUCE JAMES AT THE ORGAN.		
II.	Dance from "Othello" - - *S. Coleridge-Taylor*		
	ORCHESTRA.		
III.	(a) "Hallelujah" - - - - *Traditional*	" 5	No. 13
	(b) "Jessamine" - - - - - *Williams*	" 9	No. 23
	BAKER, MARSHALL, HARVEY, PAUL.		
	(c) "Oh Mary" - - - - - *Traditional*	" 5	No. 8
	MALE CHORUS.		
IV.	Peter Gink - - - - - *Cobb*		
	ORCHESTRA.		
V.	"I got a Robe" - - - - *Traditional*	" 4	No. 6
	CARROLL MORGAN.		
VI.	Wyoming - - - - - *Gene Williams*		
	ORCHESTRA.		
VII.	"Sinner, please doan let dis Harvest pass" *H. T. Burleigh*		
	MRS. H. KING REAVIS.		
VIII.	(a) Petite Suite de Concert, No. 2 - *S. Coleridge-Taylor*		
	(b) Russian Rag - - - - - *Cobb*		
	ORCHESTRA.		
IX.	"A Plantation Lullaby" - - *Geo. Baker*		
	ROYAL SOUTHERN SYNCOPATED SINGERS AND COMPOSER.		
X.	"Deep River" - - - - - *H. T. Burleigh*	" 9/10	No. 26
	MISS MABEL WADHAM.		
XI.	El Relicario - - - *José Padilla*		
	ORCHESTRA.		
XII.	Southland Melodies (Medley) *Arr. by Carlisle Kawbawgan*	" 12	No. 40
	ORGAN, CHORUS, and ORCHESTRA.		

Interval of ten minutes.

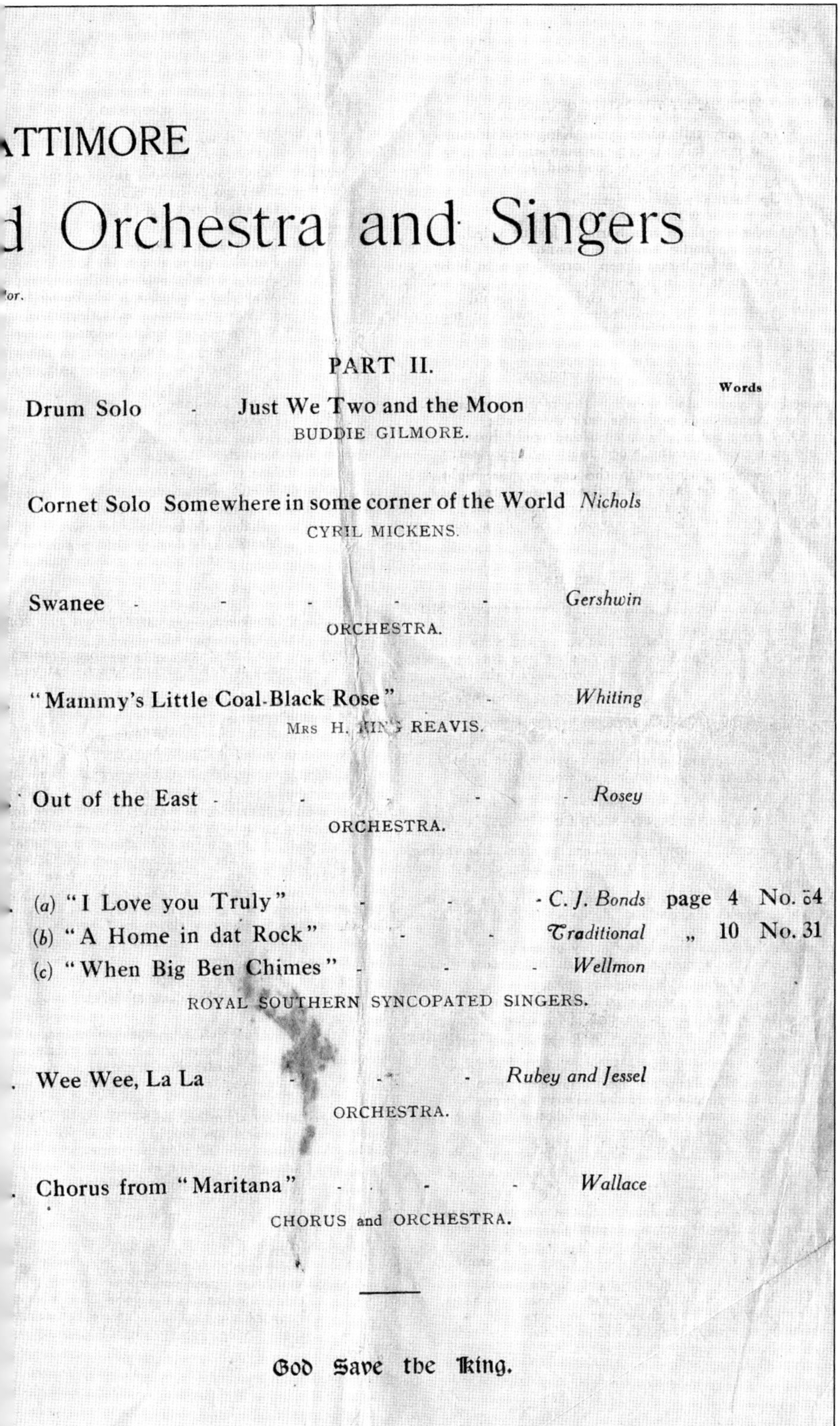

...TTIMORE

...d Orchestra and Singers

...or.

PART II.

Words

Drum Solo - Just We Two and the Moon
BUDDIE GILMORE.

Cornet Solo Somewhere in some corner of the World *Nichols*
CYRIL MICKENS.

Swanee - - - - - *Gershwin*
ORCHESTRA.

"Mammy's Little Coal-Black Rose" - *Whiting*
MRS H. KING REAVIS.

Out of the East - - - - *Rosey*
ORCHESTRA.

(*a*) "I Love you Truly" - - - *C. J. Bonds* page 4 No. 54
(*b*) "A Home in dat Rock" - - *Traditional* „ 10 No. 31
(*c*) "When Big Ben Chimes" - - - *Wellmon*
ROYAL SOUTHERN SYNCOPATED SINGERS.

Wee Wee, La La - - - *Rubey and Jessel*
ORCHESTRA.

Chorus from "Maritana" - - - - *Wallace*
CHORUS and ORCHESTRA.

God Save the King.

The Southern Syncopated Orchestra, which contained Charleston musicians, was one of the most important bands to play Europe in the early 20th century. Here are an example of the music it played and a program. (Charleston Jazz Initiative.)

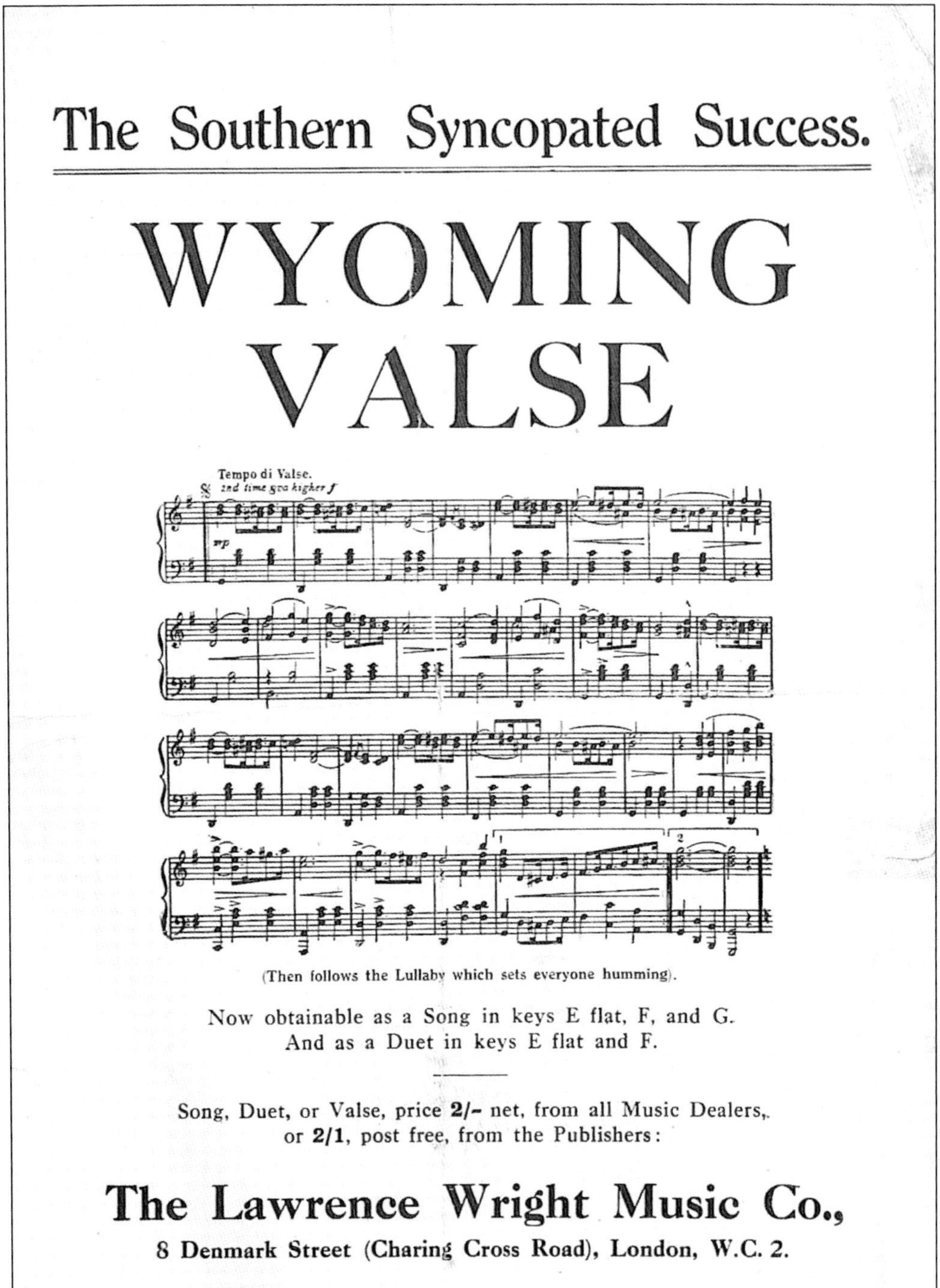

This is sheet music for a lullaby made famous by the Southern Syncopated Orchestra. All kinds of music were performed by blacks in Charleston, especially early in the 20th century. There was also a lot of crossover in terms of performance of different musical genres. The Avery Normal Institute was an excellent example of that. Classics, hymns, popular music, jazz, sacred music, and traditional music—all were performed there. (Charleston Jazz Initiative.)

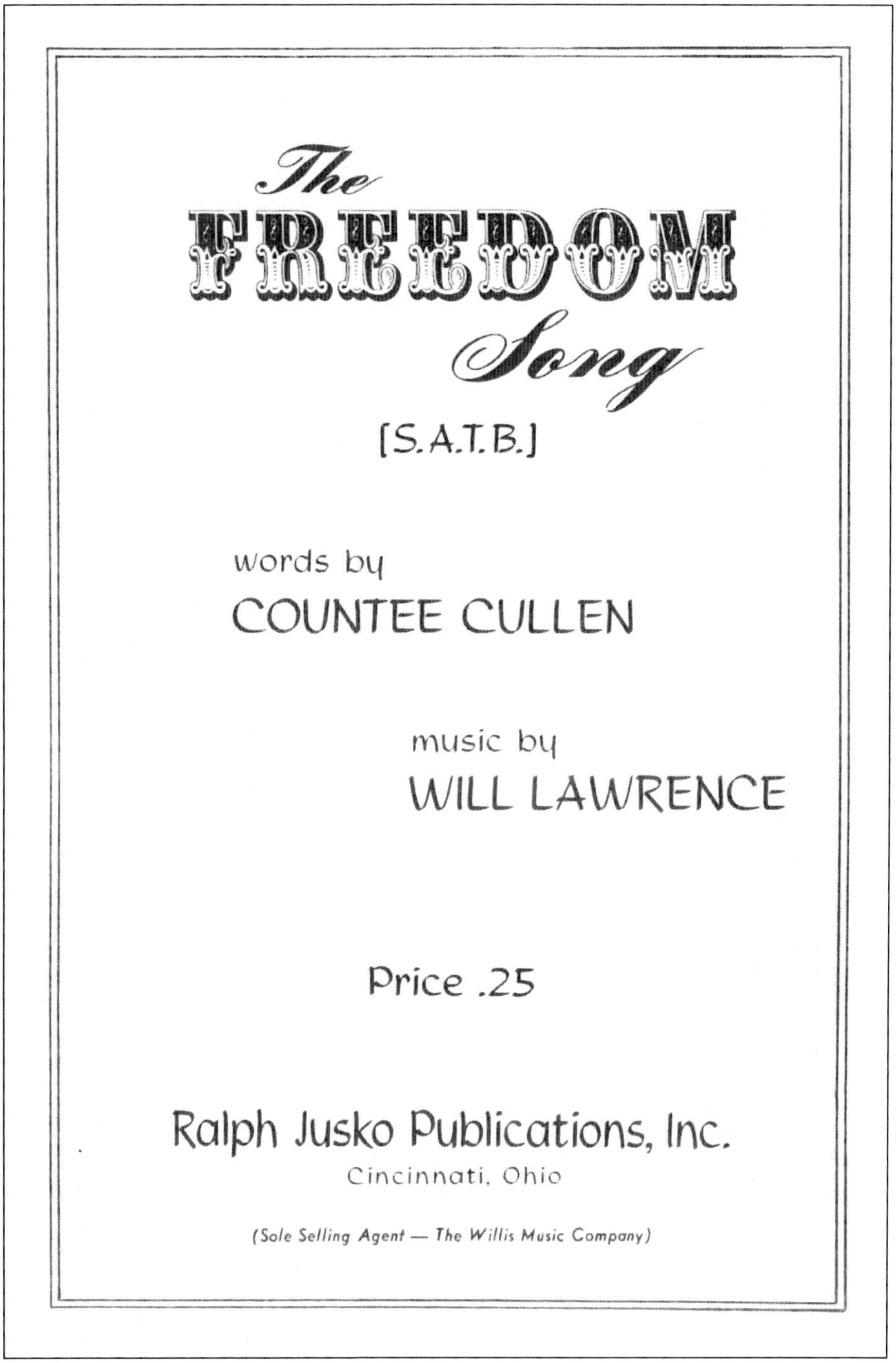

This is sheet music for a collaboration between Avery's William Lawrence and Countee Cullen. Lawrence's work with Cullen illustrates Charleston's parallel to and collaboration with the Harlem Renaissance. Cullen was a noted poet, anthologist, children's writer, and novelist who was a leading black figure for most of the first half of the 20th century. Lawrence set several of Cullen's poems to music. (Charleston Jazz Initiative.)

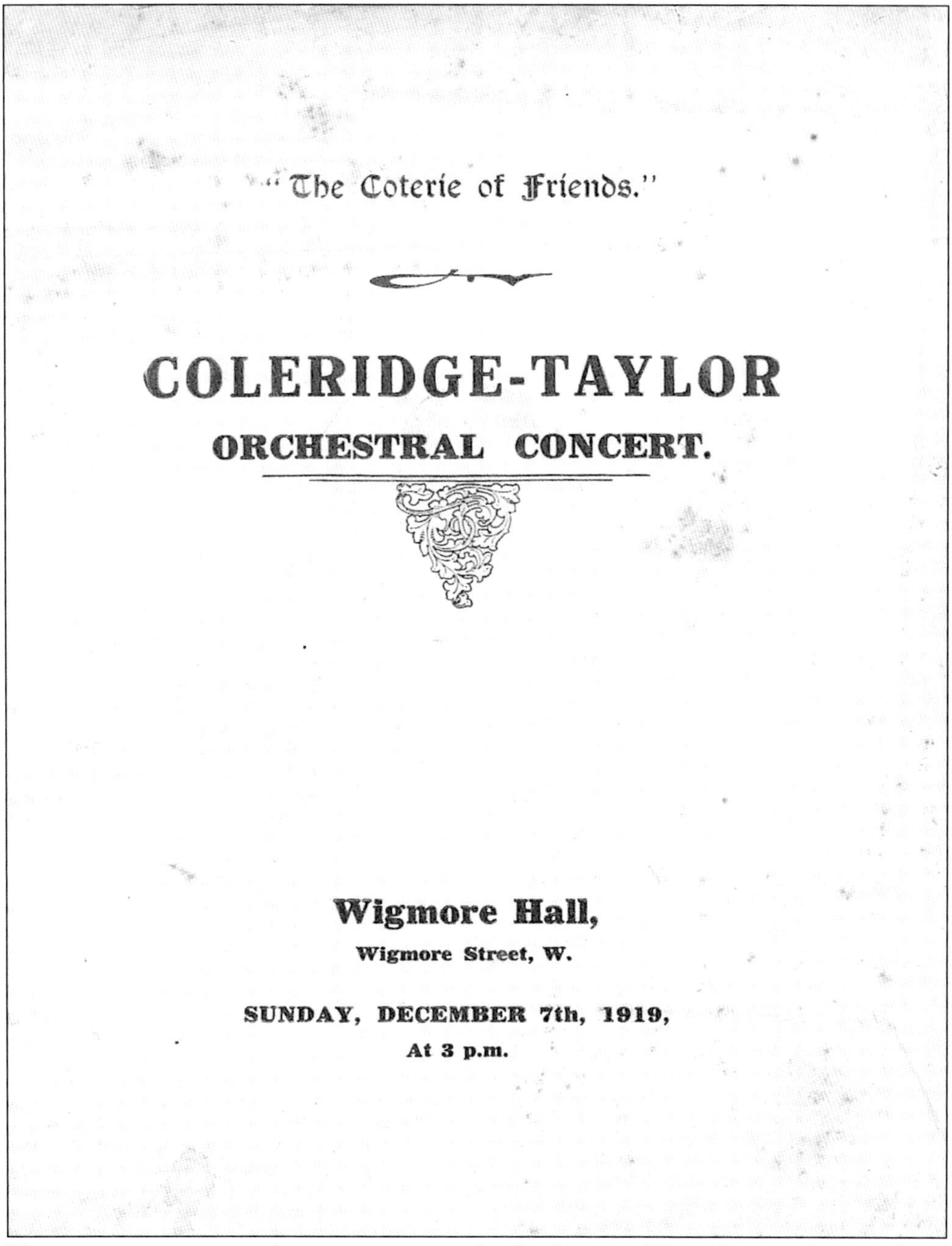

"The Coterie of Friends."

COLERIDGE-TAYLOR

ORCHESTRAL CONCERT.

Wigmore Hall,

Wigmore Street, W.

SUNDAY, DECEMBER 7th, 1919,

At 3 p.m.

This is an announcement for a concert put on by the Coterie of Friends, a London social and political organization made up of African American, African, and West Indian members that included Edmund Thornton Jenkins. The organization worked in social endeavors as well as political ones. It was a very progressive group and was made up of people instrumental in changing social and political mores in England. Music, European classical and jazz, was a large part of its activities with much time and resources devoted to its composition and performance. (Charleston Jazz Initiative.)

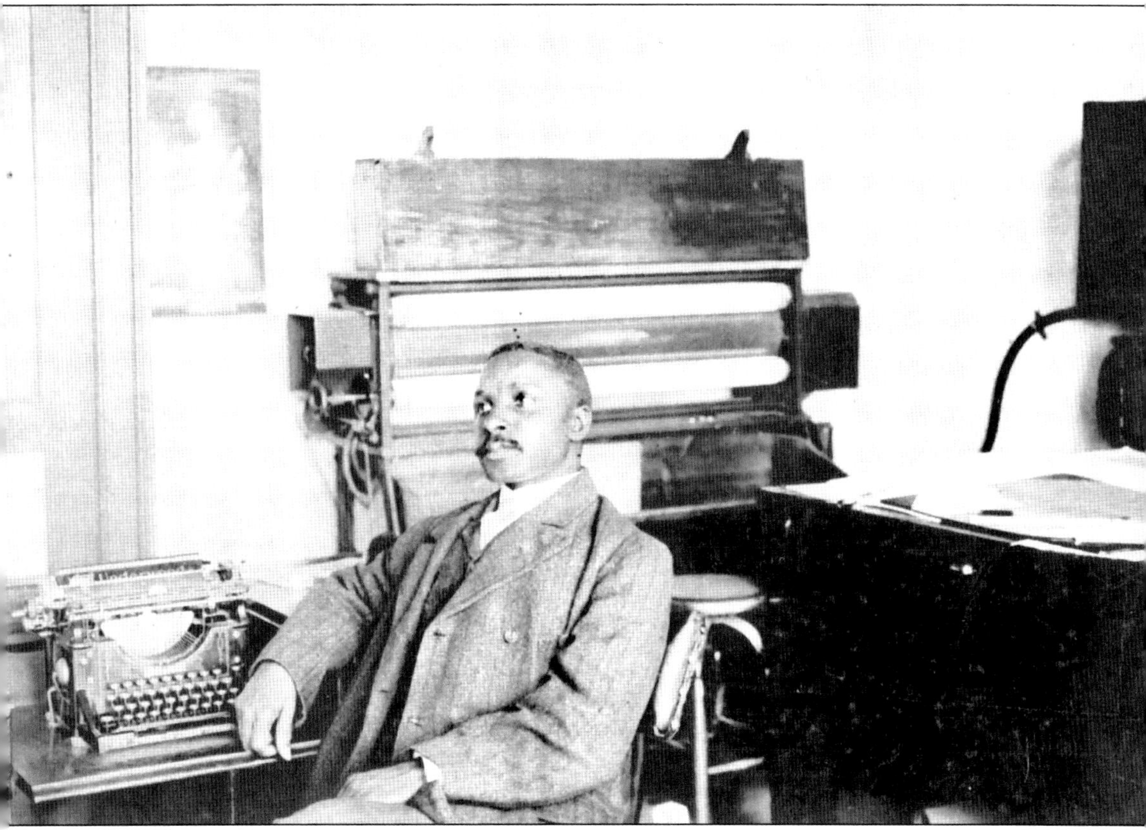

James Logan was a successful musician and educator from Avery Normal Institute. He was employed at the Charleston Naval Shipyard, where this photograph is from. Logan, like William Lawrence, was a highly regarded musician and was an example of the so-called New Negro, blacks who by their artistic endeavors and dignified demeanor dispelled myths about the stereotypical 19th-century base Negro. (Avery Research Center.)

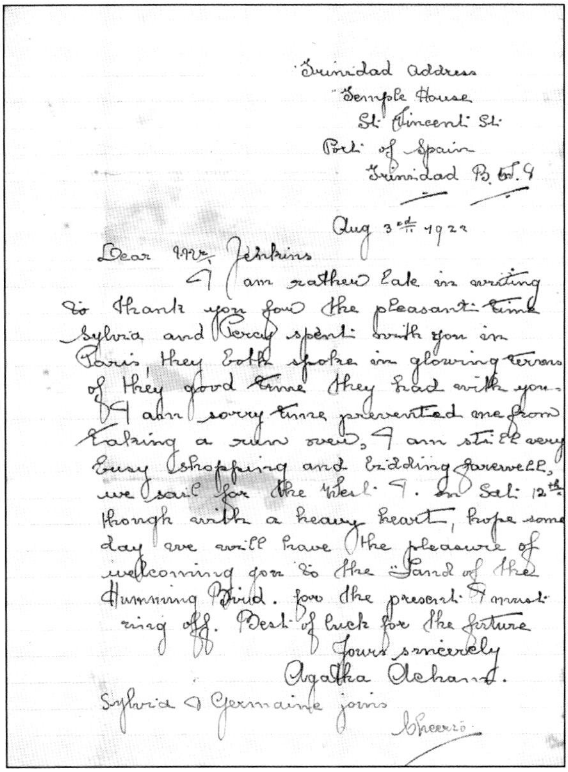

Trinidad address
Temple House
St. Vincent St.
Port of Spain
Trinidad B.W.I.

Aug 3rd 1922

Dear Mr. Jenkins

I am rather late in writing to thank you for the pleasant time Sylvia and Percy spent with you in Paris, they both spoke in glowing terms of they good time they had with you. I am sorry time prevented me from taking a run over, I am still very busy shopping and bidding farewell, we sail for the West I. on Sat. 12th though with a heavy heart, hope some day we will have the pleasure of welcoming you to the "Land of the Humming Bird". for the present I must ring off. Best of luck for the future

Yours sincerely
Agatha Acham.

Sylvia & Germaine joins
Cheerio.

This is a letter written in 1922 from Percy Achem Chen to Edmund Thornton Jenkins. He and Jenkins had become friends when Chen was studying law in London and Jenkins was a student at the Royal Academy of Music. Chen was from Trinidad. Jenkins was living in Paris at the time. The two were dear friends and involved in all kinds of matters together. (Charleston Jazz Initiative.)

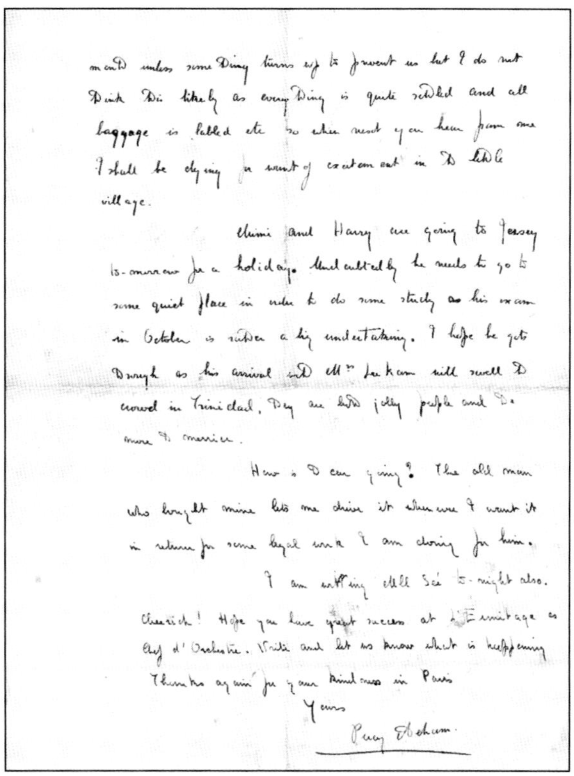

month unless something turns up to prevent us but I do not think this likely as everything is quite settled and all baggage is labled etc so when next you hear from me I shall be dying for want of excitement in the little village.

Chini and Harry are going to Jersey to-morrow for a holiday. Undoubtedly he needs to go to some quiet place in order to do some study as his exam in October is rather a big undertaking. I hope he gets through as his arrival and Mrs Jenkins will swell the crowd in Trinidad. They are both jolly people and the more the merrier.

How is the car going? The old man who bought mine lets me drive it when ever I want it in return for some legal work I am doing for him.

I am writing Mlle Sai to-night also.

Cheerioh! Hope you have great success at L'Ermitage as Chef d'Orchestre. Write and let us know what is happening. Thanks again for your kindness in Paris

Yours
Percy Acham.

ATLANTA UNIVERSITY
BENEDICT COLLEGE
BISHOP COLLEGE
FISK UNIVERSITY
HOWARD UNIVERSITY
KNOXVILLE COLLEGE
MOREHOUSE COLLEGE
SHAW UNIVERSITY
TALLADEGA COLLEGE
VIRGINIA UNION UNIVERSITY
WILBERFORCE UNIVERSITY

Association of Colleges
For Negro Youth

OFFICERS
President
BENJAMIN BRAWLEY,
Dean Morehouse College
Vice-President
C. H. MAXSON,
President Bishop College
Secretary-Treasurer
J. T. CATER,
Dean Talladega College
EXECUTIVE COMMITTEE
The Officers and
DEAN M. W. ADAMS
Atlanta University
PROF. G. M. LIGHTFOOT,
Howard University

Atlanta, Ga. Dec. 13, 1919.

My Dear Friend,

It seems a long, long time since I heard from you, and I guess you can say the same about me. I hope and pray, however, that all has been going well with you. When you wrote you were uncertain about work or returning to this country. Once more I hope that you are remaining close to all the ideals that we have cherished. Over here I have said that ~~we~~ you were the most promising musician we had in all the world.

And now what do you think? If you are still in England, as I hope you are, it is very likely that within a few weeks we may see each other. Mrs. Brawley and I are expecting to arrive in Liverpool about the end of January. What for? Well, I have on hand about the biggest thing that has ever come to me. Three responsible agencies in and near New York are sending me as their joint representative and as a teacher in Liberia College, Monrovia, Liberia. The contract is for one term only, for the school year from March to November; but I can do more with it than that if I wish. The main thing, however, is that while ostensibly I shall be a teacher my mission will have much wider scope than the work of a mere teacher. All that I could better explain in person than write to you. If all goes well, I shall arrive in Liverpool late in January and sail on to Liberia as early as possible in the next month. I am almost sure to be delayed for a few days,

ATLANTA UNIVERSITY
BENEDICT COLLEGE
BISHOP COLLEGE
FISK UNIVERSITY
HOWARD UNIVERSITY
KNOXVILLE COLLEGE
MOREHOUSE COLLEGE
SHAW UNIVERSITY
TALLADEGA COLLEGE
VIRGINIA UNION UNIVERSITY
WILBERFORCE UNIVERSITY

Association of Colleges
For Negro Youth

OFFICERS
President
BENJAMIN BRAWLEY,
Dean Morehouse College
Vice-President
C. H. MAXSON,
President Bishop College
Secretary-Treasurer
J. T. CATER,
Dean Talladega College
EXECUTIVE COMMITTEE
The Officers and
DEAN M. W. ADAMS
Atlanta University
PROF. G. M. LIGHTFOOT,
Howard University

Atlanta, Ga.

however, and in that case I should certainly not remain in Liverpool but go to London, Cambridge, Stratford, etc. At best I shall want to hurry on my way as well as I can. On my return through England some months afterwards I should want to tarry at greater length. Do you begin to catch something of the idea? If you get this letter write to me at Morehouse College at once. I shall hope to hear from you before I leave Atlanta. I shall be leaving, however, about the middle of January. If your letter is a day or two late it will be forwarded to me at New York. Meantime I shall try to keep you informed as well as I can. Let us pray and hope that we shall see each other again very soon.

Sincerely your friend,

Benjamin Brawley

This letter was written in 1919 from Benjamin Brawley, the famed black educator and author, to Edmund Thornton Jenkins, who was in England at the time to announce his getting a new job in Liberia and passing through England on the way there. Brawley wrote in the letter that Jenkins was the most gifted Negro musician in the world, in his estimation. He had taught Jenkins at Atlanta Baptist College. The letter includes the significant statement by Brawley that Jenkins was the best hope for the success of black musicians in the world—no small idea from one so highly regarded. (Avery Research Center.)

A SACRED CONCERT

WILL BE GIVEN BY

809 BAND ASSOCIATION

ASSISTED BY

LOCAL TALENTS

AT THE LINCOLN THEATRE

Sunday Afternoon, May 31st, 1925

AT 5:30 O'clock

Invocation	Mr. W. G. Kinard
Selection	809 Band
Vocal Solo	Mrs. Ida Lewis
Instrumental Solo	Mr. P. Daniels, Jr.
Selection	The Utopian Orchestra
Vocal Solo	Mrs. W. G. Kinard
Instrumental Solo	Mr. P. Poinsett
Duett	Messrs Chapman and Groves
Selection	809 Band
Vocal Solo	Mrs. E. C. Jenkins
Recitation	Miss M. St. Marks
Instrumental Solo	Miss L. Mayers
Selection	The Utopian Orchestra
Vocal Solo	Mrs. H. H. Green
Remarks	Mrs. E. G. Baker
Selection	809 Band

B. B. St. Marks, Chairman; Wm. A. Evans, Secretary

Wm. Dickinson, Ex-officio; J. R. Logan, Director

SILVER OFFERING TAKEN AT THE DOOR.

J. R. Harlee Print, 104 Line St.
Carpenters' Hall

This is a program of musical entertainment staged at Charleston's Lincoln Theater in 1925 featuring Charleston bands and soloists. The Lincoln Theater building stood on King Street until the late 1980s. It was a movie theater as well as a stage theater and was one of the more unique black businesses in Charleston catering to blacks during segregation. (Avery Research Center.)

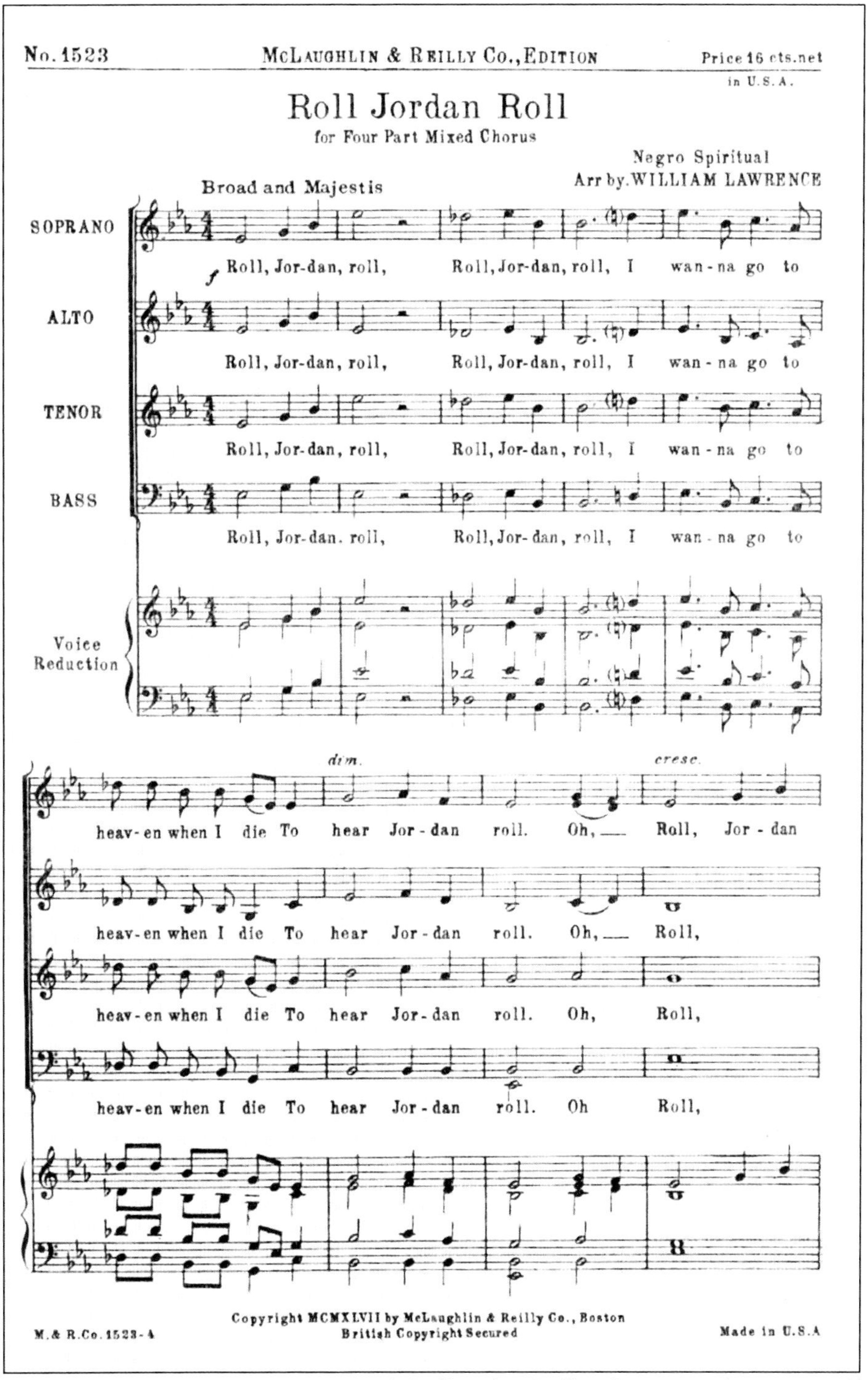

This is William Lawrence's arrangement of "Roll Jordan Roll." This spiritual is a song of hope for enslaved Africans, literally and figuratively. It expresses a desire to go to heaven after death and shows a deep faith in God and the afterlife in spite of horrific conditions on Earth. (Avery Research Center.)

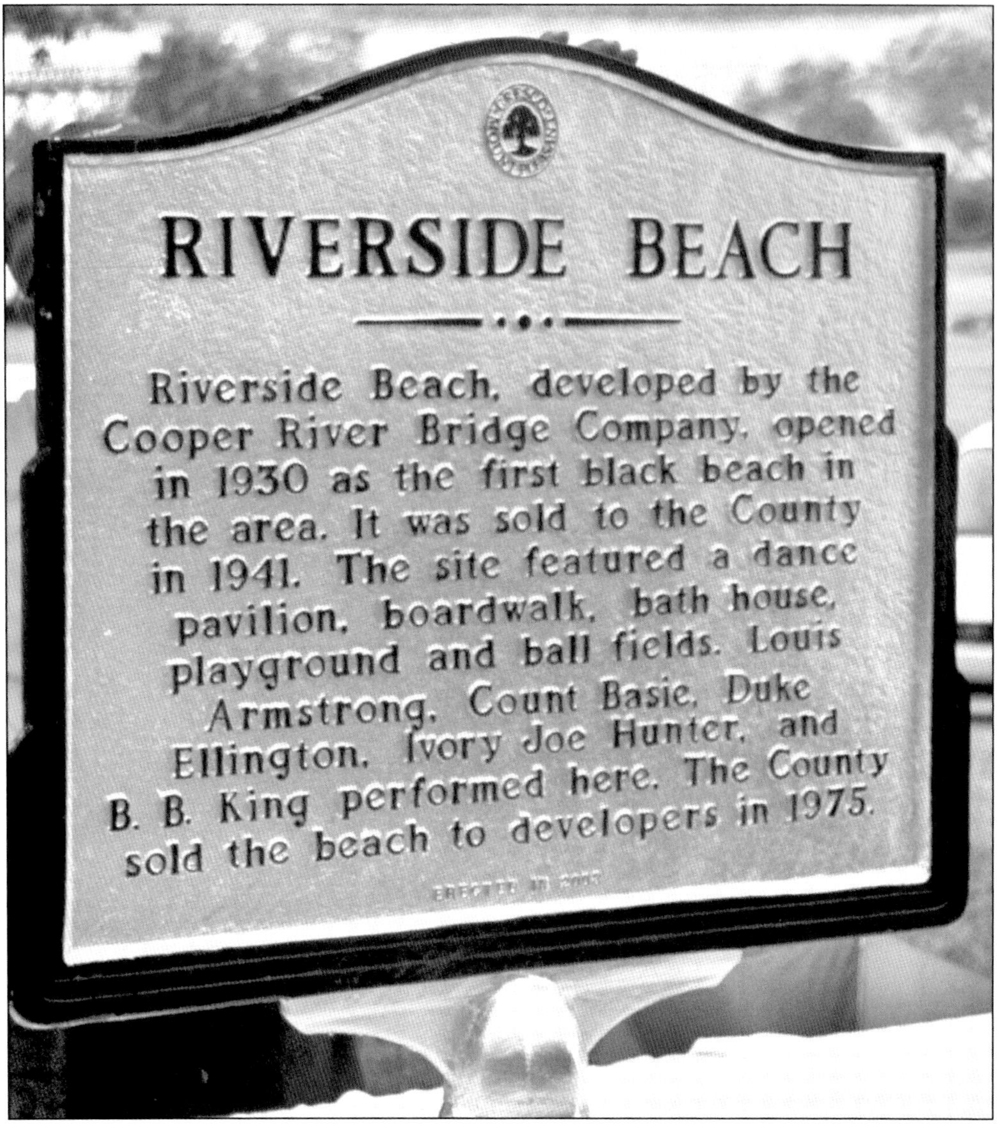

This marker shows the importance of the old Riverside Beach Pavilion as a venue in the Charleston area important to jazz by local and national acts. Many of the great bands played there, including Louis Armstrong. The most significant touring band from Charleston, the Carolina Cottonpickers, also played there. Riverside Beach was one of the most popular entertainment spots for locals and lasted well into the 20th century. It was also worked by rhythm-and-blues acts including James Brown and Famous Flames. (*Post and Courier.*)

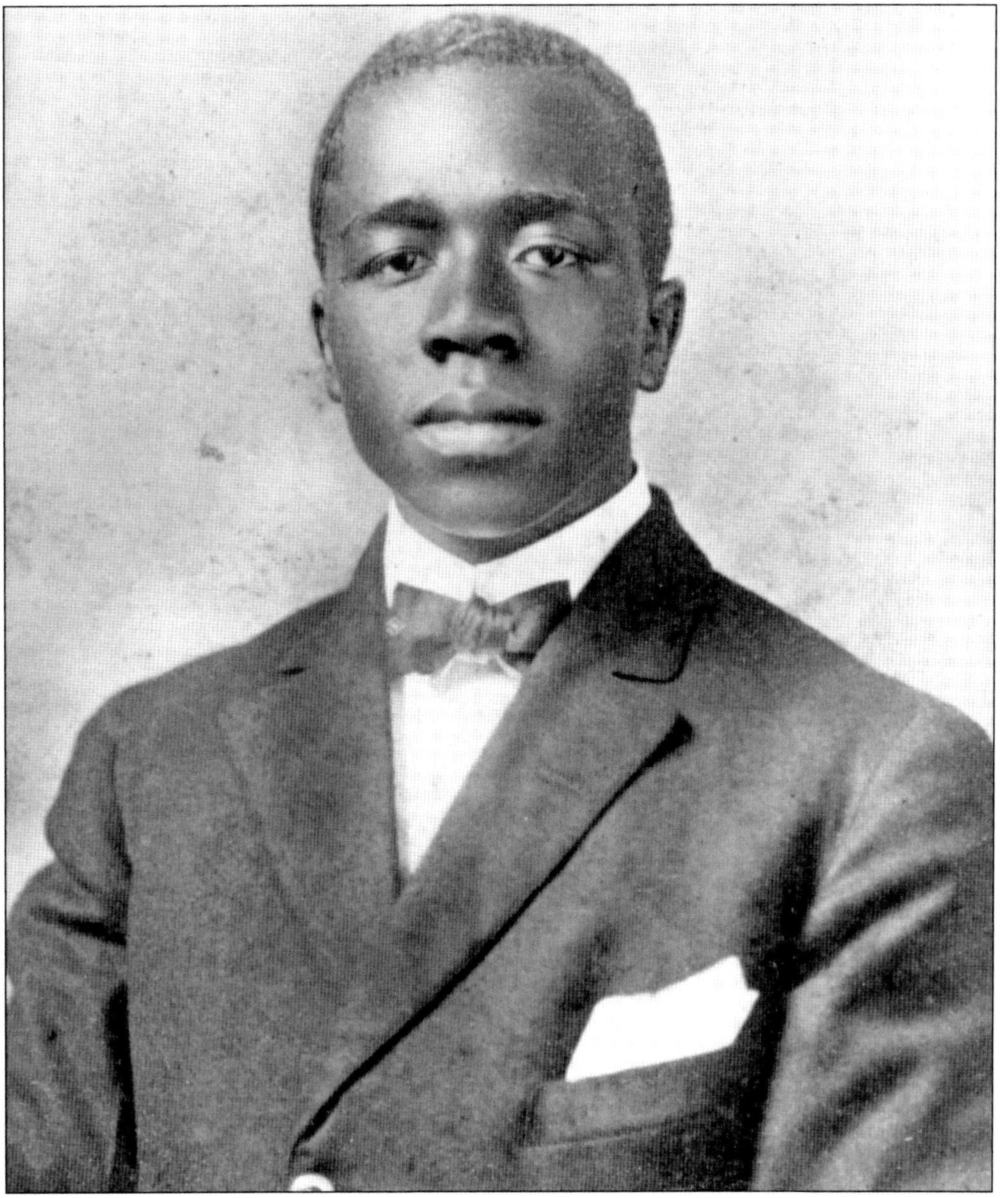

Edmund Thornton Jenkins, the seventh son of the Reverend Daniel Joseph Jenkins, founder of Jenkins Orphanage, only lived to be 32 years old and died in 1926 as an expatriate in Paris. This picture is believed to have been taken in 1913. He was a prize-winning composer and performer who wrote and played all kinds of music. He graduated with honors from the Royal Academy of Music in London and went on to teach there. He performed all over Europe, produced entertainment events, and was involved in British politics. The themes in Edmund Jenkins's works are said to be based on black Charleston themes, folk life, and such. Some recordings of his jazz work with English band director Jack Hylton, known as the British Paul Whiteman, have recently been released. Jenkins attempted to return to Charleston once in his life, wanting to establish a music school and music publishing company. (Charleston Jazz Initiative.)

GREAT EFFORTS

...ON THE....

Part of Some of of The Leading Women of Charleston to Raise $100.00 by an Entertainment,

Mon. Evening, October 16th

At The New Tabernacle Fourth Church, Palmetto St. to help relieve the immediate needy conditions at the Jenkins Orphanage

ADMISSION, ADULTS, 25C CHILDREN 15C

Every man, woman and child interested in the poor children and their needy condition ought to be there Monday night.

....PROGRAMME....

1 Opening Song .... By children of Jenkins Orphanage
2 Selection My country tis of the ......Jenkins Orphan Band
3 Selection........ Lyceum Orchestra, Prof. Wilson Director
4 Recitation .... Miss. J. A. Moore
5 Selection.......................Jenkins Orphan Band
6 Selection......................Lyceum Orchestra
7 Paper ....Mrs. H, Williams
8 Solo. ..."When the rest of the world don't want you'....... . Mr. Alonzo Mills
9 Brass Quartette ....Messrs Mills, Brown, Aiken & Holme
10 Violin Solo.............................Prof Saxton Wilson
11 Address Subject ....Training children Prof. Wm. Dubois
12 Selection.................. By the Lyceum Orchestra
13 Selection ....By the Jenkins Orphan Band
14 Competitive Drill ....By Orphan Band Boys
15 Recitation by.................Miss. Blanche Jamison
16 Clarinet Solo .... Mr. Alonzo Mills
17 REMARKS
Why the Band Boys were arrested in the North and detained nearly two months. By the President Rev. D. J. Jenkins
18 Closing selection...."God be with you until we meet Again" By Band and Orchestra. Competition between Band and Orchestra.

This flier announces a fund-raiser at the old New Tabernacle Fourth Baptist Church on Palmetto Street, probably from the 1930s. The program included a talk by the Reverend Daniel Joseph Jenkins on why one of his bands had been arrested in the North. Occasionally Jenkins Orphanage bands were detained—once in London, England—for causing a disturbance on public streets, given the attention they got when they performed on street corners. (Charleston Jazz Initiative.)

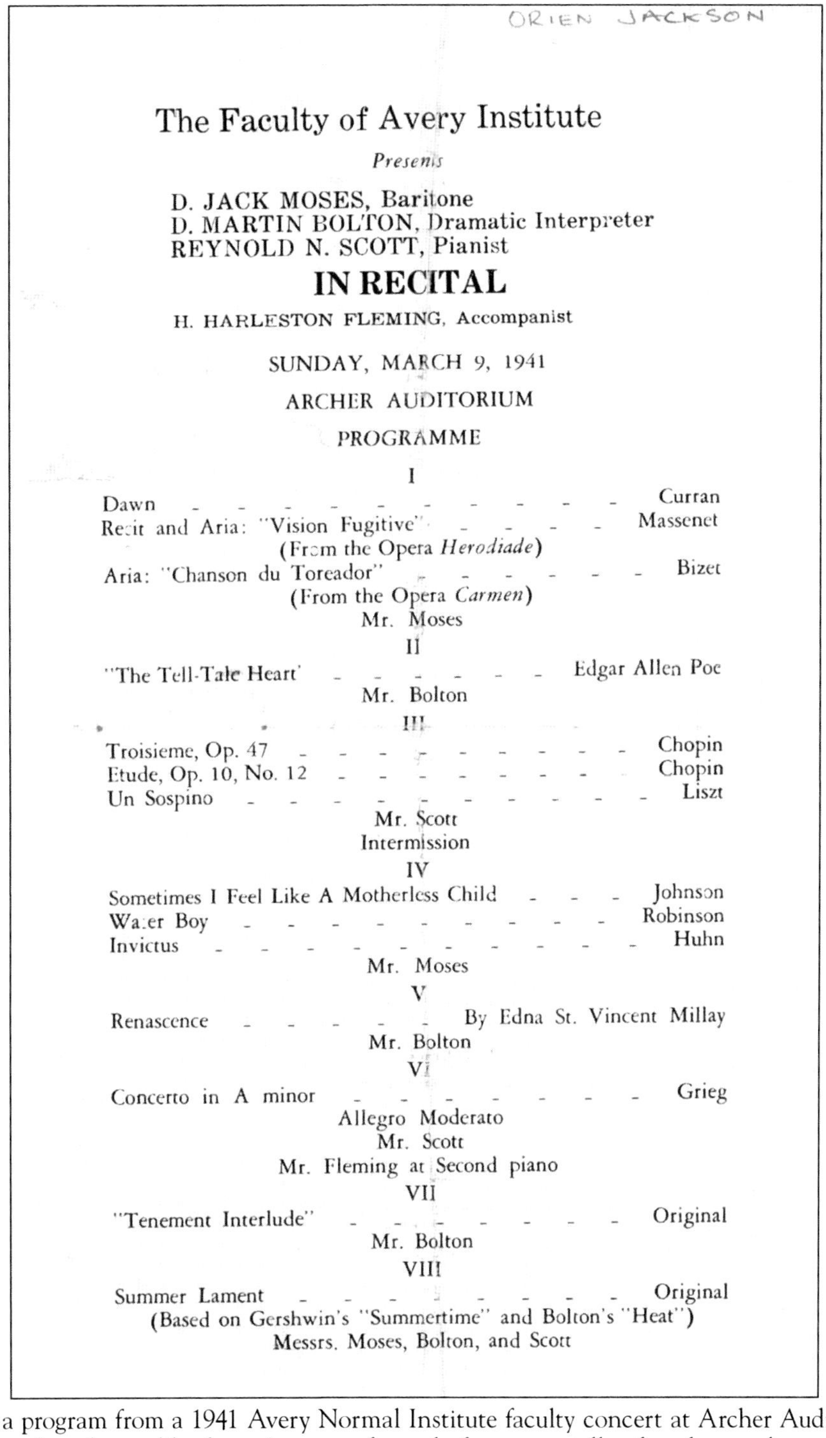

ORIEN JACKSON

The Faculty of Avery Institute

Presents

D. JACK MOSES, Baritone
D. MARTIN BOLTON, Dramatic Interpreter
REYNOLD N. SCOTT, Pianist

IN RECITAL

H. HARLESTON FLEMING, Accompanist

SUNDAY, MARCH 9, 1941

ARCHER AUDITORIUM

PROGRAMME

I

Dawn - - - - - - - - - - - - - Curran
Recit and Aria: "Vision Fugitive" - - - - - Massenet
(From the Opera *Herodiade*)
Aria: "Chanson du Toreador" - - - - - - - Bizet
(From the Opera *Carmen*)
Mr. Moses

II

"The Tell-Tale Heart" - - - - - - - Edgar Allen Poe
Mr. Bolton

III

Troisieme, Op. 47 - - - - - - - - - - Chopin
Etude, Op. 10, No. 12 - - - - - - - - Chopin
Un Sospino - - - - - - - - - - - - Liszt
Mr. Scott
Intermission

IV

Sometimes I Feel Like A Motherless Child - - - Johnson
Water Boy - - - - - - - - - - - - Robinson
Invictus - - - - - - - - - - - - - Huhn
Mr. Moses

V

Renascence - - - - - - By Edna St. Vincent Millay
Mr. Bolton

VI

Concerto in A minor - - - - - - - - - - Grieg
Allegro Moderato
Mr. Scott
Mr. Fleming at Second piano

VII

"Tenement Interlude" - - - - - - - - - Original
Mr. Bolton

VIII

Summer Lament - - - - - - - - - - - Original
(Based on Gershwin's "Summertime" and Bolton's "Heat")
Messrs. Moses, Bolton, and Scott

This is a program from a 1941 Avery Normal Institute faculty concert at Archer Auditorium. Faculty and students alike from Avery performed often, especially after the arts became more emphasized at the school in the 1920s. Archer Auditorium was also important to music in black Charleston. Many musicians who became performers later in life learned music and played in school bands there. (Avery Research Center.)

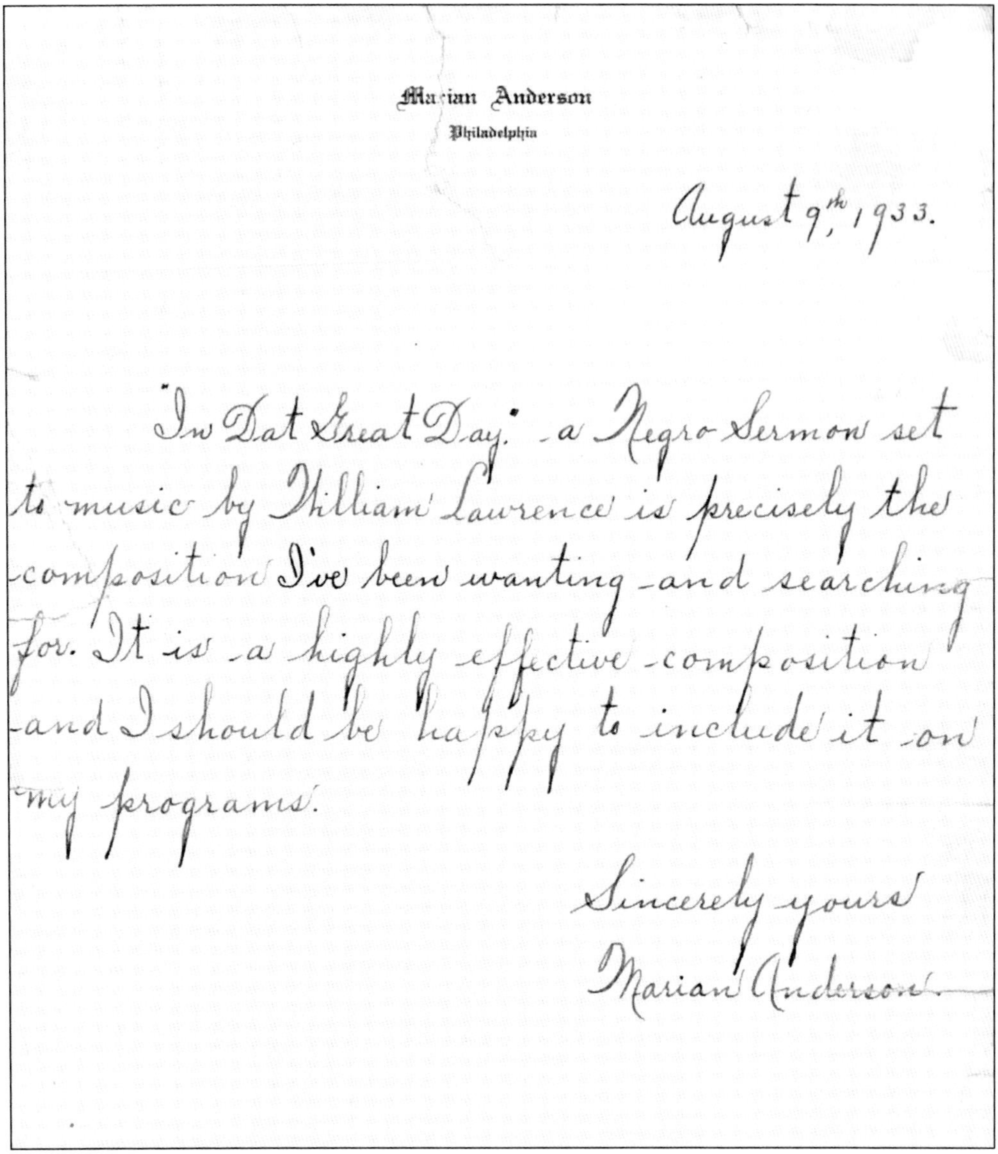

Marian Anderson

Philadelphia

August 9th, 1933.

"In Dat Great Day" - a Negro Sermon set to music by William Lawrence is precisely the composition I've been wanting - and searching for. It is a highly effective composition and I should be happy to include it on my programs.

Sincerely yours

Marian Anderson

Shown here is a 1933 letter from legendary singer Marian Anderson lauding the composition skills of Charleston's William Lawrence. Lawrence was known around the country as a composer and was among the ranks of other composers such as Charles Marsh, Virgil Thomson, William Schuman, Margaret Bonds, Clarence Cameron White, Emerson Whithorne, and Noel DaCosta. (Avery Research Center.)

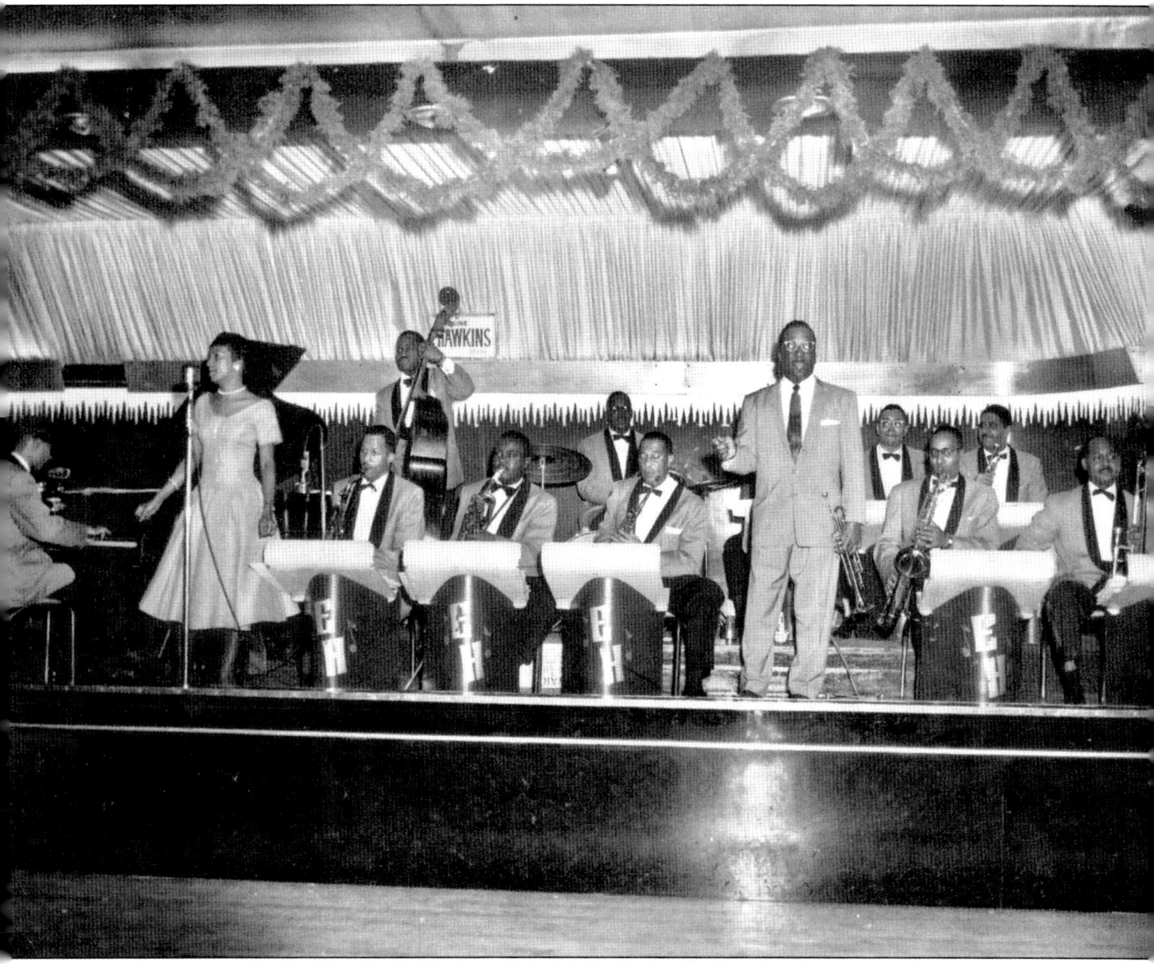

The Erskine Hawkins Orchestra featured Charleston's St. Julian Dash. The orchestra was one of the most famous and important jazz orchestras in American history. It started at Alabama State College in Montgomery, Alabama, and was originally known as the Collegians. Dash went to Alabama State, where he joined the band, after graduating from Avery. Dash left the school to go to New York City, where he rejoined the band after it got there under Hawkins's name. For a long time, the orchestra was one of the house bands at the Savoy Ballroom, one of the most important and popular dance halls in New York City. (Charleston Jazz Initiative.)

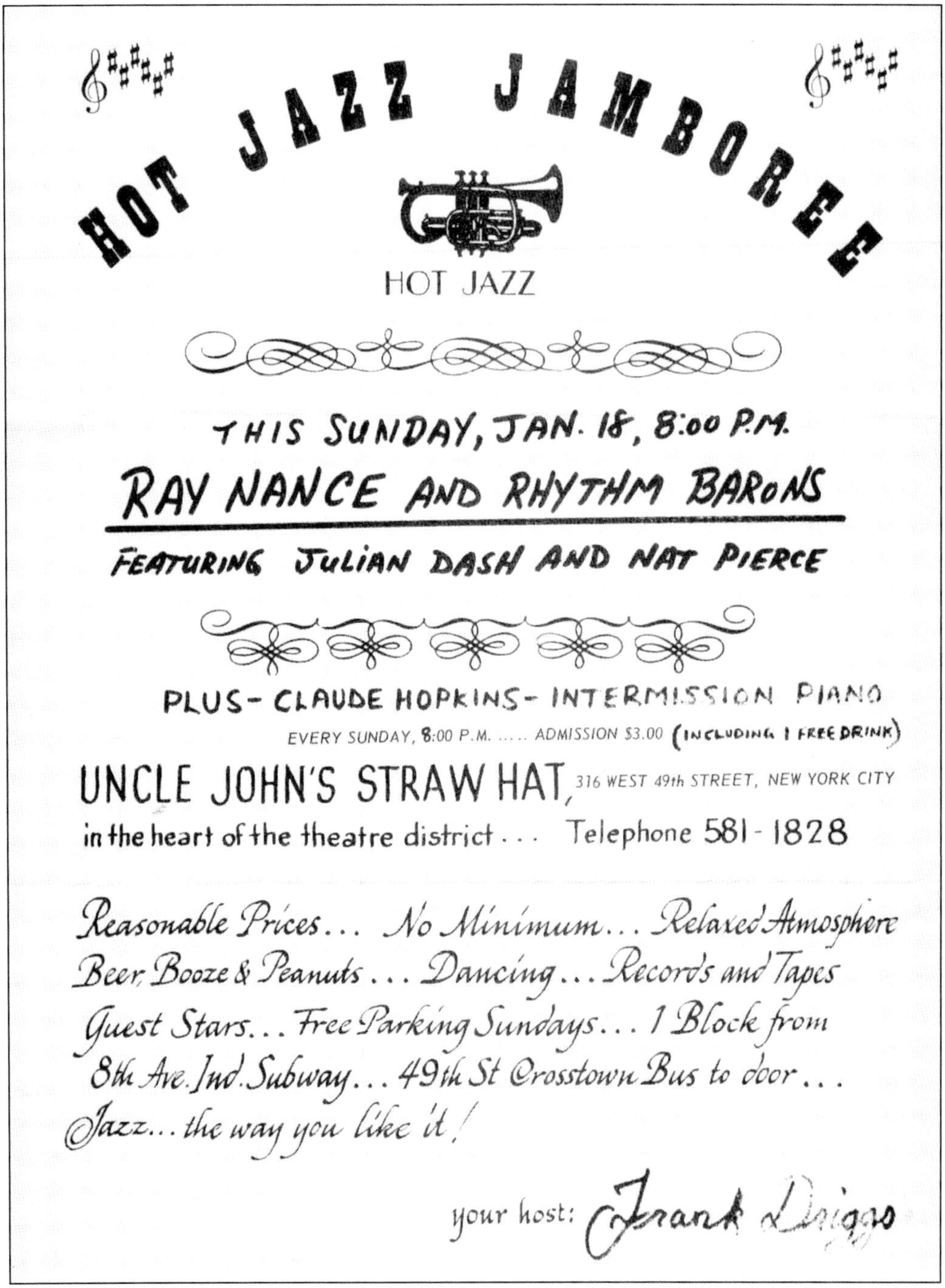

This is a flier for a jazz dance in New York City (probably in the 1950s) that included Charleston's St. Julian Dash. Typical of musicians from Charleston, Dash did other work for a living. While recording and performing music in New York City, he had a career working for Merrill Lynch. (Charleston Jazz Initiative.)

St. Julian Bennett Dash

(JULIAN DASH)

I was born April 9, 1916 in Charleston, South Carolina. I attended Avery Institute, graduating in 1934. During my junior and senior year at Avery, I played with the Night Hawks Orchestra...at that time, Charleston's leading orchestra.

After graduating from Avery, I attended Alabama State Teachers College in Montgomery, Alabama on a music scholarship. While attending Alabama State I was a member of the Collegians, the number one jazz orchestra of the three jazz outfits on the campus; a member of the symphony band and the marching band. These bands traveled throughout the states playing for dances, concerts, basketball and football games.

In 1939 in collaboration with Erskine Hawkins and William Johnson, "Tuxedo Junction" was composed. The Erskine Hawkins Orchestra used this tune as their theme song. "Tuxedo Junction" was later made into a standard hit by the late Glenn Miller and his band. "Tuxedo Junction" has been recorded by over 50 bands, singers and various musical groups since its introduction.

In 1952 I became a member of the American Society of Composers, Authors and Publishers.

During my association with Erskine Hawkins Orchestra I was the featured tenor saxophone soloist.

Aside from recording with Erskine Hawkins, I've recorded with Buck Clayton and Jimmie Rushing plus recording numerous titles under my name. Some of the record companies I've recorded for are Mercury, Signature, Mello-Roll, Sittin In and Vee Jay.

...Discography...

"My Silent Love" ....Signature, Mello-Roll
"Goin Along" ....Signature, Mello-Roll
"Zig-Zag" ....Vee Jay
"Zero" ....Vee Jay
"So Let It Be" ....Vee Jay
"Rhythm Punch" ....Vee Jay
"Deacon Dash" ....Mercury
"Fire-eater" ....Mercury
"Blue Velvet" ....Mercury
"Hot Rod" ....Sitin In
"Holiday In Cuba" ....Sitin In
"No Soap" ....Bluebird
"Double Shot" ....King
"Creamin" ....Signature, Mello-Roll

This is a biography composed by St. Julian Dash. He comes from a very prominent and well-thought-of family in Charleston. Formal education was very important in their lives, and everyone strove for excellence no matter their individual endeavors. They have all made marks in life and are proud of their Charleston heritage. Dash's niece, Julie Dash, is a world-renowned filmmaker, probably best known for *Daughters of the Dust*, set in the South Carolina Lowcountry. (Charleston Jazz Initiative.)

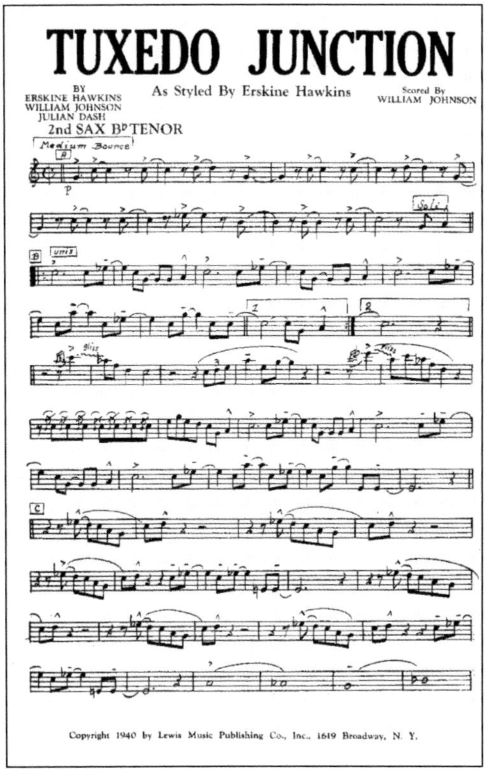

This is sheet music for "Tuxedo Junction," a big 1940s hit for the famous Erskine Hawkins Orchestra cowritten in 1939 by Charleston's St. Julian Dash. The song is named after a section of Birmingham, Alabama, that featured eateries, nightclubs, and other businesses. It is believed that the area got its name from a clothing store located just down the street from the main pavilion where the bands would play. The story goes that partygoers would emerge from the streetcars wearing their work clothes, unacceptable attire for the majority of clubs in Tuxedo Junction. People wanted to put on their best clothes when they went to Tuxedo Junction. A clothing store in the area would rent tuxedos to those who were not properly dressed. These people would, in turn, trade in the clothes they had on as collateral. Thus the area came to be known as the streetcar junction where a person could get a tuxedo. (Charleston Jazz Initiative.)

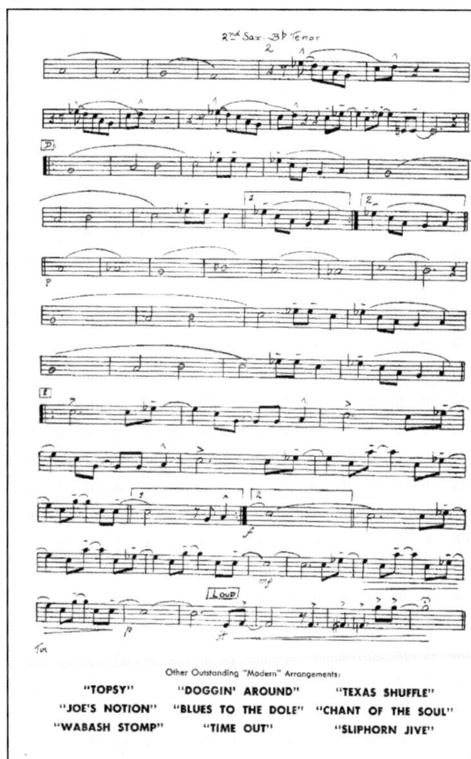

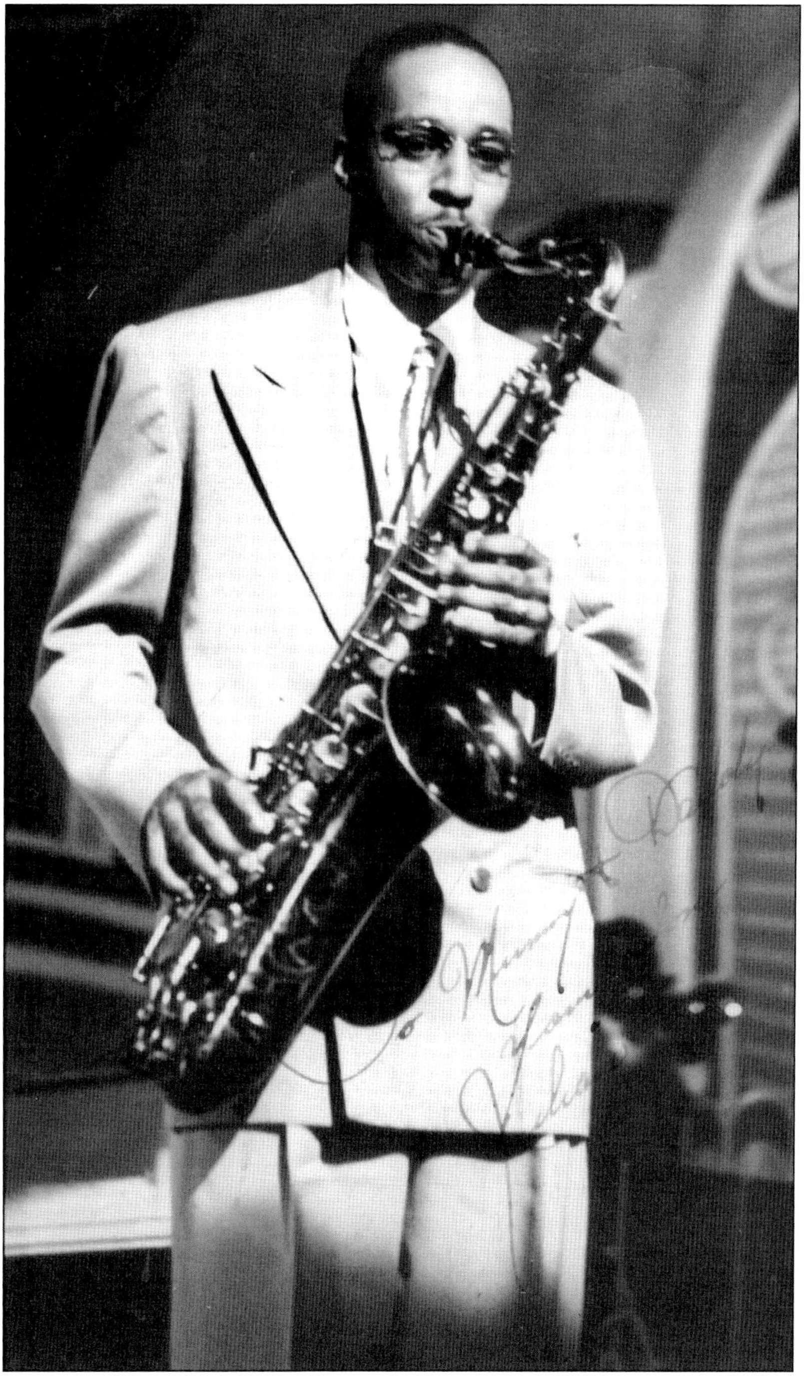

This is a portrait of St. Julian Dash. He was known to be mild mannered, deliberate in his demeanor, and rational in thought and delivery of his music. He was regarded by his musical contemporaries as one of the strongest tenor saxophone soloists in the country. He was a stalwart in the Erskine Hawkins Orchestra, but he played and recorded with many other musicians. He was much appreciated in Europe as well. Critics appreciated the way he resolved musical ideas in his solos. (Charleston Jazz Initiative.)

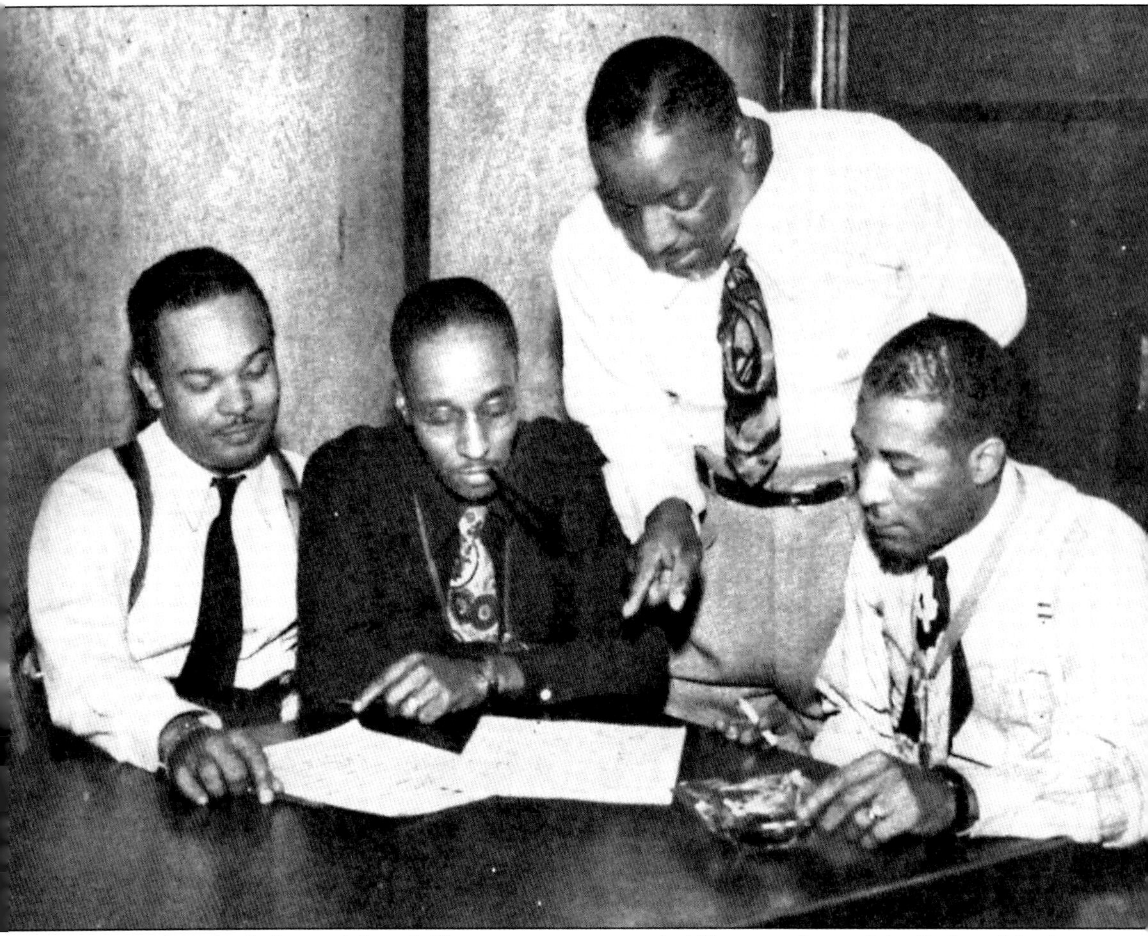

St. Julian Dash (second from left) goes over music with fellow members of the Erskine Hawkins Orchestra. Dash was well within the tradition of Charleston musicians in that he could write and play music with the best of them. His skills were respected by his colleagues and contemporaries. (Charleston Jazz Initiative.)

This is the cover of the sheet music for the big-band jazz evergreen "Tuxedo Junction," cowritten by Charlestonian St. Julian Dash. The song came out of the Erskine Hawkins Orchestra but it got most exposure from the famous Glenn Miller Orchestra, the toast of the World War II big-band era. (Charleston Jazz Initiative.)

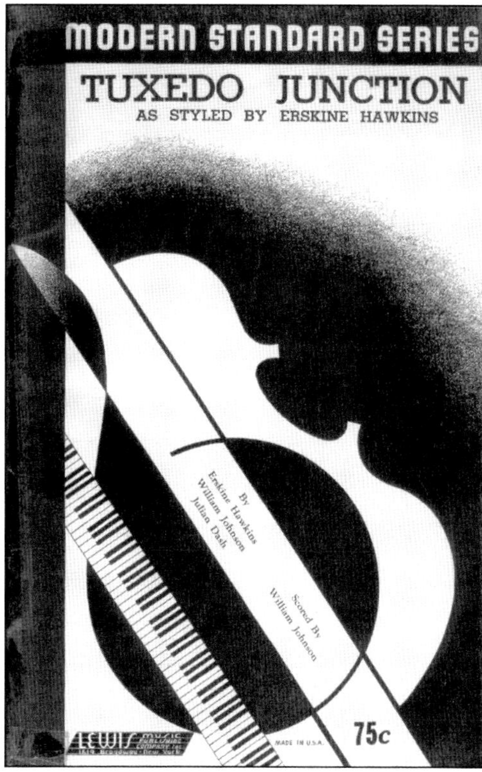

1867 "BROADENING THE HORIZONS OF MIND, HEART AND SPIRIT" 1967

TALLADEGA COLLEGE

TALLADEGA, ALABAMA 35160

ALUMNI - PUBLIC RELATIONS
OFFICE OF THE DIRECTOR

July 30, 1969

AREA CODE 205
TELEPHONE 362-3230

Dear St. Julian:

It was very good seeing you again - at the Eastern Alumni Regional last weekend at Vassar.

Because of your long affiliation with the college, and your obvious interest in it and the many friends you have who attended Talladega College, the thought occurs that you just ought to be on our mailing list for graduates, former students and employees, and those who work with and through our alumni clubs.

This letter comes, then, to advise that if there is no objection on your part, you are hereafter an adopted Talladegan and are invited and expected to participate in all gatherings and activities of the Alumni Club in your area, and will hereafter get such mailings as we make from time to time to Talladegans.

Meanwhile, welcome aboard and thanks very much for having made the Vassar annual such a marvelous occasion.

Sincerely,

John H. McCray

John H. McCray, Director
Alumni-Public Relations

JHMcC:bm

Mr. St. Julian Dash
522 W. 157th St., Apt. 2-C
New York, New York 10032

UNDER THE AUSPICES OF THE AMERICAN MISSIONARY ASSOCIATION

This is a letter inviting St. Julian Dash to become an honorary alumnus of Talladega College by John McCray, a noted Charleston journalist. Talladega, located in Alabama, was founded by the American Missionary Association, which founded Avery Normal Institute in Charleston as well as other black institutions of higher learning in the South. (Charleston Jazz Initiative.)

'E The People Sept 22/69 Vol 23 No 15

Two veteran jazzmen bring special verve to Home Office

Dash, Benford led distinguished musical careers in '40s, '50s

Jazz is alive and well at Merrill Lynch. Indeed, two MLers, Julian Dash and Tommy Benford, are playing, talking, and thinking in terms of the original American art form everyday.

"Actually," says Julian, who's head receptionist on 70 Pine Street's tenth floor, "it can be said that I lead two lives. First, there's my Merrill Lynch world by day, and then my world of music during the evenings and on weekends."

Both Tommy and Julian are well known figures in the jazz music field. Tommy, an EDP messenger, has been a drummer with several jazz greats—Coleman Hawkins and Jelly Roll Morton to name just two. Julian spent the greater part of his music career playing tenor sax with the Erskine Hawkins band. He is the co-composer of "Tuxedo Junction," a number made famous by the late Glenn Miller.

Julian and Tommy are still active in the contemporary jazz scene and frequently play at concerts, dances, and private parties. In addition, Juli-

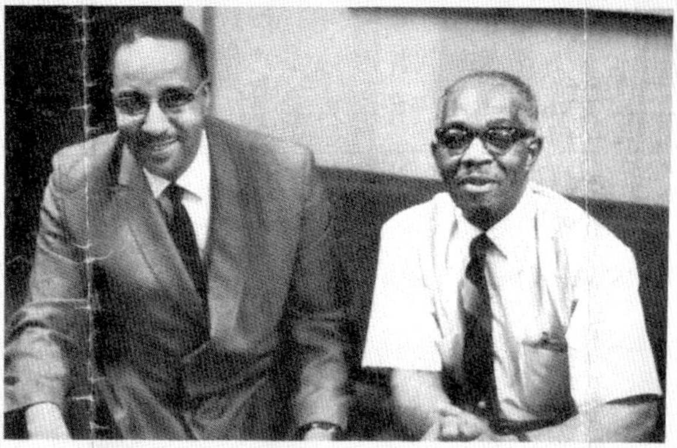

Julian Dash (l.) and Tommy Benford sitting in tenth floor reception area of 70 Pine St. Both men were mentioned in recent New York Times article on old-time jazz greats which said that many jazz musicians are now working on Wall Street.

He is also president of a scholarship aid group in Charleston, S. C. which gives college grants to students from minority groups.

Julian still finds time to make recordings (his latest is "Gee Baby, Ain't I Good to You" on the "Master Jazz" label) and to talk about jazz: "How many of us realize," he asks, "that jazz is America's only original contribution to the musical art form? ... that all Americans can be proud of."

Tommy Benford

Tommy began playing drums at the age of nine. While still a teenager, he toured Europe with the Jenkens Orphanage band. "The greatest thrill was being invited to Buckingham Palace," he says. "We played for the entire royal family, including the young princesses, Elizabeth and Mar-

in 1930, opened Ben Marten's ... era with Eddie South, the "Dark ... gel of the Violin." He played ... Fats Waller before leaving for a ... of Europe in 1932 with Eddie Sr... Django Rhinehart, and Willie L... "In 1940," says Tommy, "we ... caught in Belgium when the ... man army invaded. As soon as ... escaped, we began working our ... to Lisbon where we were able to ... a ship back to the United State...

During the next few years ... toured U.S. military camps with E... Blake and Noble Sissle. In the ... maining years he played and re... ed with Sidney Bechet, Cole... Hawkins, Benny Carter, Wild Bill ... ison, Willie "The Lion" Smith, ... Muggsy Spanier. His last Euro... tour was in 1960 with the "... Train."

Tommy, who joined the firm ... 1963, has dreams of forming a... band. "You can't imagine how m... musical talent there is in M... Lynch," he says. "We could ge... gether a great group — musi... known throughout the jazz wor... know of at least 15 accompli...

St. Julian Dash (left) and Tommy Benford were two of the most important jazz musicians to come out of Charleston in the mid-20th century. They are profiled here in a 1969 edition of *We The People*. Dash was a saxophonist who gained prominence with the Erskine Hawkins Orchestra, while Benford was a drummer who traveled the world with the likes of Louis Armstrong and is credited by some with teaching drumming to the famous Chick Webb. (Charleston Jazz Initiative.)

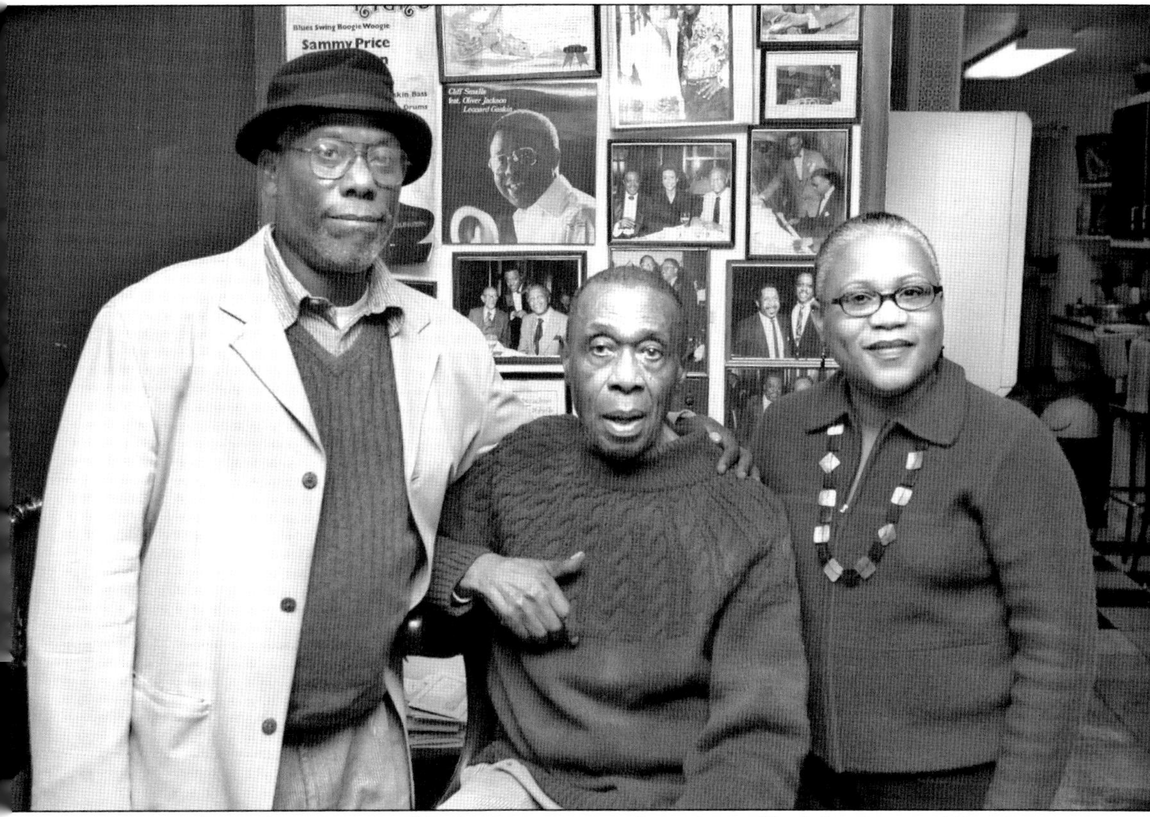

Cliff Smalls (center), an 87-year-old Charleston piano player, hosted Jack McCray and Dr. Karen Chandler of the Charleston Jazz Initiative at his home in Brooklyn, New York, in 2006. Smalls has played with many of the jazz greats, beginning in the 1930s. For a long time, he was Billy Eckstine's musical director, and he was later musical director for William "Smokey" Robinson. Smalls, a trombonist and pianist, learned music from his father in Charleston, where he attended Burke High School. He was also a member of the Carolina Cottonpickers, a territorial band from Charleston that toured the country in the 1930s and 1940s. Smalls played for many years with the Sy Oliver Orchestra. He still plays and directs a band in Brooklyn, New York. (Charleston Jazz Initiative.)

ORPHAN AID SOCIETY BOARD

MRS. E. C. JENKINS, PRESIDENT
MRS. F. A. DICKINSON, SECRETARY
REV. P. G. DANIELS, V-PRES. & TREAS.
J. E. DOWLING, SUPT.
MISS D. McLEOD
MR. W. P. HAMILTON
MR. F. R. BLANCHARD
MR. T. M. FURMAN, CHR.

ALL MONEY IS FIRST DEPOSITED IN CAROLINA SAVINGS BANK AND DRAWN ON CHECKS MADE OUT BY SECRETARY AND SIGNED BY TREASURER.

Jenkins Orphanage Institute

Founded December 16, 1891

THE ORPHAN AID SOCIETY

(Incorporated Name)

REV. D. J. JENKINS, Founder

Box 851

CHARLESTON, S. C.

OUR ADVISORY BOARD OF LEADING WHITE CITIZENS

MR. W. H. COGSWELL, JR.
MR. JOHN I. COSGROVE
MR. I'ON RHETT
MR. S. M. DOYLE
MR. L. A. R. NELSON
MR. SIDNEY RITTENBURG
MR. A. J. RILEY, SECRETARY
MR. J. F. RILEY, CHAIRMAN
MR. C. L. VANN, CERTIFIED ACCOUNTANT AUDITOR

FOR REFERENCE
EX-MAYOR THOS. P. STONEY

June 24, 1941

TO WHOM THIS MAY CONCERN:

This is to certify that the Bearer, Wilbur Carter, (Musician) is hereby honorably released from the Jenkins Orphanage, to take up custody with his mother, Mrs. Caroline Brown, who resides at 146 Coming Street, Charleston, South Carolina.

He carries with him the prayers of the Management of the Institution.

Signed: ORPHAN AID SOCIETY

Eloise C. Jenkins PRES.
Paul G. Daniels V. PRES.
Florence A. Dickinson SEC'Y.
J. E. Dowling SUPT.

This is a 1941 certificate of release from the Jenkins Orphanage for Wilbur Carter, a trumpeter in the orphanage bands. Carter settled in Schenectady, New York, upon release from Jenkins, where he had a successful career as a jazz player. He and his sister, Elizabeth, resided at the orphanage in the 1920s and 1930s as children. Carter could not walk until a benefactor paid for an operation that enabled him to get on his feet on crutches. His late sister told the story of a wealthy woman driving by one day who, upon seeing Carter crawling on the ground, inquired about his health and decided to help him. (Charleston Jazz Initiative.)

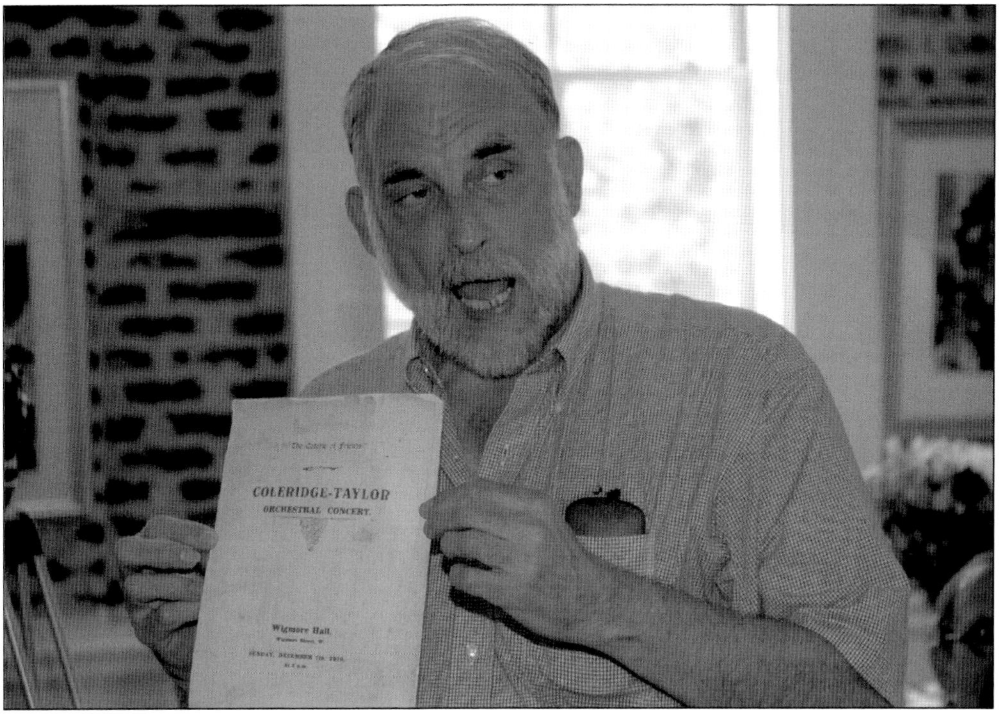

Author Jeffrey Green visited Charleston in 2005 to participated in the Charleston Jazz Initiative's annual conference. Here he explains how Edmund Thornton Jenkins admired and used the work of composer Samuel Coleridge-Taylor early in the 20th century in England. (Charleston Jazz Initiative.)

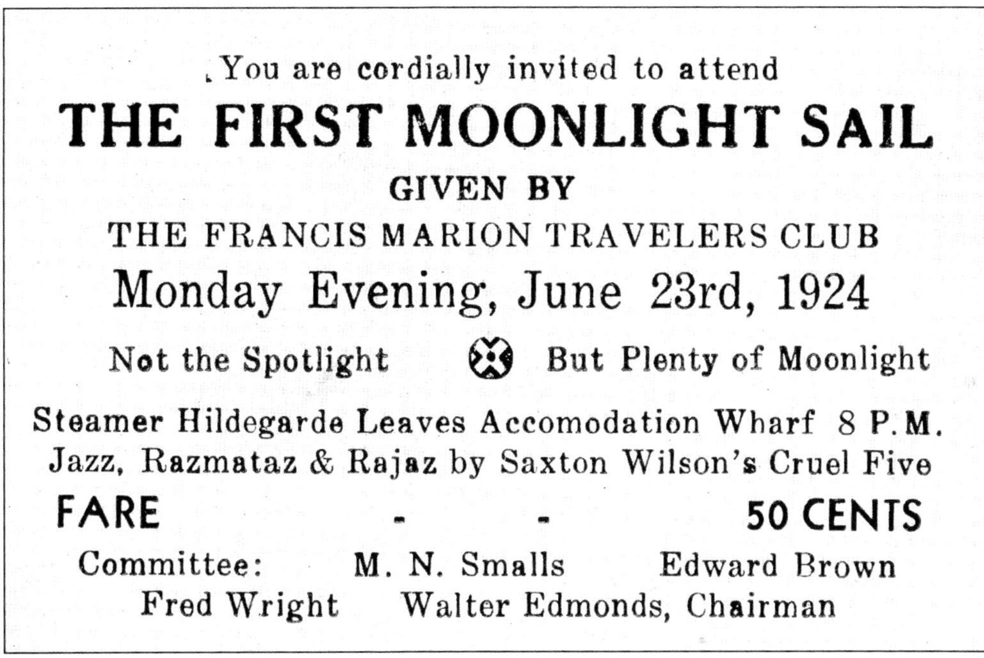

You are cordially invited to attend

THE FIRST MOONLIGHT SAIL

GIVEN BY

THE FRANCIS MARION TRAVELERS CLUB

Monday Evening, June 23rd, 1924

Not the Spotlight ✠ **But Plenty of Moonlight**

Steamer Hildegarde Leaves Accomodation Wharf 8 P. M.

Jazz, Razmataz & Rajaz by Saxton Wilson's Cruel Five

FARE - - 50 CENTS

Committee: M. N. Smalls Edward Brown
Fred Wright Walter Edmonds, Chairman

Social clubs were very popular in Charleston over much of the 20th century, as were boat rides. This 1924 venture happened at night and probably packed them in. (Avery Research Center.)

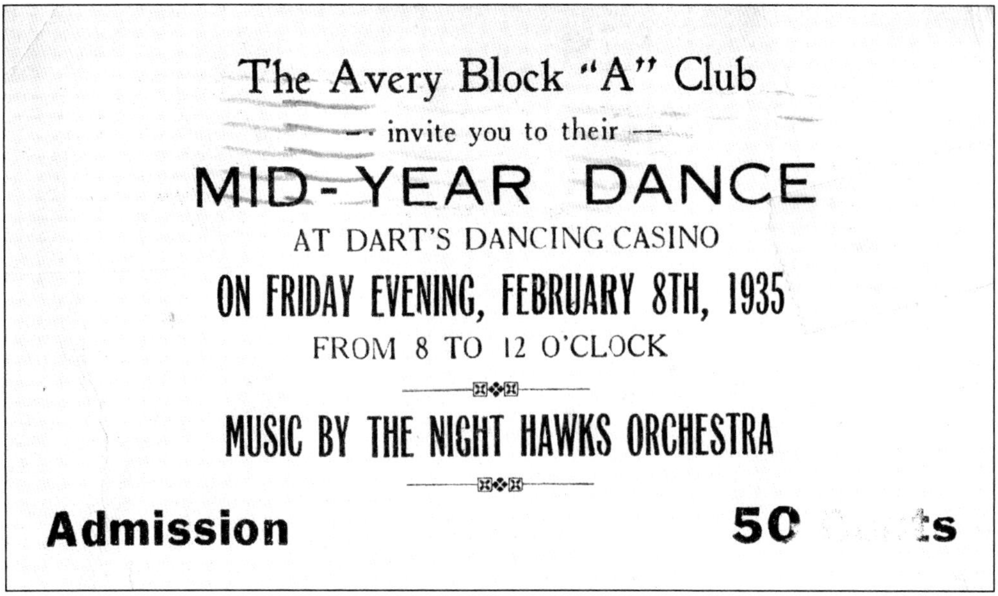
The Avery Block "A" Club

— invite you to their —

MID-YEAR DANCE

AT DART'S DANCING CASINO

ON FRIDAY EVENING, FEBRUARY 8TH, 1935

FROM 8 TO 12 O'CLOCK

MUSIC BY THE NIGHT HAWKS ORCHESTRA

Admission **50 C[illegible]ts**

As well as providing top-notch education to its students, the Avery Normal Institute provided off-campus social outlets for them was well. This dance was held at Dart's Dancing Casino, located across town from the Bull Street school. (Avery Research Center.)

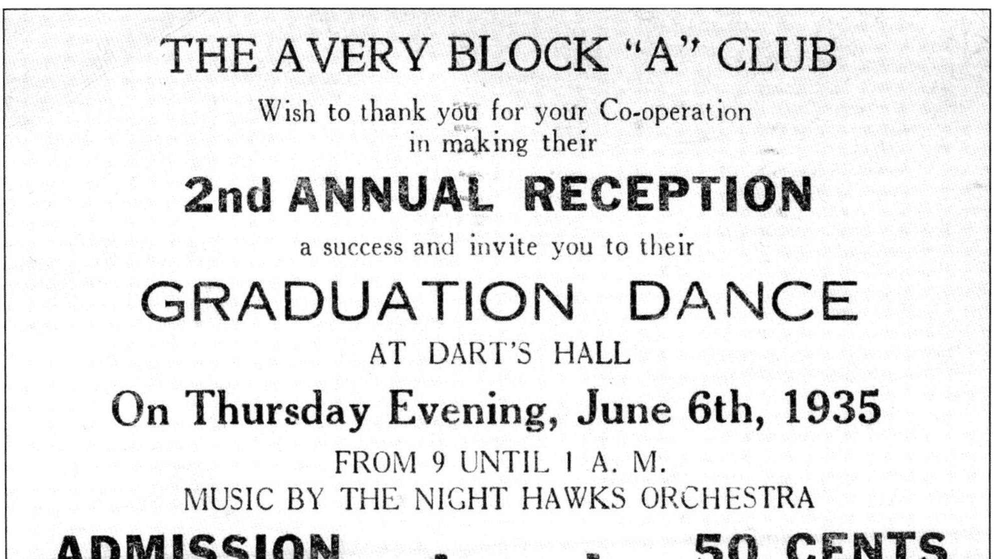
THE AVERY BLOCK "A" CLUB

Wish to thank you for your Co-operation
in making their

2nd ANNUAL RECEPTION

a success and invite you to their

GRADUATION DANCE

AT DART'S HALL

On Thursday Evening, June 6th, 1935

FROM 9 UNTIL 1 A. M.

MUSIC BY THE NIGHT HAWKS ORCHESTRA

ADMISSION - - 50 CENTS

The Avery Block A Club held many social events. This one celebrated graduation in 1935 and featured the Night Hawks band. (Avery Research Center.)

African American improvisation is present in the concept for this event. As sophisticated as Charleston blacks were, this group adopted a country theme for its 1921 dance. The music by Prof. W. Saxton Wilson's Orchestra undoubtedly had a country flavor, although it was known for jazz and popular music. This event also included a country costume contest. (Avery Research Center.)

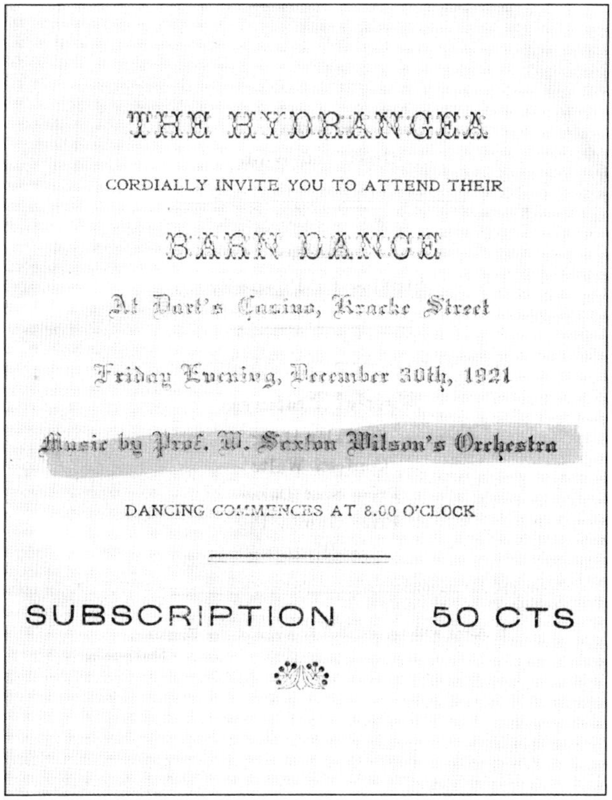
THE HYDRANGEA

CORDIALLY INVITE YOU TO ATTEND THEIR

BARN DANCE

At Dart's Casino, Kracke Street

Friday Evening, December 30th, 1921

Music by Prof. W. Saxton Wilson's Orchestra

DANCING COMMENCES AT 8.00 O'CLOCK

SUBSCRIPTION 50 CTS

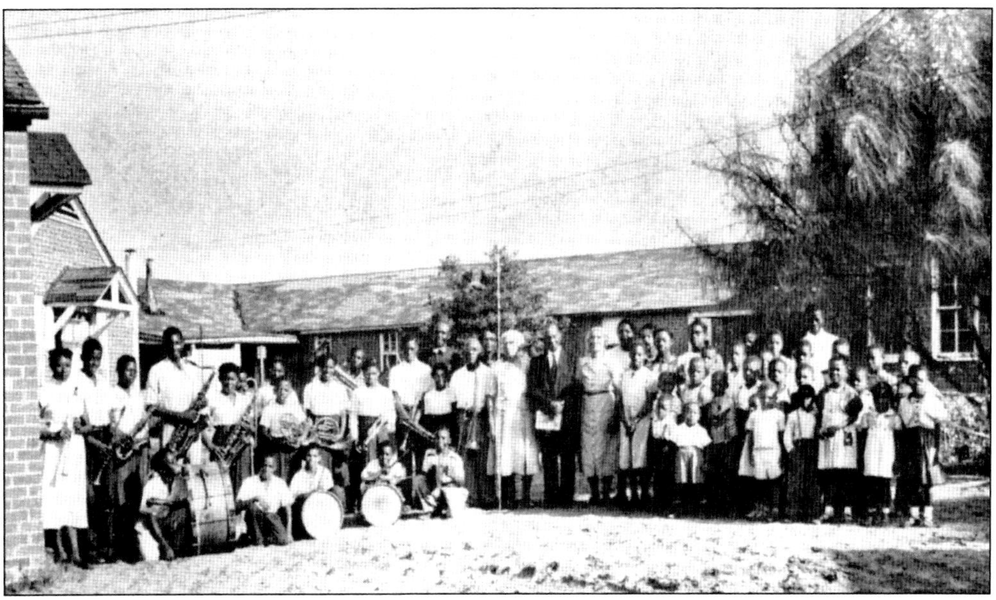

Jenkins Orphanage band members, other residents, and staff are pictured in 1954 on the North Charleston campus. Eloise C. Jenkins (center, left of the man in a suit), widow of the Reverend Daniel Joseph Jenkins, had worked with the organization since 1902. She was president from 1938, a year after Reverend Jenkins died, until 1941, when she resigned. She stayed on as a clerical worker. (Avery Research Center.)

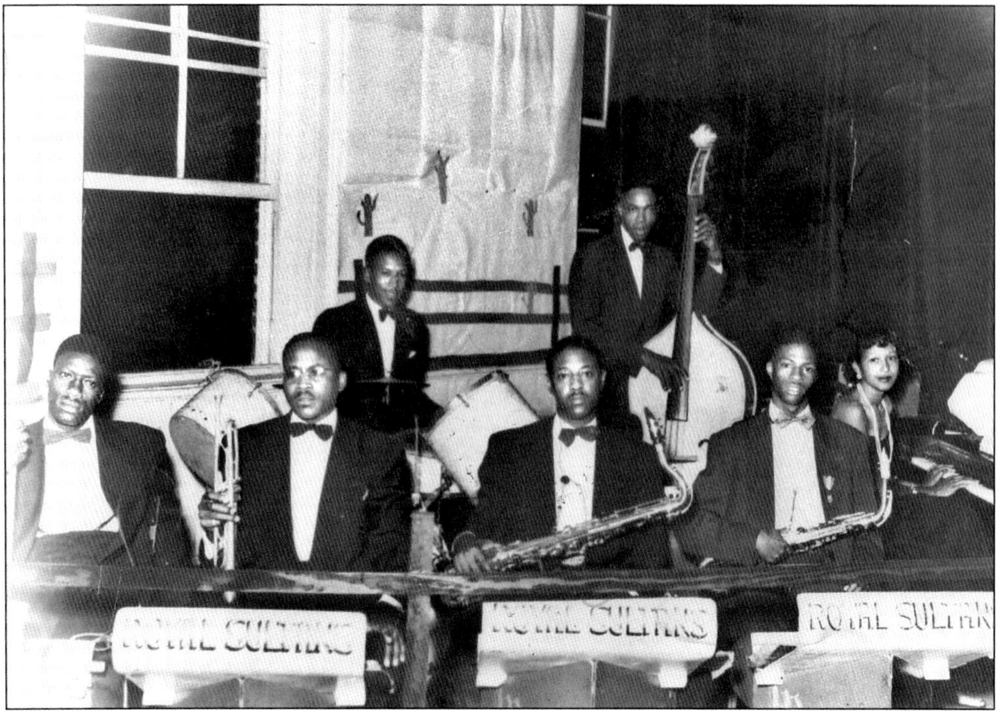

The Royal Sultans in 1951 comprised (from left to right) James Lawrence, Fletcher Linton, E. Green, W. Perrineau, William Louis Gilliard, unidentified, and C. Peters. (Avery Research Center.)

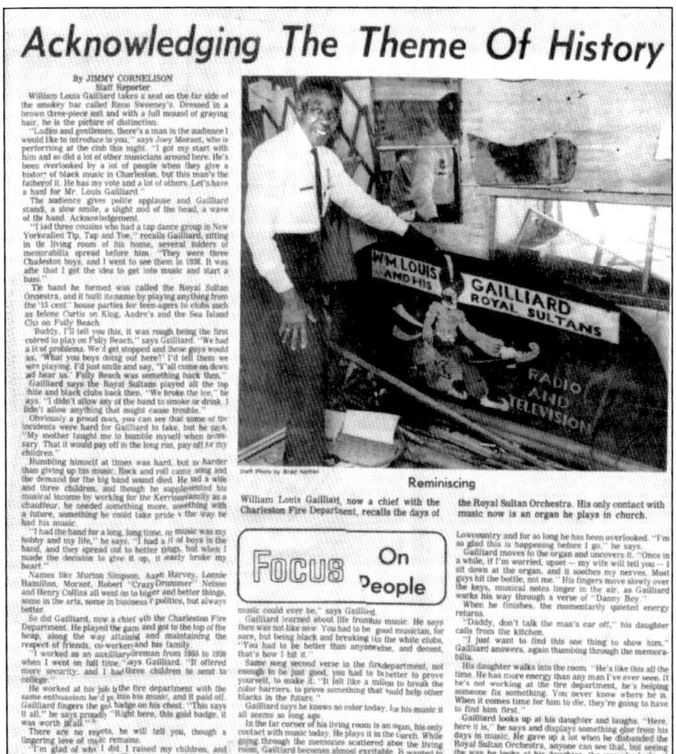

Acknowledging The Theme Of History

By JIMMY CORNELISON
Staff Reporter

William Louis Gailliard takes a seat on the far side of the smokey bar called Reno Sweeney's. Dressed in a brown three-piece suit and with a full mound of graying hair, he is the picture of distinction.

"Ladies and gentlemen, there's a man in the audience I would like to introduce to you," says Joey Morant, who is performing at the club this night. "I got my start with him and so did a lot of other musicians around here. He's been overlooked by a lot of people when they give a history of black music in Charleston, but this man's the father of it. He has my vote and a lot of others. Let's have a hand for Mr. Louis Gailliard."

The audience gives polite applause and Gailliard stands, a slow smile, a slight nod of the head, a wave of the hand. Acknowledgement.

"I had three cousins who had a tap dance group in New York called Tip, Tap and Toe," recalls Gailliard, sitting in the living room of his home, several folders of memorabilia spread before him. "They were three Charleston boys, and I went to see them in 1938. It was after that I got the idea to get into music and start a band."

The band he formed was called the Royal Sultan Orchestra, and it built its name by playing anything from the "15 cent" house parties for teen-agers to clubs such as Ielene Curtis on King, Andre's and the Sea Island Club on Folly Beach.

"Buddy, I'll tell you this, it was rough being the first colored to play on Folly Beach," says Gailliard. "We had a lot of problems. We'd get stopped and these guys would ask, 'What you boys doing out here?' I'd tell them we were playing. I'd just smile and say, 'Y'all come on down and hear us.' Folly Beach was something back then."

Gailliard says the Royal Sultans played all the top white and black clubs back then. "We broke the ice," he says. "I didn't allow any of the band to smoke or drink. I didn't allow anything that might cause trouble."

Obviously a proud man, you can see that some of the incidents were hard for Gailliard to take, but he says, "My mother taught me to humble myself when necessary. That it would pay off in the long run, pay off for my children."

Humbling himself at times was hard, but no harder than giving up his music. Rock and roll came along and the demand for the big band sound died. He had a wife and three children, and though he supplemented his musical income by working for the Kerrison family as a chauffeur, he needed something more, something with a future, something he could take pride in the way he had his music.

"I had the band for a long, long time, my music was my hobby and my life," he says. "I had a lot of boys in the band, and they spread out to better things, but when I made the decision to give it up, it nearly broke my heart."

Names like Murton Simpson, Aaron Harvey, Lonnie Hamilton, Morant, Robert "Crazy Drummer" Nelson and Henry Collins all went on to bigger and better things, some in the arts, some in business or politics, but always better.

So did Gailliard, now a chief with the Charleston Fire Department. He played the game and got to the top of the heap, along the way attaining and maintaining the respect of friends, co-workers and his family.

"I worked as an auxilliary fireman from 1955 to 1959 when I went on full time," says Gailliard. "It offered more security, and I had three children to send to college."

He worked at his job in the fire department with the same enthusiasm he'd put into his music, and it paid off. Gailliard fingers the gold badge on his chest. "This says it all," he says proudly. "Right here, this gold badge, it was worth it all."

There are no regrets, he will tell you, though a lingering love of music remains.

"I'm glad of what I did. I raised my children, and they've turned out good. That's more fulfilling than music could ever be," says Gailliard.

Gailliard learned about life from his music. He says then was not like now. You had to be a good musician, for sure, but being black and breaking into the white clubs, "You had to be better than anyone else, and decent, that's how I hit it."

Same song second verse in the fire department, not enough to be just good, you had to be better to prove yourself, to make it. "It felt like a million to break the color barriers, to prove something that would help other blacks in the future."

Gailliard says he knows no color today, like his music it all seems so long ago.

In the far corner of his living room is an organ, his only contact with music today. He plays it in the church. While going through the memories scattered about the living room, Gailliard becomes almost excitable. He wanted to be remembered for his contribution to music in the Lowcountry and for so long he has been overlooked. "I'm so glad this is happening before I go," he says.

Gailliard moves to the organ and uncovers it. "Once in a while, if I'm worried, upset — my wife will tell you — I sit down at the organ, and it soothes my nerves. Most guys hit the bottle, not me." His fingers move slowly over the keys, musical notes linger in the air, as Gailliard works his way through a verse of "Danny Boy."

When he finishes, the momentarily quieted energy returns.

"Daddy, don't talk the man's ear off," his daughter calls from the kitchen.

"I just want to find this one thing to show him," Gailliard answers, again thumbing through the memorabilia.

His daughter walks into the room. "He's like this all the time. He has more energy than any man I've ever seen. If he's not working at the fire department, he's helping someone fix something. You never know where he is. When it comes time for him to die, they're going to have to find him first."

Gailliard looks up at his daughter and laughs. "Here, here it is," he says and displays something else from his days in music. He gave up a lot when he disbanded the Royal Sultan Orchestra, anyone can see that, but seeing the way he looks at his daughter, the way she looks at him, it's as Gailliard says, "It was worth it."

Staff Photo by Brad Nettles

Reminiscing

William Louis Gailliard, now a chief with the Charleston Fire Department, recalls the days of the Royal Sultan Orchestra. His only contact with music now is an organ he plays in church.

Focus On People

A 1980 edition of the *News and Courier*, the morning paper forerunner of today's *Post and Courier*, published a feature story on Louis William Louis Gilliard, leader of the Royal Sultans. Gilliard was also a well-known Charleston Fire Department captain, and he blazed many trails in Charleston during his lifetime. He was a very congenial person and widely respected and loved around Charleston. Most people smile when they think of him today. (Avery Research Center.)

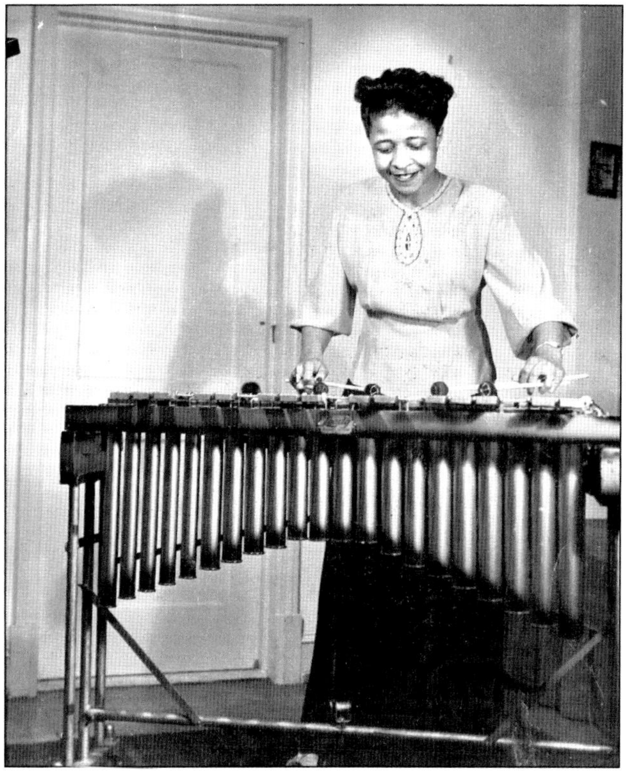

Ray Carter was vibraphonist with the Royal Sultans in 1950, an example of the role of women in Charleston's jazz tradition. Inclusion of the vibes in bands in Charleston also shows the sophistication of the music scene in Charleston. The vibraphone is not a basic instrument and certainly not one found in many early bands. (Avery Research Center.)

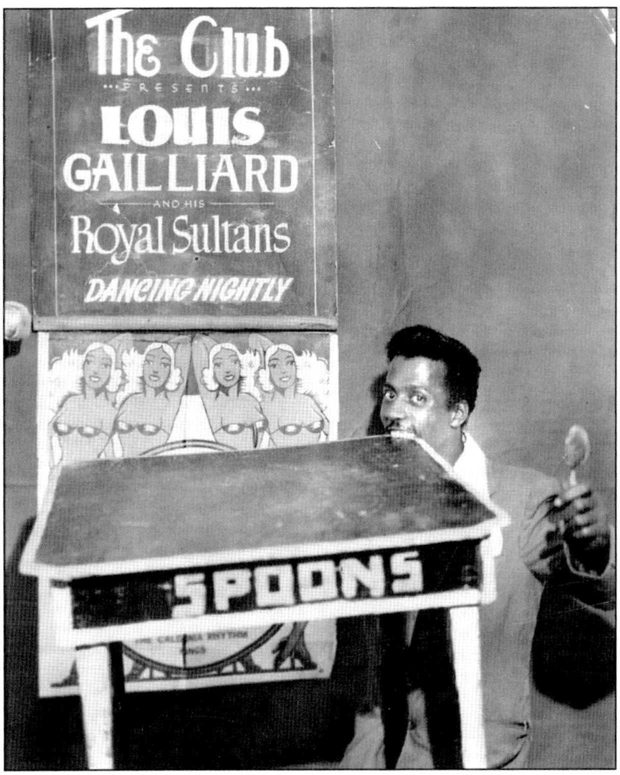

Music can be made from almost anything, and it's certainly in the Southern African American musical tradition to use all sorts of household implements to make music. Kitchen spoons were a favorite around the South, and Charleston was no exception. The musician here was known as "Spoons," and in 1950 he worked The Club with the Royal Sultans. (Avery Research Center.)

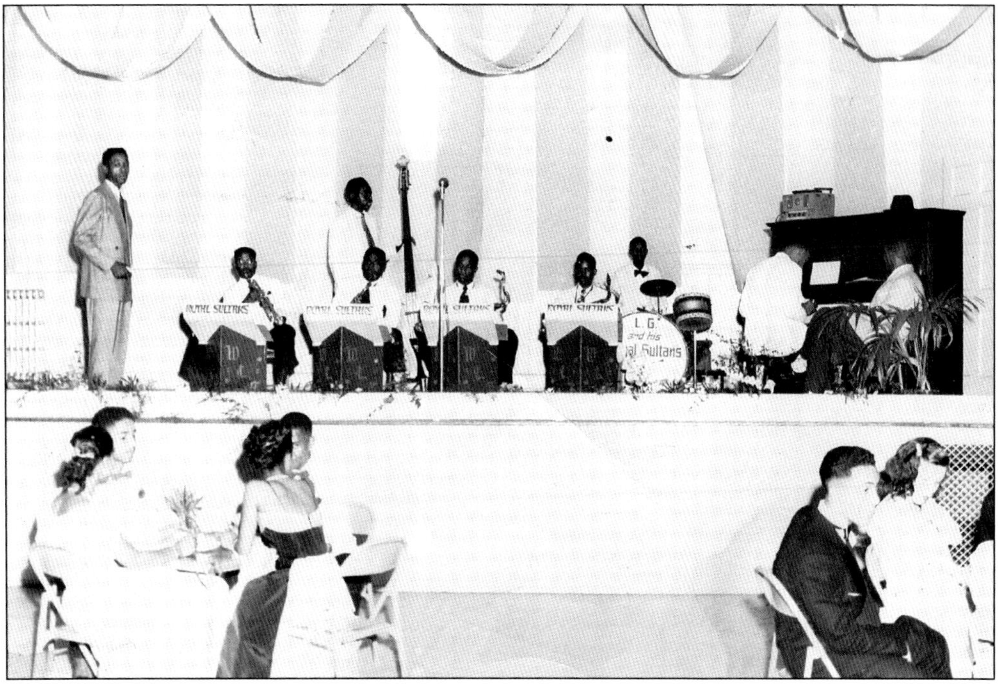

The Royal Sultans performed at the high school prom of the Immaculate Conception School, a Charleston Catholic school for blacks on Coming Street. (Avery Research Center.)

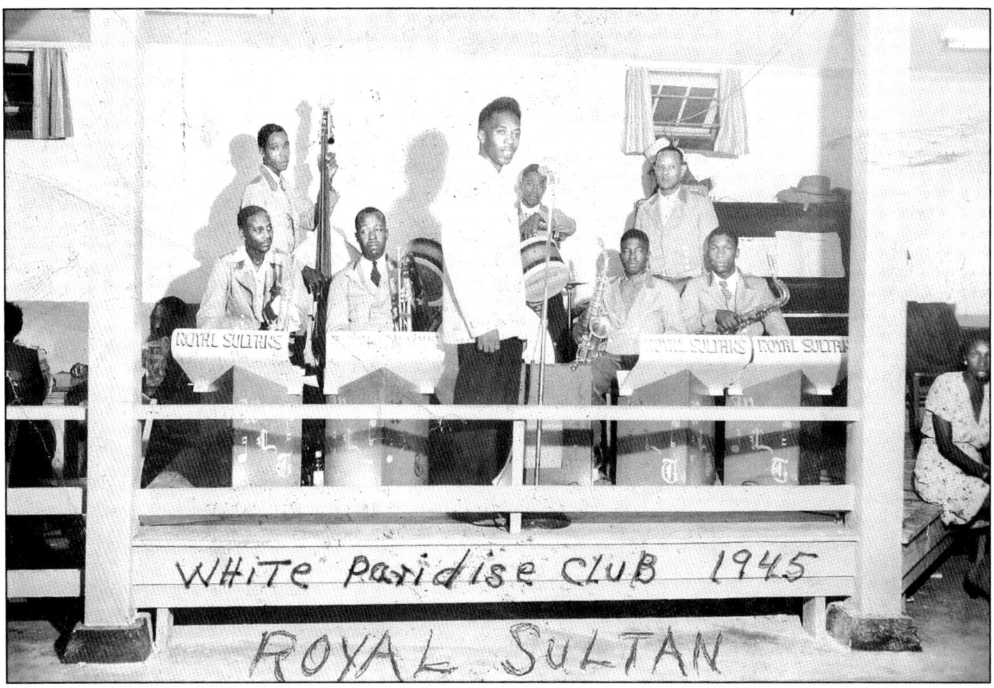

White's Paradise was a popular music venue located east of the Cooper River in the Charleston area. The Sultans was one of many bands that worked the nightspot. It also hosted touring bands, including some of the big-name acts of the times. James Brown performed there in the 1950s, early in his career. (Avery Research Center.)

Four

The Golden Age

Jazz in Charleston flowered from the 1940s through the middle of the century, laying the groundwork for today's energetic scene. The city by the sea shared what many jazz historians call the golden age of jazz, the Swing Era, from 1930 through 1950. It was the heyday of the big bands. Much of the groundwork for the glamour days was laid by the famous Fletcher Henderson Band, which had Charleston players such as trumpeters Gus Aitken and Herbert "Peanuts" Holland. Charleston's Bertha "Chippie" Hill, an important blues singer and contemporary of Mamie Smith, Ma Rainey, and Bessie Smith, also worked with Henderson, whose arrangements did as much as anyone for the success of the Benny Goodman Orchestra, including Goodman himself, the so-called King of Swing.

Many journeymen musicians form Charleston living and working in New York City during this period, such as trombonist Julius "Bankhead" Watson, populated pit bands at large theaters and Broadway shows for years. Mostly because of the teachings at Jenkins Orphanage and instruction by teachers who learned there, Charleston musicians were legendary for their ability to sight-read and play any kind of music. Many of them were section leaders and played first chair on their instruments not only because of their ability to swing but because they were extremely proficient technically.

By the 1950s, the smaller ensemble returned to the fore in jazz, and Charleston bands flourished. William Louis Gilliard and his Royal Sultans, the Metronome All-Stars, the Carolina Stompers, the Night Hawks Orchestra, and the Royal Entertainers were among the top bands in the third quarter of the 20th century. As colorful as band names were during this time, they had a lot to build on from what came before in the Lowcountry. For instance, a 1924 band named Saxton Wilson's Cruel Five (apparently a smaller ensemble drawn from the 1921 Professor William Saxton's Orchestra) played a type of music described as "jazz, razmatazz and rajazz."

Charleston bands were in step with the times in terns of slang, too. Gilliard worked a dance whose ticket was emblazoned across the top with "GET HIP! GET WISE!" then underneath "Say Diddy Bops Stick to the Jive," then the name of the event "A Rockin and Rollin Dance." This event was held at the now-gone Hotel James on Spring Street near the Ashley River. It was the segregation-era hotel for African Americans, including the black celebrities of the day who stopped in downtown Charleston.

The hotel's Azalea Ball Room, where the dances, concerts, and receptions were held, had a mezzanine-level bandstand that literally made the live music swing to the rafters. Other well-known venues for black music in the Charleston area included the 52-20 Club in Summerville; Grant Hall and the RVA Club in the Neck Area; Zanzibar, Harlem Club, and Bacardi's Rose Room in North Charleston; Riverside Beach Park, a beachfront pavilion, and White's Paradise, at Remley's Point; and downtown Charleston's Harleston Hall, Lincoln Theater, Dash Hall,

Moulin Rouge, Charleston County Hall, RVA Club (later the Village), Dart Hall (also known as Dart's Dancing Casino), Colonial Cabin, Cadillac Club, Kozy Korner, Ponderosa, and the D.P.O. Hall. There were also many outdoor venues for picnics where black music was featured, as well as harbor or river cruises.

Charleston, among the smaller jazz cradles in the United States (compared to Kansas City, Memphis, Chicago, and New Orleans) even had a territorial band, a band that stayed on the road covering the entire United States, including the West Coast. It was called the Carolina Cottonpickers. The band was formed in the 1930s and traveled through the 1950s, playing Los Angeles, New Orleans, Jacksonville, New York City, Chicago, and all points in between. The band grew out of a Jenkins Orphanage band that decided to stay on the road after some financial success while away from the orphanage. Trumpeter William "Cat" Anderson was a Cottonpicker, as was St. Julian Bennett Dash, eventual lead tenor saxophonist with the famed Erskine Hawkins Orchestra. A very important Charleston pianist, Clifton Smalls, was a Cottonpicker. Smalls was also musical director for singer Billy Eckstine, pianist for 10 years with Sy Oliver at New York City's Rainbow Room, and musical director for William "Smokey" Robinson. He has worked with Chicago and Los Angeles jazz impresario Gerald Wilson, singer Brook Benton, and vocalist Dinah Washington. Smalls is still a working musician, teaching, composing and leading the Cliff Smalls Septet in Brooklyn. Some may remember him giving a cameo performance as a piano player in the movie *Cotton Club* starring Richard Gere.

The 1950s generation of Charleston musicians eventually gave way to a group that is still around today. They also represent another important aspect of the musicians that came out of the Charleston area. Almost all of them are educators and they, like many before them, excelled at endeavors other than music. It explains why some Charleston jazz musicians did not attain celebrity: they knew how to do other things. As an example, Watson was a printer, a skill he learned at Jenkins Orphanage. Tommy Benford, who many critics and historians believe to be one of the best jazz drummers ever, also did administrative work at the New York City Merrill Lynch office.

One player from the 1950s–1960s era, Lonnie Hamilton III, went on to chair Charleston County Council. The county's main administrative building is named after him. He was a career educator, working in both the classroom and administration, as well as a professional musician. There are also saxophonist and pianist Oscar Rivers, multi-instrumentalist George Kenny, trombonist Raymond Rhett, bassist Leon Chisolm, trumpeters Bob Ephiram, Sykes Garvin, and Joey Morant, bassist and vibraphonist St. Julian German, drummer Bob "Stinky" Nelson, saxophonist Melvin Hodges, bassist William Rivers, and saxophonist Snookie Rivers, William's brother.

This period was the height of Charleston's modern jazz scene before integration. Although television had gone much further since it came on the scene the 1950s toward keeping people at home for entertainment instead of going out to theaters and nightclubs, folks in Charleston still flocked to the venues mentioned above for live music, not to mention other social events such as wedding receptions, anniversaries, and house parties, all of which still had live music.

Also by this time, some of the younger musicians who had been taught and mentored by the likes of Hodges, Hamilton, Kenny, and others were relocating to other places. New York City still beckoned as it did 50 years earlier, and Atlanta, Georgia, had emerged as an attraction for Charleston jazz musicians. Hodges moved there to teach and play in the clubs, as did saxophonists Raymond Alston, Richard Smalls, and Leonard Chisolm. For a time, the Charleston sound dominated Atlanta's famed Hunter Street venues, Paschal Brothers Hotel and Don Clendenon's.

It was also during this time many Charlestonians made their mark in military bands and at South Carolina State College, now South Carolina State University in Orangeburg, South Carolina. In fact, musicians had been going to State since the early days, when the Reverend Daniel Joseph Jenkins sent players from his orphanage. John Williams, an Orangeburg native, State graduate, and baritone saxophone player in the Count Basie Orchestra since 1973, was a schoolmate of some of the guys. As he did in a Jenkins Orphanage Band documentary produced by South Carolina Educational Television, Williams sings the praises of musicians from Charleston. He played in a jazz band at State called the Collegians, which was led by Kenny.

The Department of Music

of

Avery Institute

Presents Its

ANNUAL CONCERT

The Archer Auditorium — December 8, 1940

D. Jack Moses, *Director* Reynold N. Scott, *Accompanist*

———Soloists———

Helen M. Holton, *Soprano*

Nathaniel A. James, *Tenor*

Catherine A. Heyward, *Pianist*

———P R O G R A M———

I

(a) The Kerry Dance - - - - - - - - - Molloy
(b) To A Wild Rose - - - - - - - - McDowell
(c) Carmena - - - - - - - - - - - Wilson

Mixed Chorus

II

(a) Dear Land of Home (Finlandia) - - - Sibelius
(b) Brothers, Sing On - - - - - - - - Grieg

Boy's Glee Club

III

(a) Sleep, Kentucky Babe - - - - - - - Barnby
(b) Plenty Good Room - - - - - - Arr. by Moses
(c) Heaben - - - - - - - - - - Arr. by Moses

Male Quintette

IV

(a) Solvejg's Song - - - - - - - - - Grieg
(b) Ave Maria - - - - - - - - - - Schubert

Girls' Glee Club, R. N. Scott, Director

V

(a) Lo, How a Rose E'er Blooming - - - Praetorius
(b) Every Time I feel the Spirit - - - Arr. by Moses
(c) Great Day - - - - - - - - - Arr. by Moses

A Cappella Choir

VI

(a) Waltz C Minor - - - - - - - - - - Chopin
(b) Prelude G Minor - - - - - - - Rachmaninoff

Catherine A. Heyward

VII

(a) Po' Ol' Laz'rus - - - - - - - - - - Work
(b) Battle of Jericho - - - - - - - Arr. by Moses

Boy's Glee Club

VIII

Negro Spirituals and Jubilees - - - - - Arr. by Moses

(a) Steal Away
(b) My Good Lord
(c) My Lord, What A Morning
(d) Study War No More

—Mixed Chorus

This is a program form a 1940 concert at Avery Normal Institute. The concerts at Avery were well attended by the community at large. Its reputation for the performing arts was excellent and reached far and wide. People looked forward to them, especially for their variety. (Avery Research Center.)

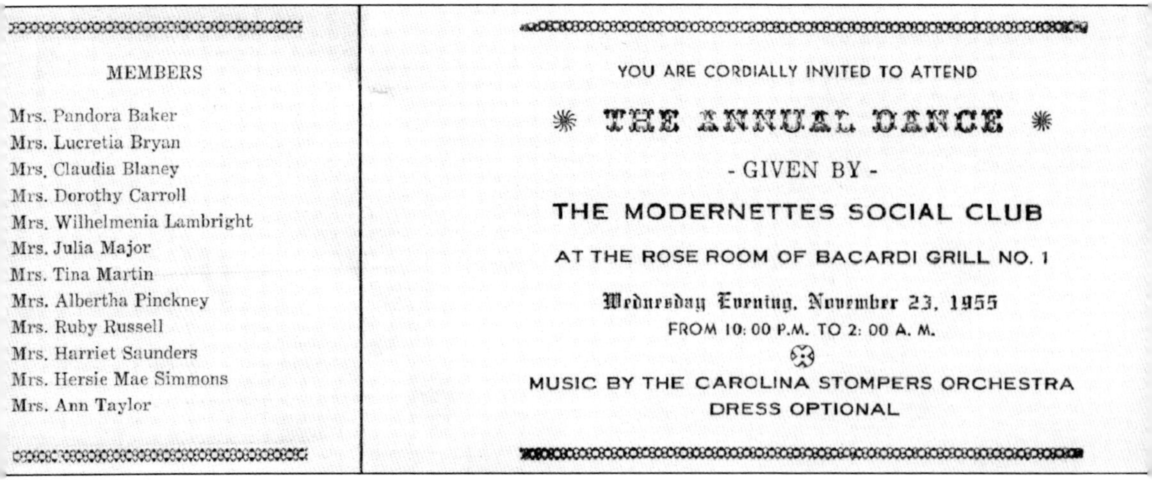

MEMBERS

Mrs. Pandora Baker
Mrs. Lucretia Bryan
Mrs. Claudia Blaney
Mrs. Dorothy Carroll
Mrs. Wilhelmenia Lambright
Mrs. Julia Major
Mrs. Tina Martin
Mrs. Albertha Pinckney
Mrs. Ruby Russell
Mrs. Harriet Saunders
Mrs. Hersie Mae Simmons
Mrs. Ann Taylor

YOU ARE CORDIALLY INVITED TO ATTEND

THE ANNUAL DANCE

- GIVEN BY -

THE MODERNETTES SOCIAL CLUB

AT THE ROSE ROOM OF BACARDI GRILL NO. 1

Wednesday Evening, November 23, 1955

FROM 10: 00 P.M. TO 2: 00 A. M.

MUSIC BY THE CAROLINA STOMPERS ORCHESTRA

DRESS OPTIONAL

This is a ticket for a dance in 1955 at Bacardi's Rose Room in North Charleston announcing music by the Carolina Stompers, one of the most popular jazz bands in Charleston in the 1950s. (Avery Research Center.)

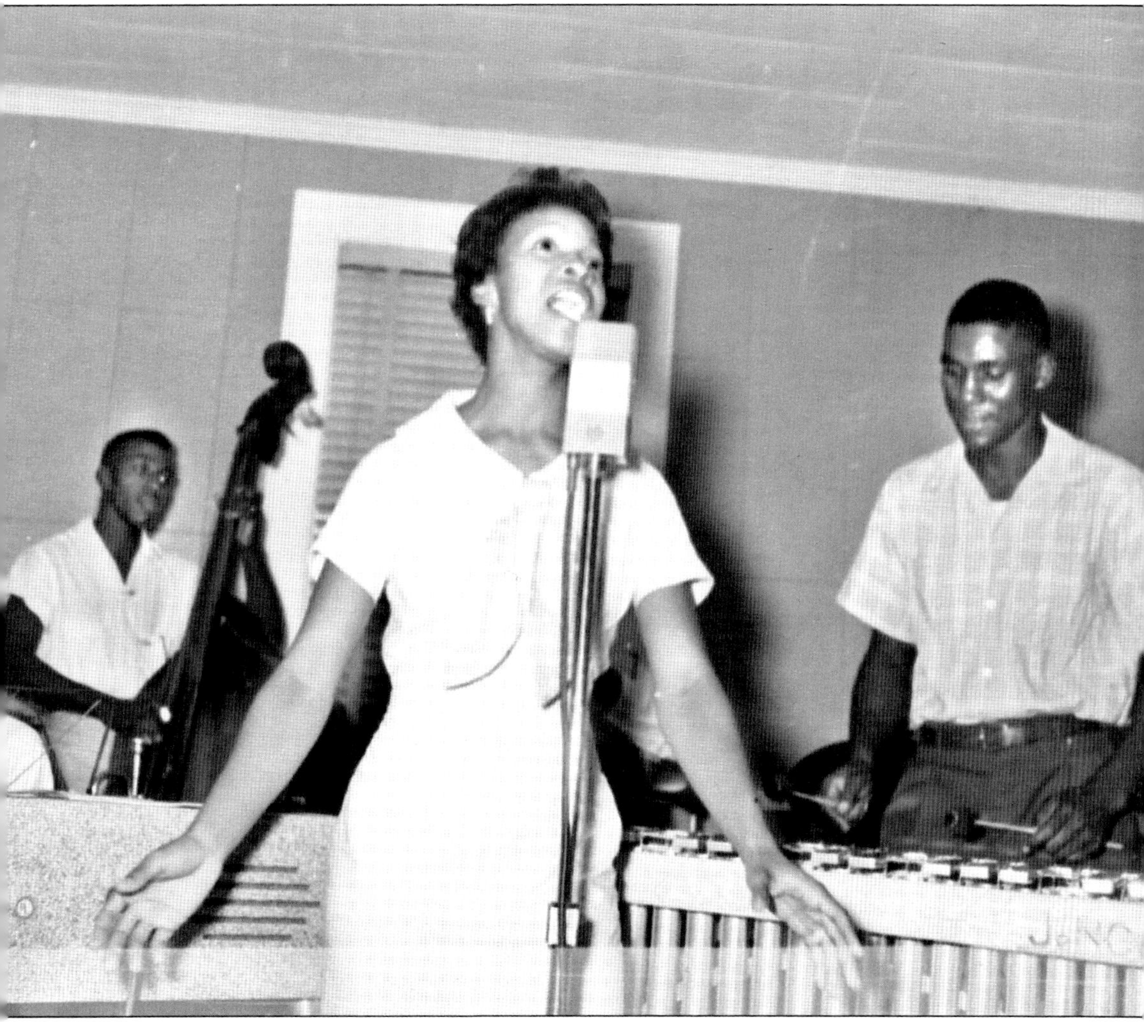

A singer takes a solo in front of a radio studio band in the 1960s. In early jazz and blues, soloists weren't all that prominently featured, especially women. One of the women to change the trend was Bertha "Chippie" Hill, a Charlestonian who left to go to New York to become a contemporary of Ma Rainey and Bessie Smith. When female singers started in front of big bands it was mostly window dressing. By this time, female singers were just as important to a band as the individual musicians. (George Kenny.)

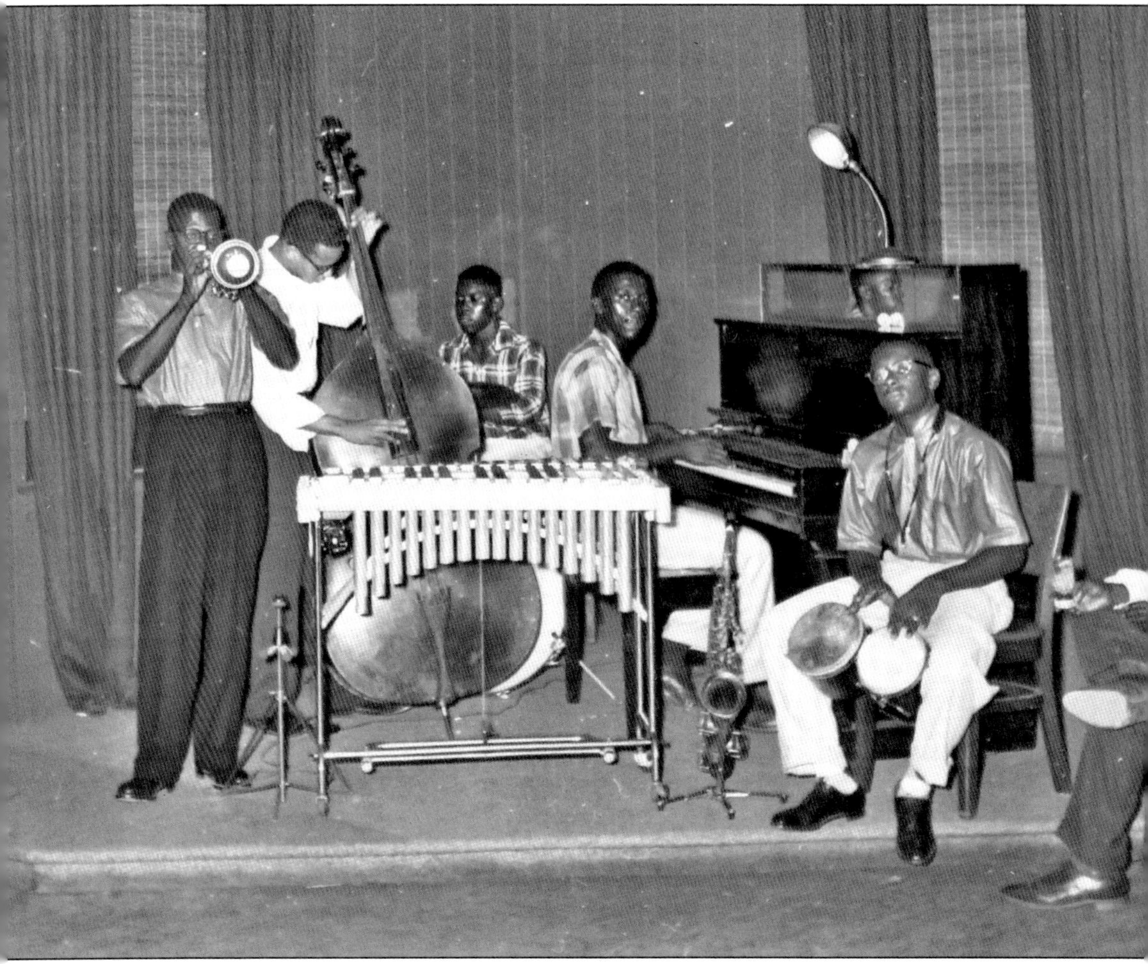

Percussion instruments, such as the bongos, were often included in jazz bands. St. Julian German leads here on the piano. There is a long tradition in Charleston of percussion instruments, through brass bands, military bands, and fife-and-drum corps all the way back to the 18th century. Rhythm is fundamental to jazz music, and the Charleston sound is very rhythmic, with heavy accents and syncopation. This has a lot to do with the African origins of the people here. (George Kenny.)

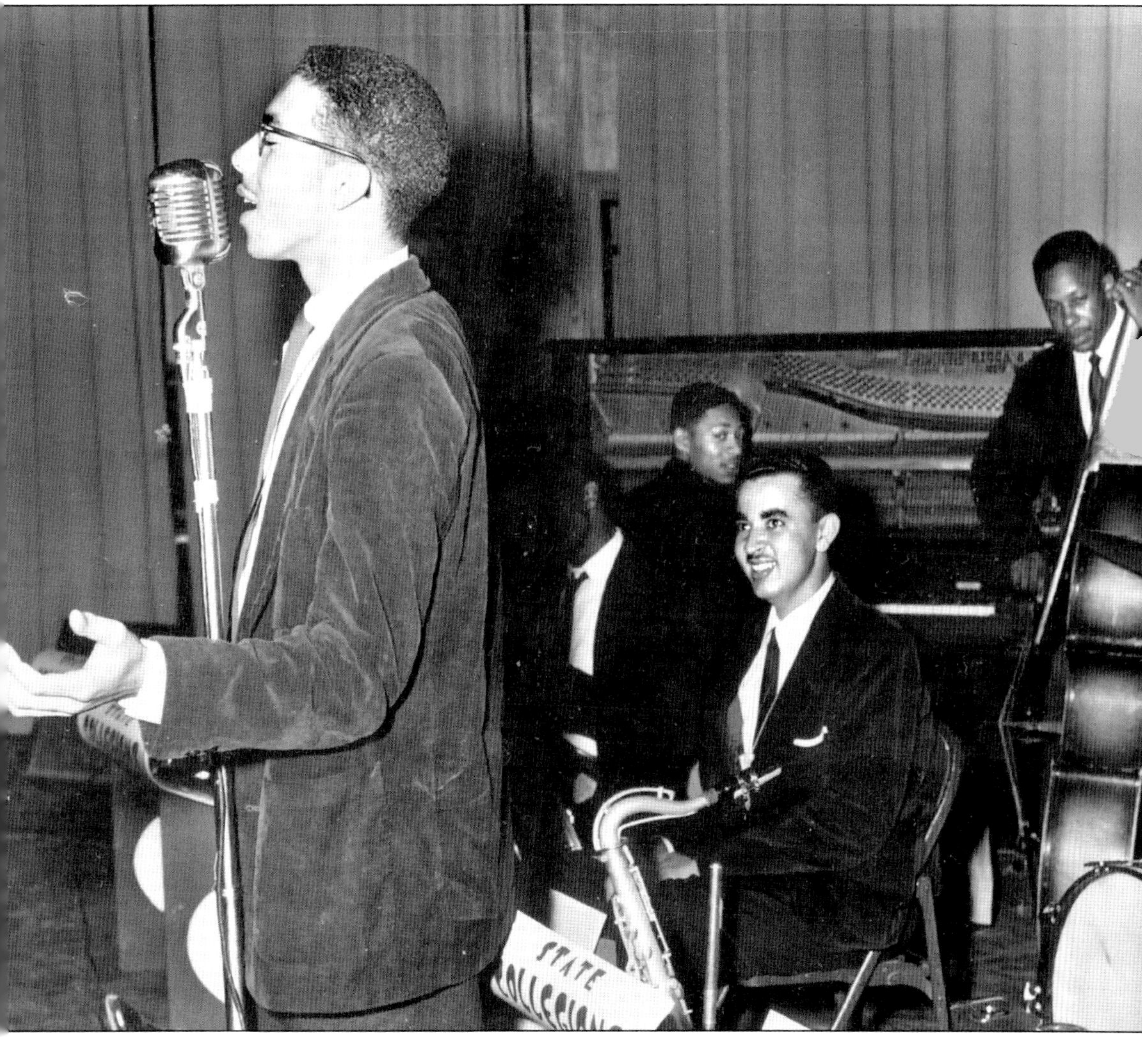

George Kenny (right) is a great Charleston multi-instrumentalist. Known for his saxophone playing, he is shown here in the 1950s on bass while a student at South Carolina State College. South Carolina State College accepted many musicians from Charleston over the years. (George Kenny.)

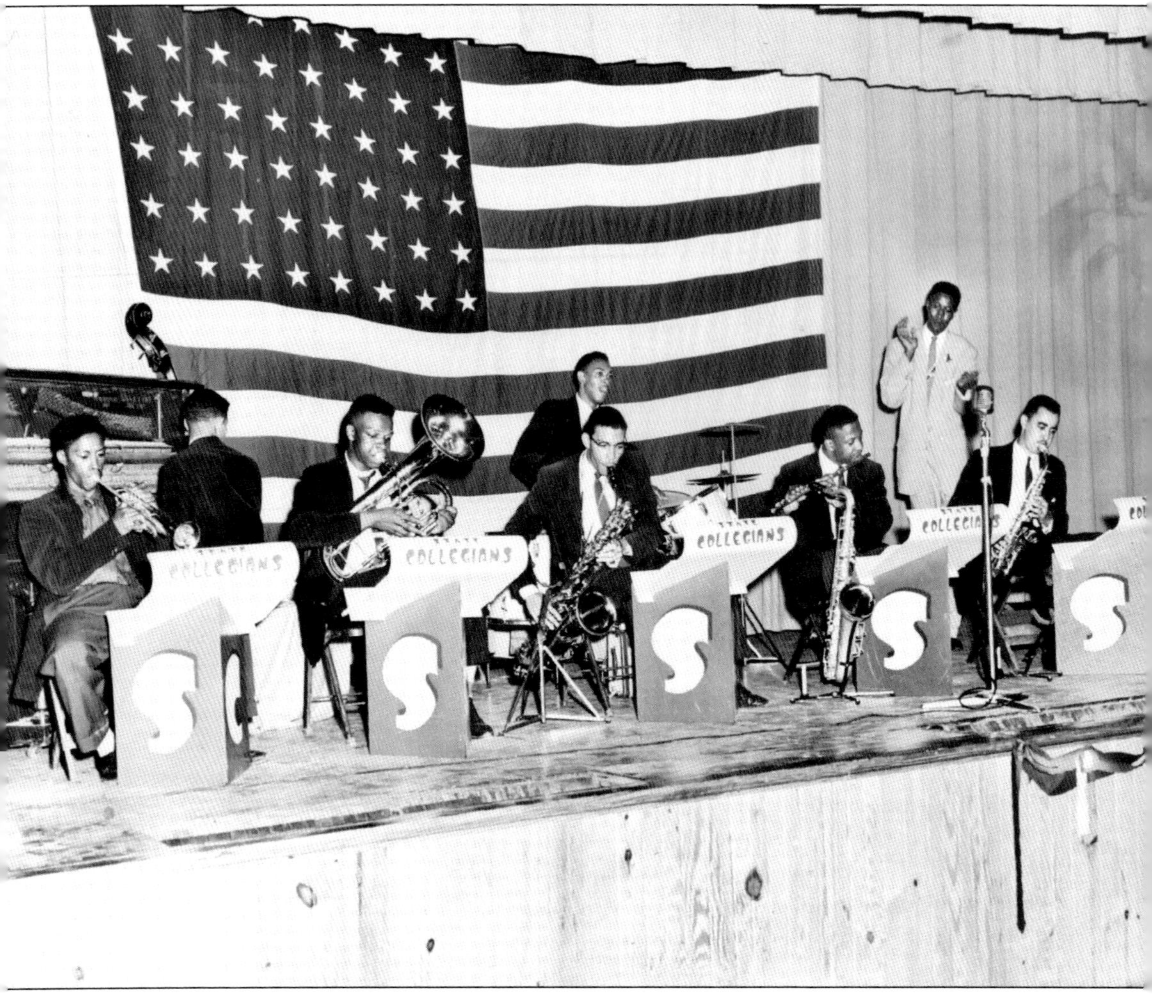

George Kenny is also adept at the flute, as he demonstrates here in the South Carolina State College jazz band. He went on to be an important music educator in Charleston, teaching at area public schools, giving private lessons, and teaching at the famed Jenkins Orphanage. (George Kenny.)

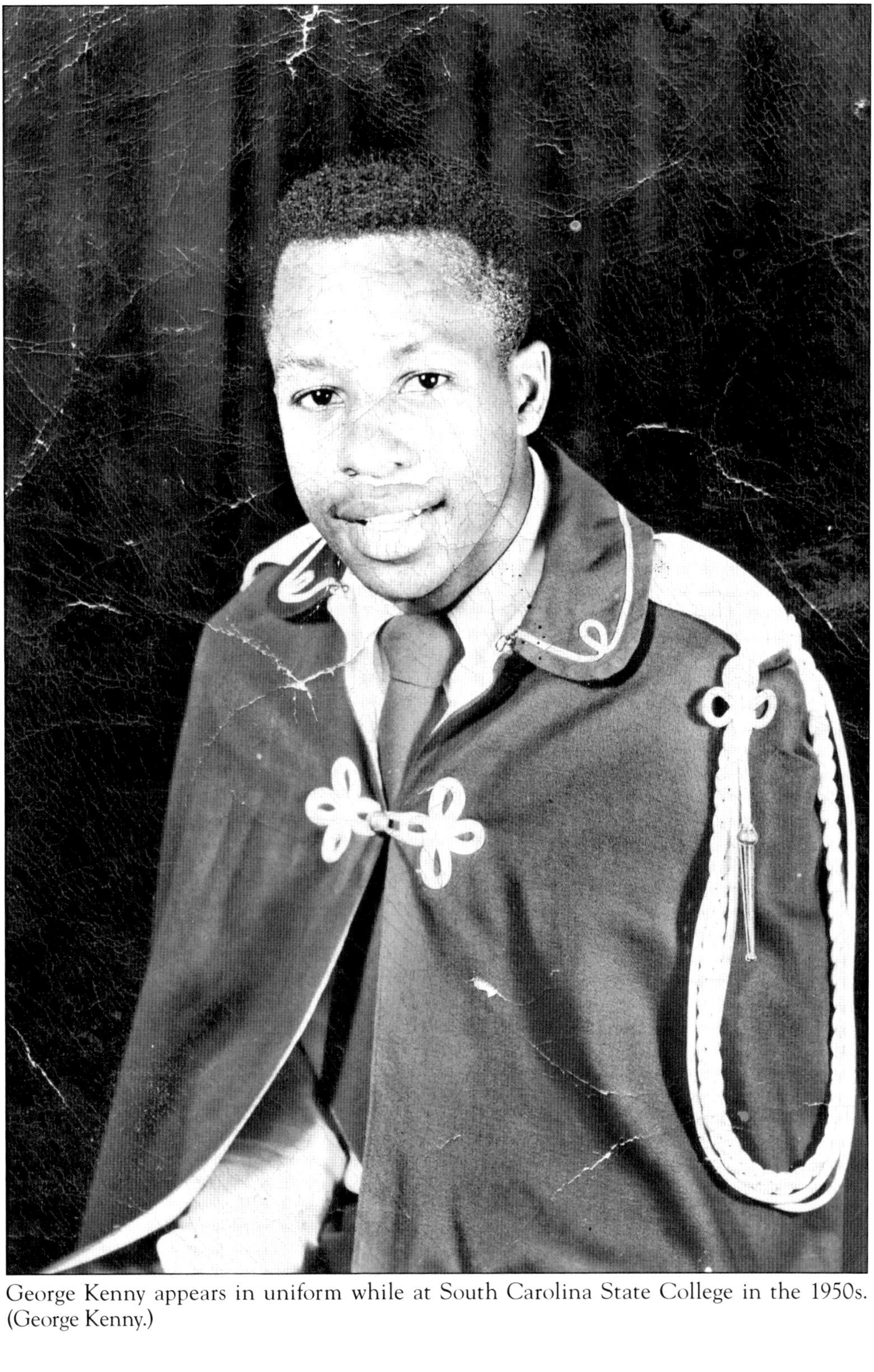

George Kenny appears in uniform while at South Carolina State College in the 1950s. (George Kenny.)

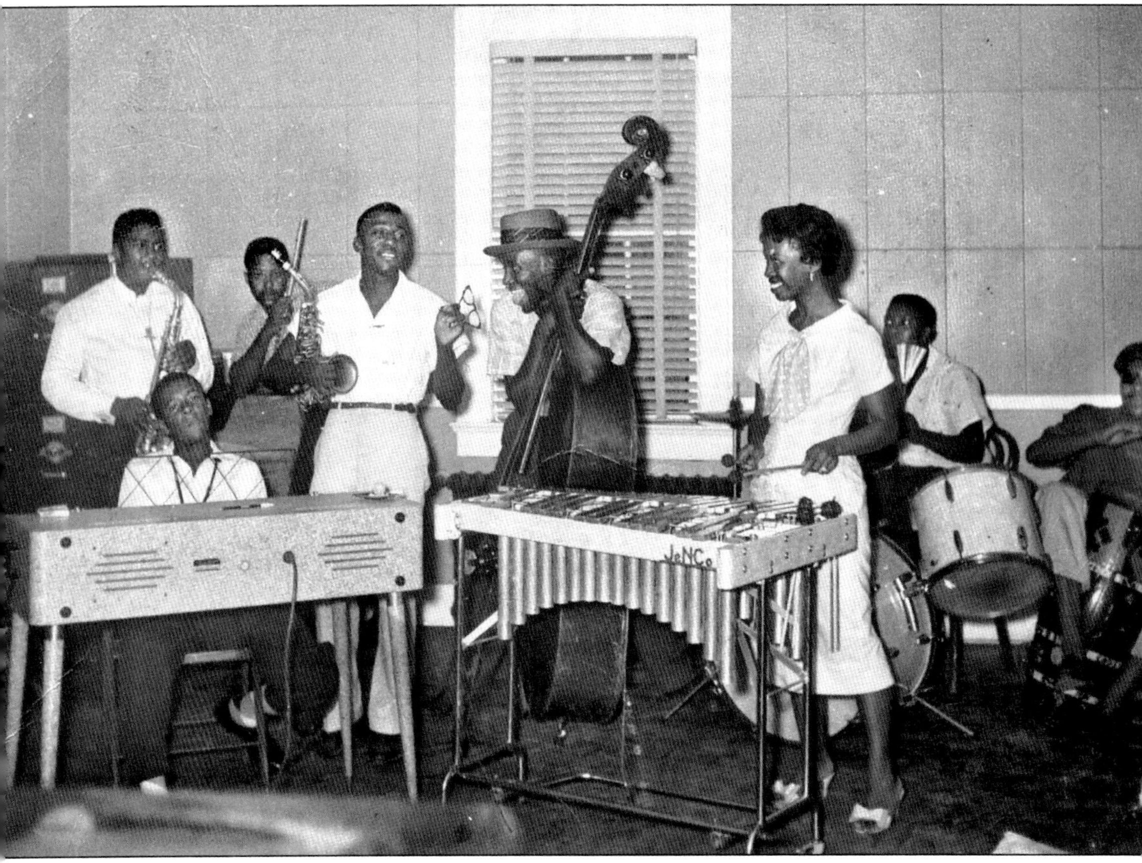

A young Oscar Rivers (at piano) is among many Charleston musicians at a jam session in the 1950s. Rivers attended Burke High School and South Carolina State College and has taught in public schools here. Rivers lived and worked for years in Chicago, becoming a major force on the local scene there on alto saxophone. He has since taken on the piano. Over the years, he has worked with the likes of Nancy Wilson, Lou Rawls, and Sonny Stitt. (George Kenny.)

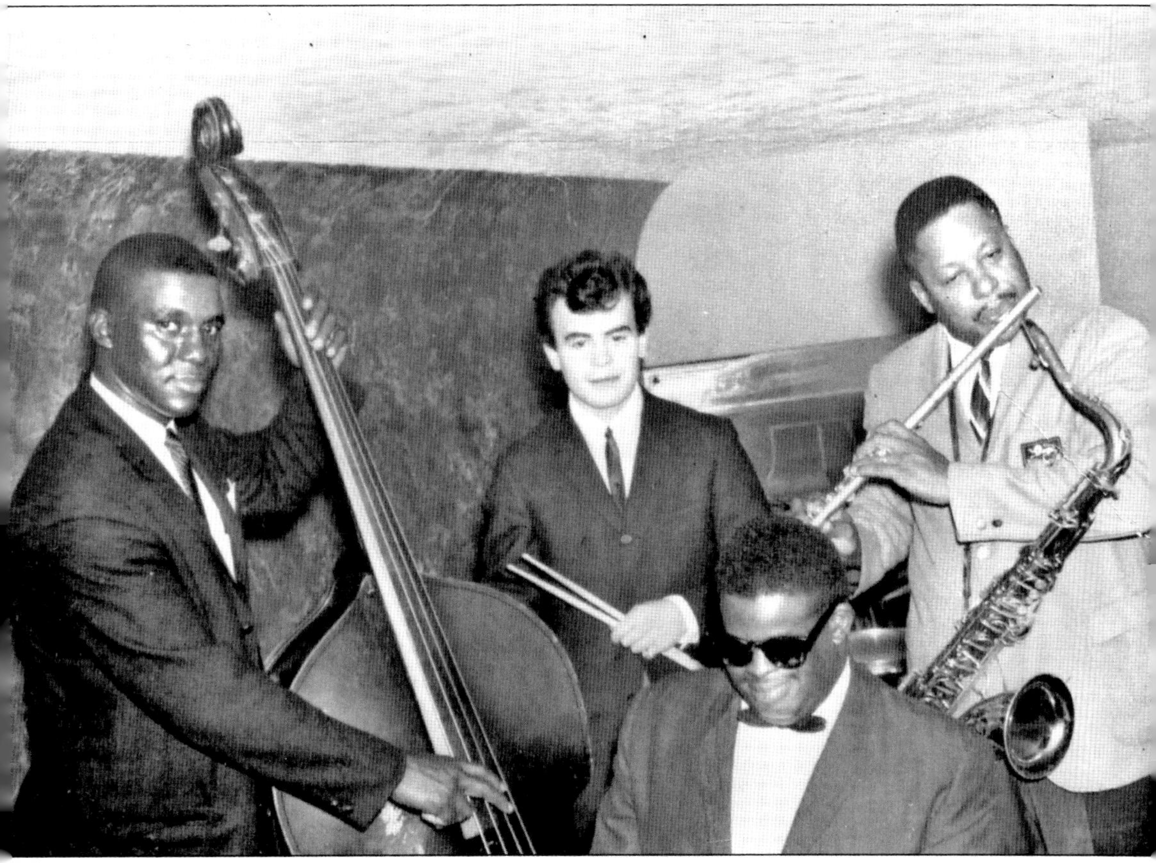

St. Julian German (left) played bass for many years in Charleston. He is also a fine vocalist and vibraphone player. For a long time, he and family members backed singer Ann Caldwell at venues around town. Over several decades, German worked most of the public and private spots in the Lowcountry, drawing all kinds of attention. He was a musician's musician and highly respected in the Charleston musician community. (George Kenny.)

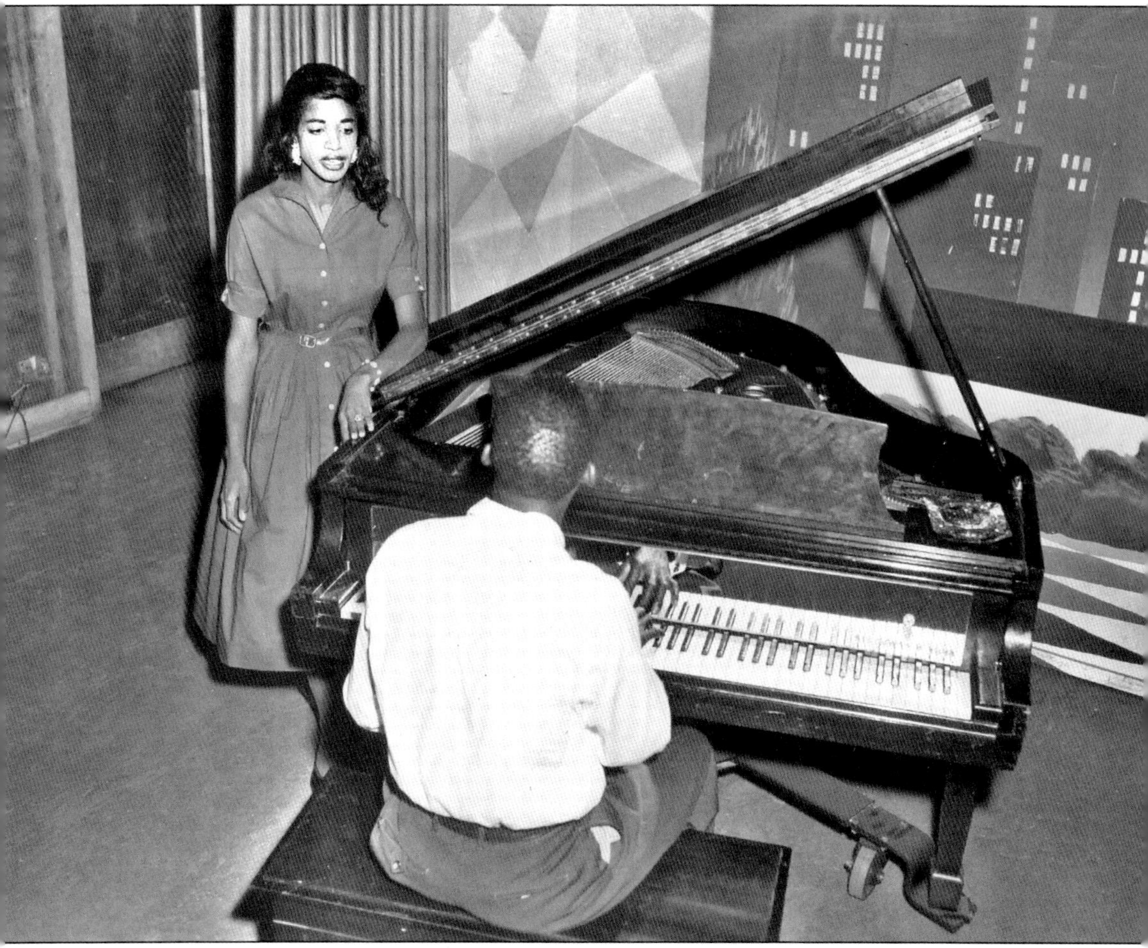

The big-city backdrop gave an air of sophistication to this Charleston performance. Jazz was always thought of as a sophisticated music, almost to the point of being elitist. Small towns like Charleston always aspired at least to be seen as having a big-city air when they needed to, such as in this performance. (George Kenny.)

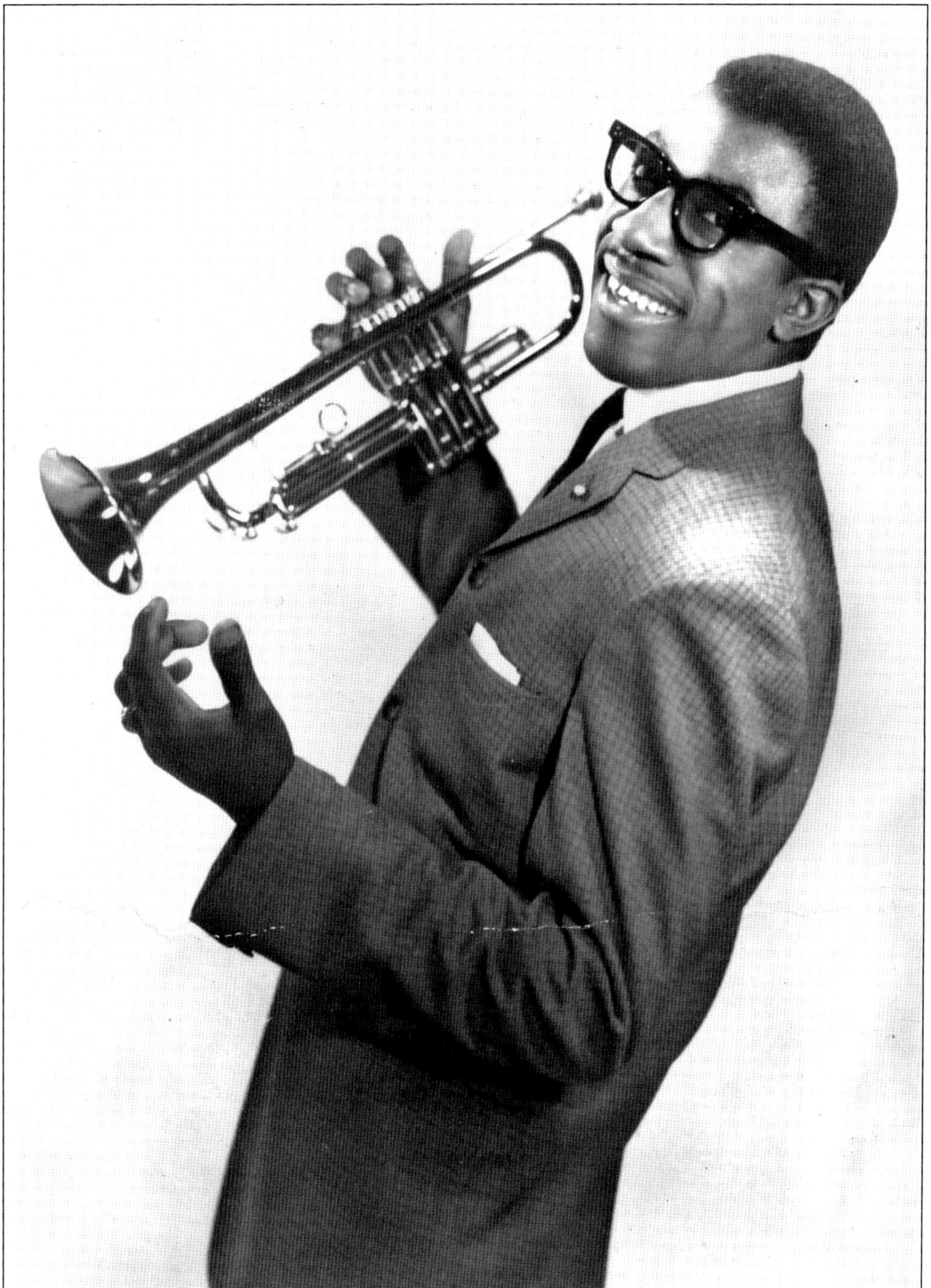

Joey Morant, shown here in the 1960s, left Charleston for the Northeast and Canada in the 1960s to seek fame and fortune. He has played around the world, and many believe there aren't too many trumpeters better than him anywhere. He is a representative of the Charleston high-note tradition, like Leo Sheperd and William "Cat" Anderson. Morant is also a noted multi-instrumentalist. He plays flugelhorn, trombone, baritone horn, and tuba. (George Kenny.)

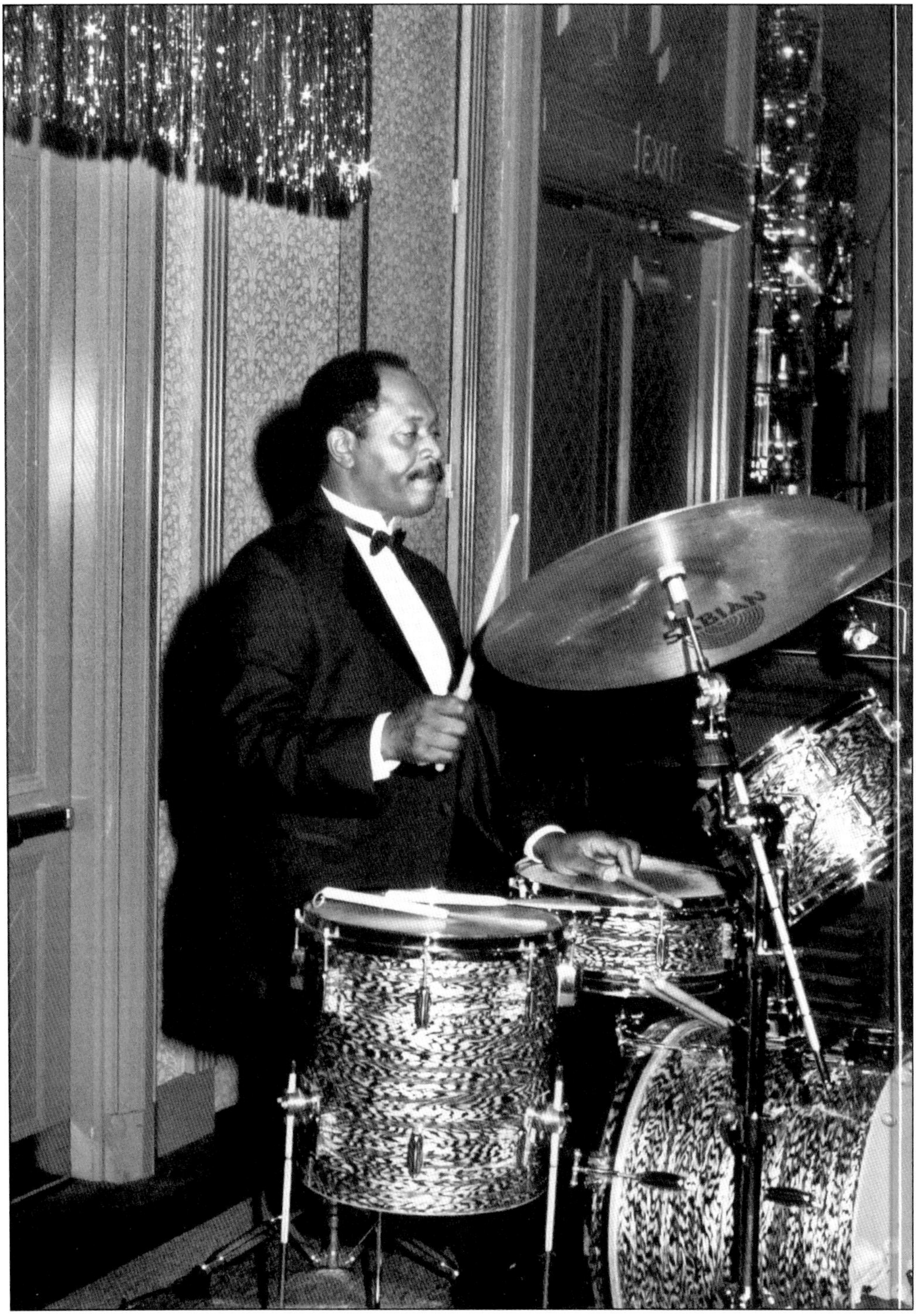

Leroy Chisolm was a drummer and bandleader in Charleston in the 1950s. His colleagues consider him to have been one of the best musicians around town during his time. They all aspired to be in his bands. (George Kenny.)

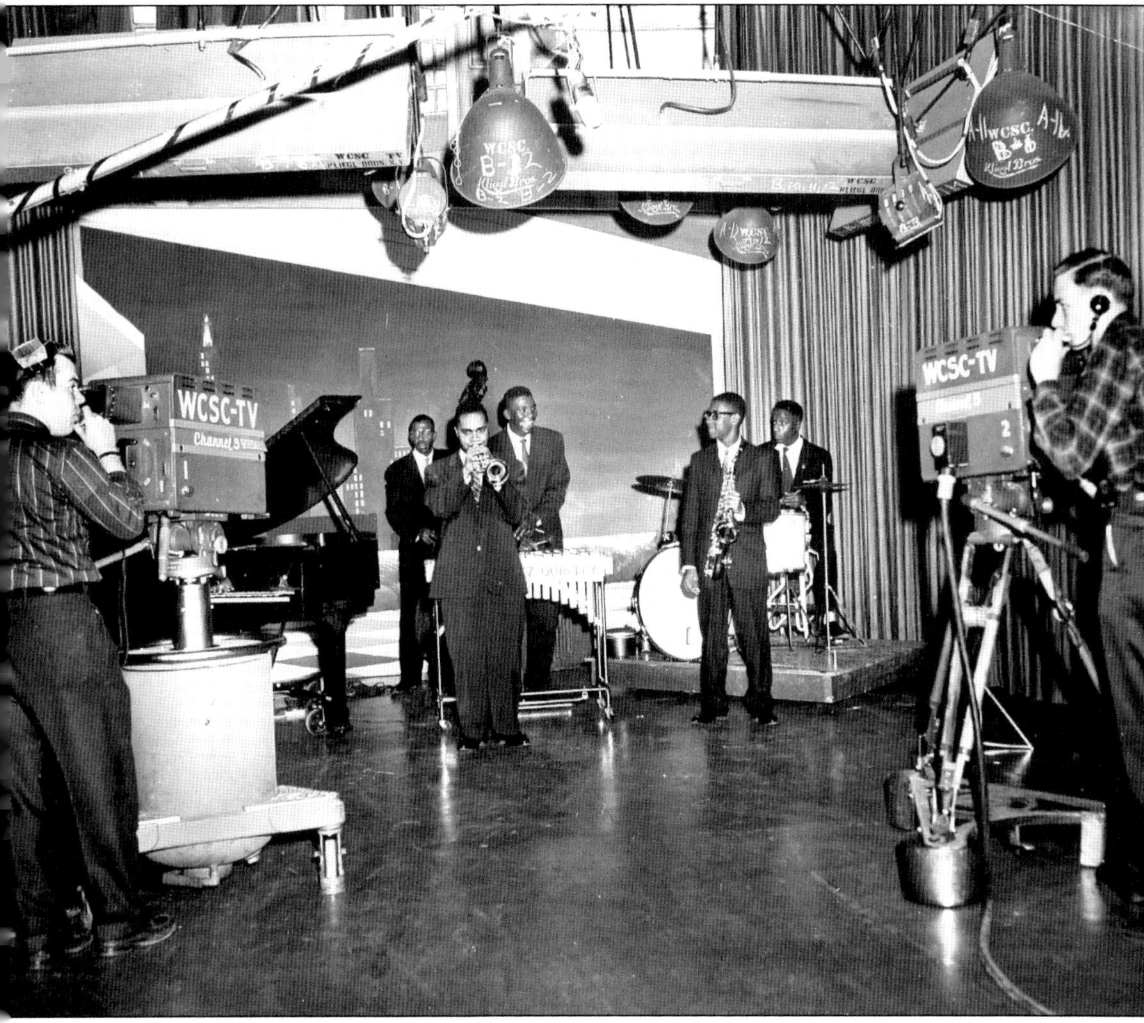

WCSC-TV hosted live jazz in Charleston through the 1960s. Many singers and instrumentalists graced its studios, much to the delight of viewers of the new entertainment medium starting in the 1950s. The station was the first to go on the air in Charleston, and it provided exposure to many jazz musicians over the years. (George Kenny.)

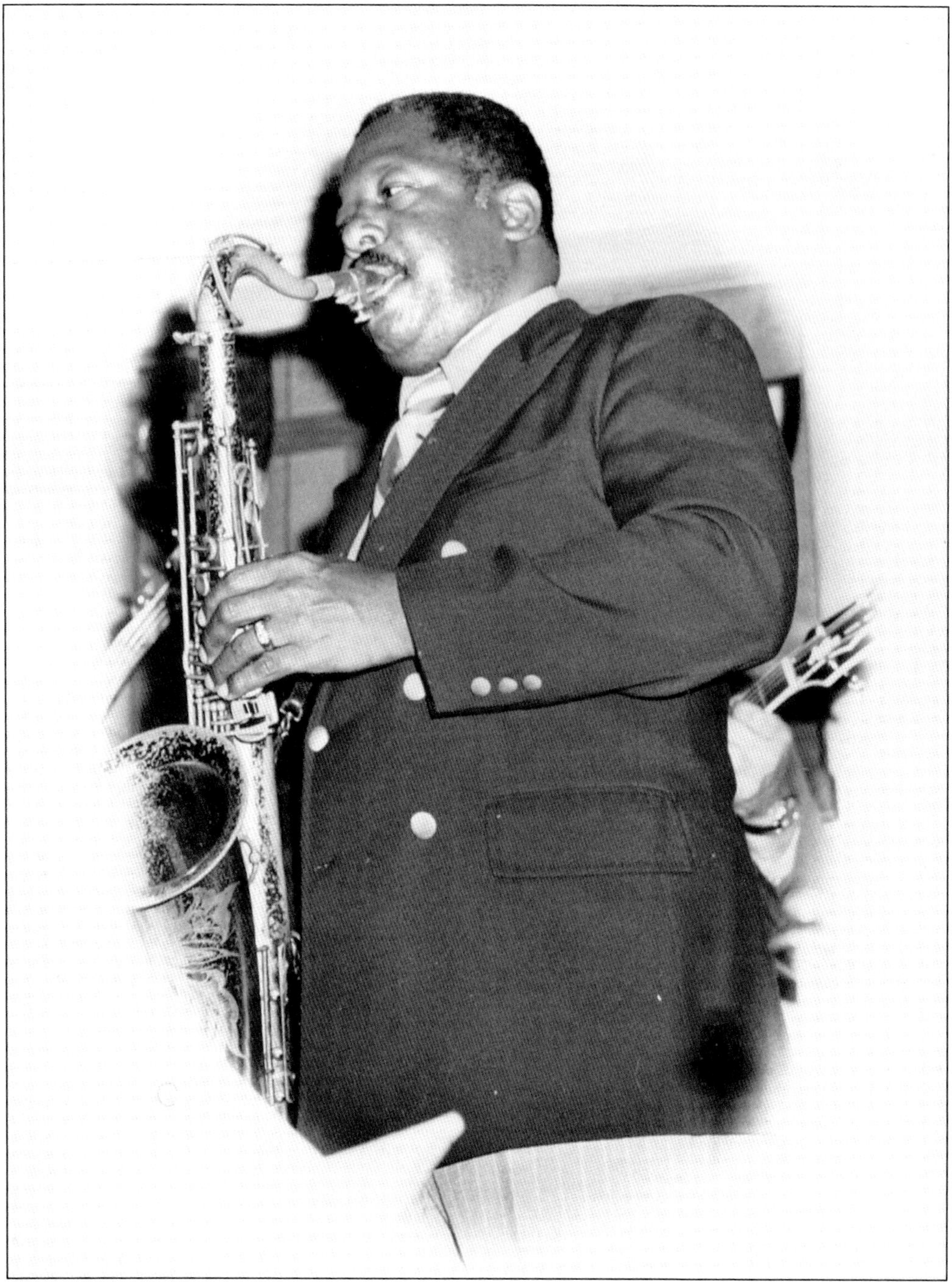

George Kenny dresses as well as he plays the saxophone. Charleston jazz musicians have been known for their style in dress as well as on their instruments. How you dress can be improvised on just like music can. Jazz musicians from Charleston have always been known for their natty attire, a point of personal pride as well as an important part of showmanship. (George Kenny.)

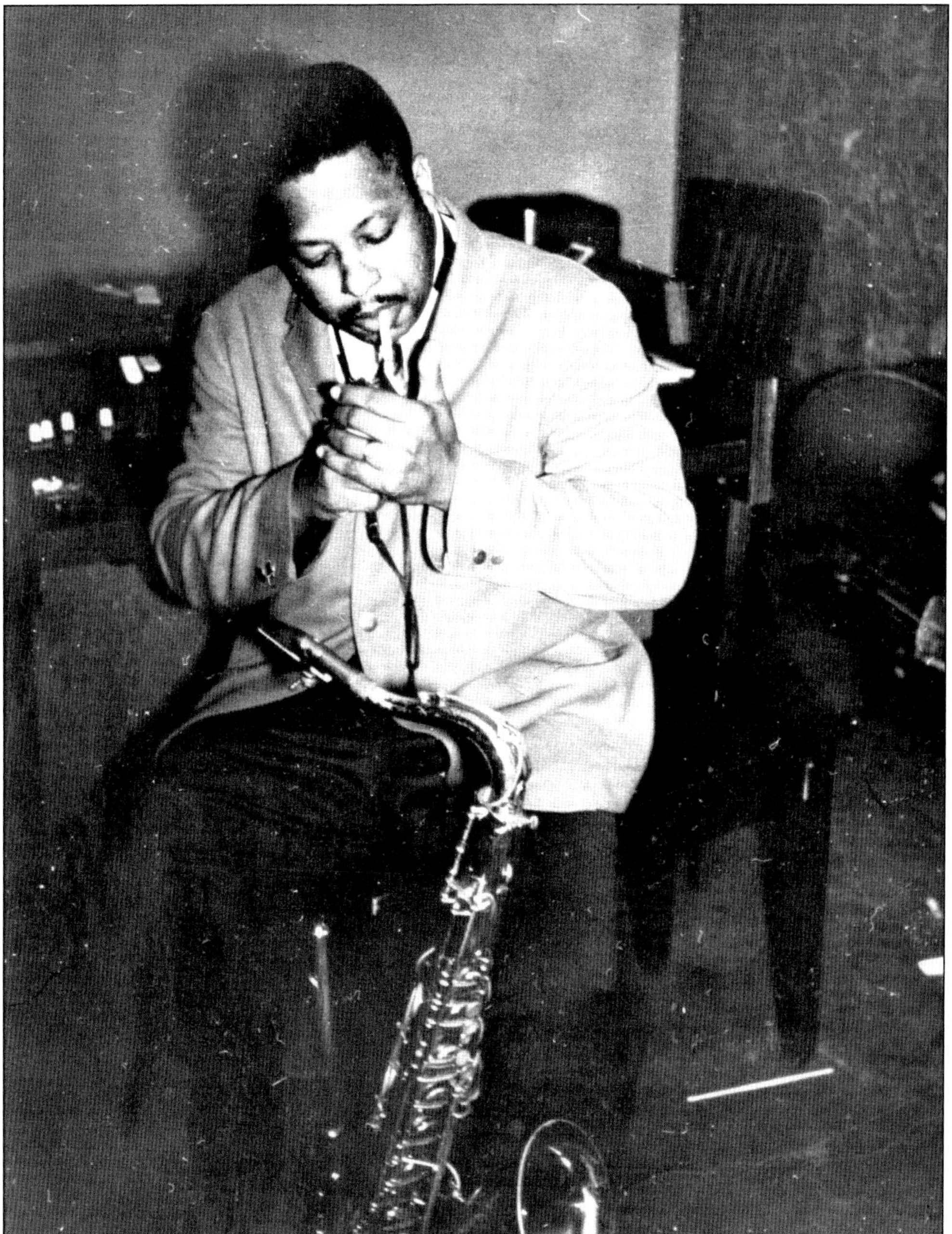

George Kenny enjoys a moment off the bandstand in this 1960s photograph. As intensely as he sometimes plays, Kenny is known for his cool reserve. He knows the ins and outs of his instruments and he can interpret the most intricate charts, but through it all he remains unflappable. It is a trait that also makes him a good teacher. Jazz is often associated with cool, and players from Charleston are no exception. (George Kenny.)

SOUTH CAROLINA TRICENTENNIAL COMMISSION and
The CHARLESTON SYMPHONY ORCHESTRA ASSOCIATION presents

SOUTH CAROLINA TRICENTENNIAL
1670-1970

PORGY and BESS

Music by GEORGE GERSHWIN

Book by DUBOSE HEYWARD

Lyrics by DUBOSE HEYWARD and IRA GERSHWIN

(Founded on the play "PORGY" by DuBose and Dorothy Heyward)

LUCIEN De GROOTE
Musical Director and Conductor

JAMES EDWARDS
Choral Director

NEIL STANNARD
Assistant to the Conductor

JON FROSCHER
Production Stage Manager

WILLIAM S. TAYLOR
Production Consultant

Scenery Designed by
EMMETT ROBINSON

Lighting by
NORMAN WEBER

FITZHUGH HAMRICK
and LOUIS CONDON
Producers for the Symphony Orchestra

Entire Production Directed by
ELLA GERBER

"PORGY AND BESS" is presented by arrangement with

Shown here is a copy of the program for the highly regarded 1970 Tricentennial production of *Porgy and Bess* put on by the Charleston Symphony Orchestra. The opera, based on the novel by Dorothy and Dubose Heyward, depicts African American life in Charleston at the turn of the 20th century, including the Jenkins Orphanage bands. George Gershwin wrote the music for the opera and his brother Ira the libretto with assistance from Dubose Heyward. George Gershwin came to Charleston in the 1930s to gather material and immerse himself in Lowcountry music to prepare for the project. Among other things, he visited black churches to experience the "jazzy" rhythms and melodies of the Charleston area. The opera plays around the world to this day and is considered to be the greatest American opera of all time. (Avery Research Center.)

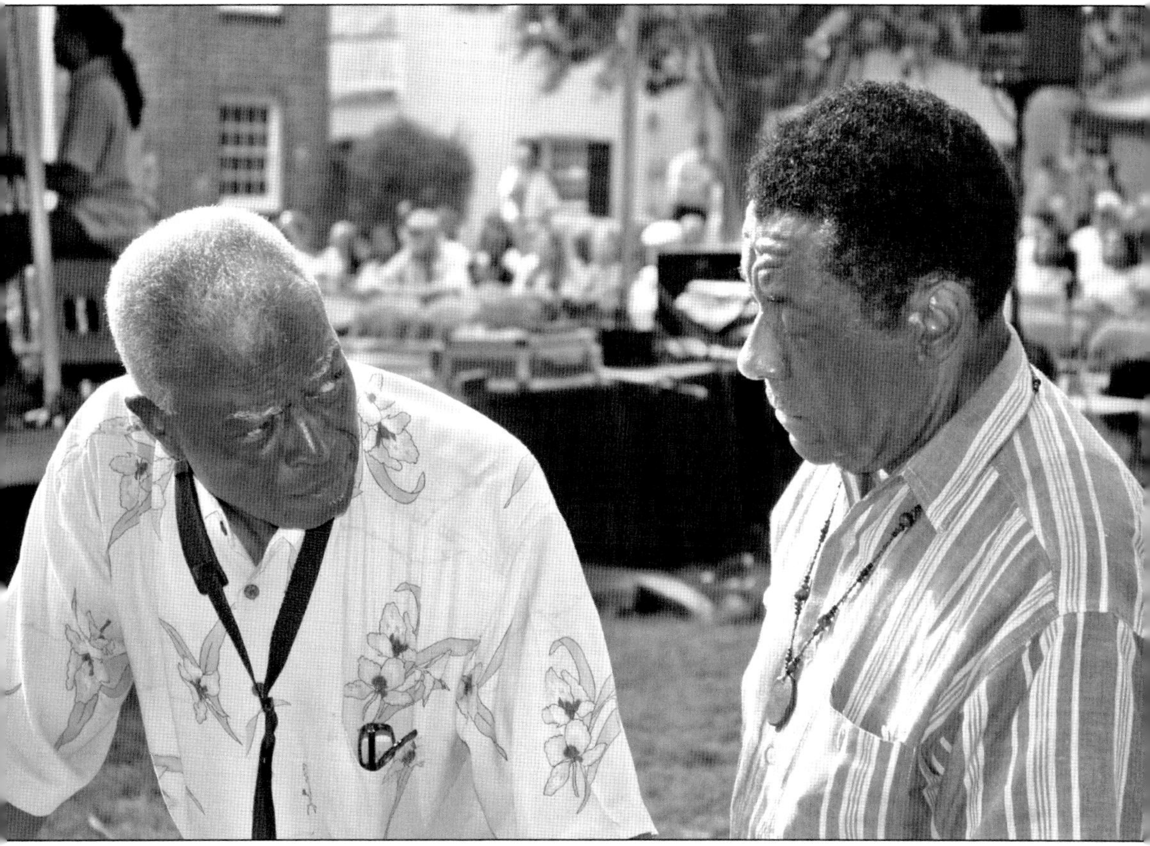

Charleston jazz giants Lonnie Hamilton (left), saxophonist, and Oscar Rivers, pianist, prepare to take the stage at the Jazz Picnic at Robert Mills Manor, site of the original home of the Jenkins Orphanage, in June 2005. The picnic is a tribute to the legacy of Charleston musicians, especially those who attended Jenkins Orphanage. Hamilton and Rivers have been important players on the Charleston scene for decades, and both have serious ties to Jenkins Orphanage. (Charleston Jazz Initiative.)

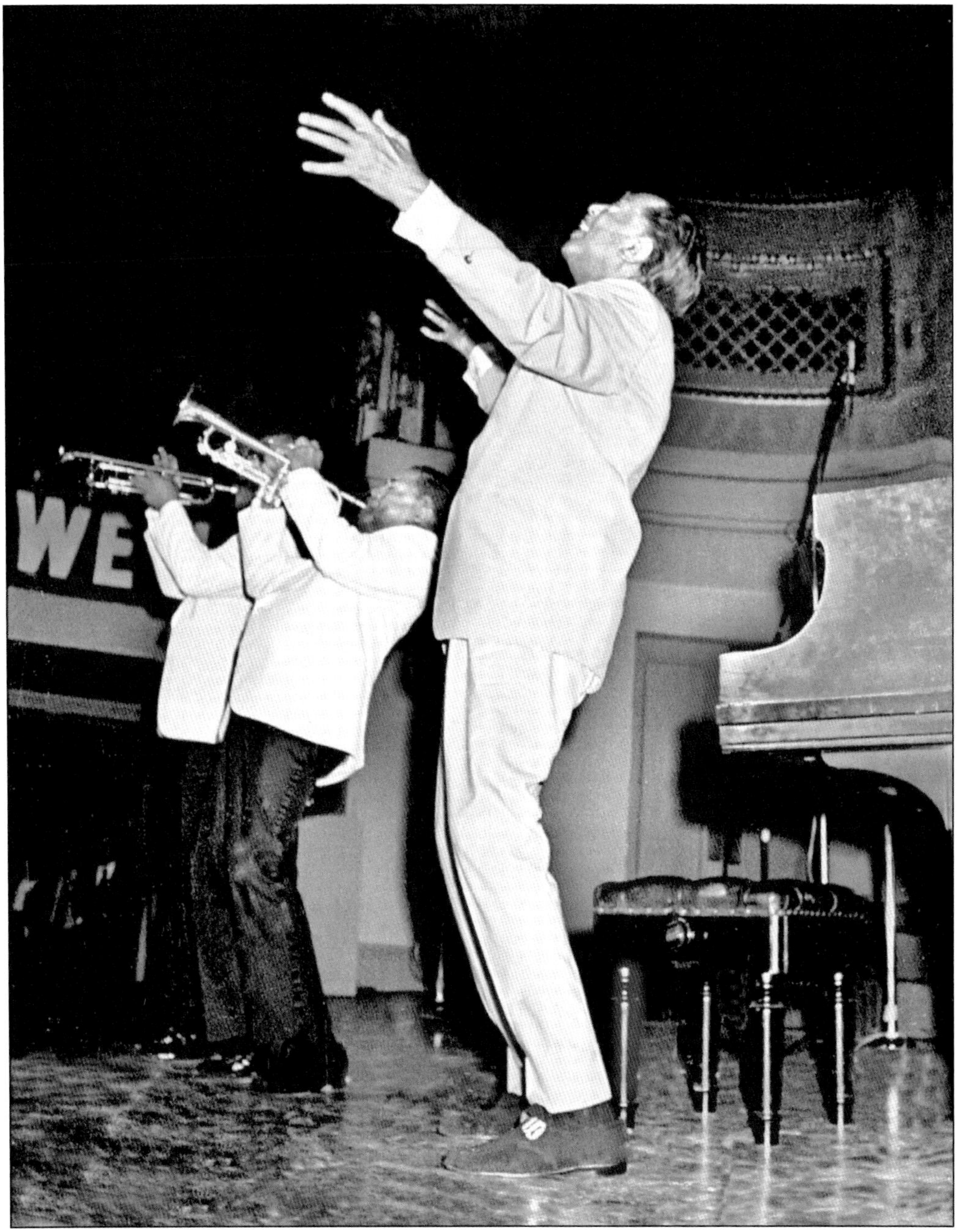

Cat Anderson (center) of the Duke Ellington Orchestra was a high-note specialist, a trademark of trumpet players taught at Jenkins Orphanage. Anderson played with Ellington (right) for many years. He was born in Greenville and ended up in Jenkins as a child. He made many records, some on his own, and led Ellington's trumpet section for years. (Charleston Jazz Initiative.)

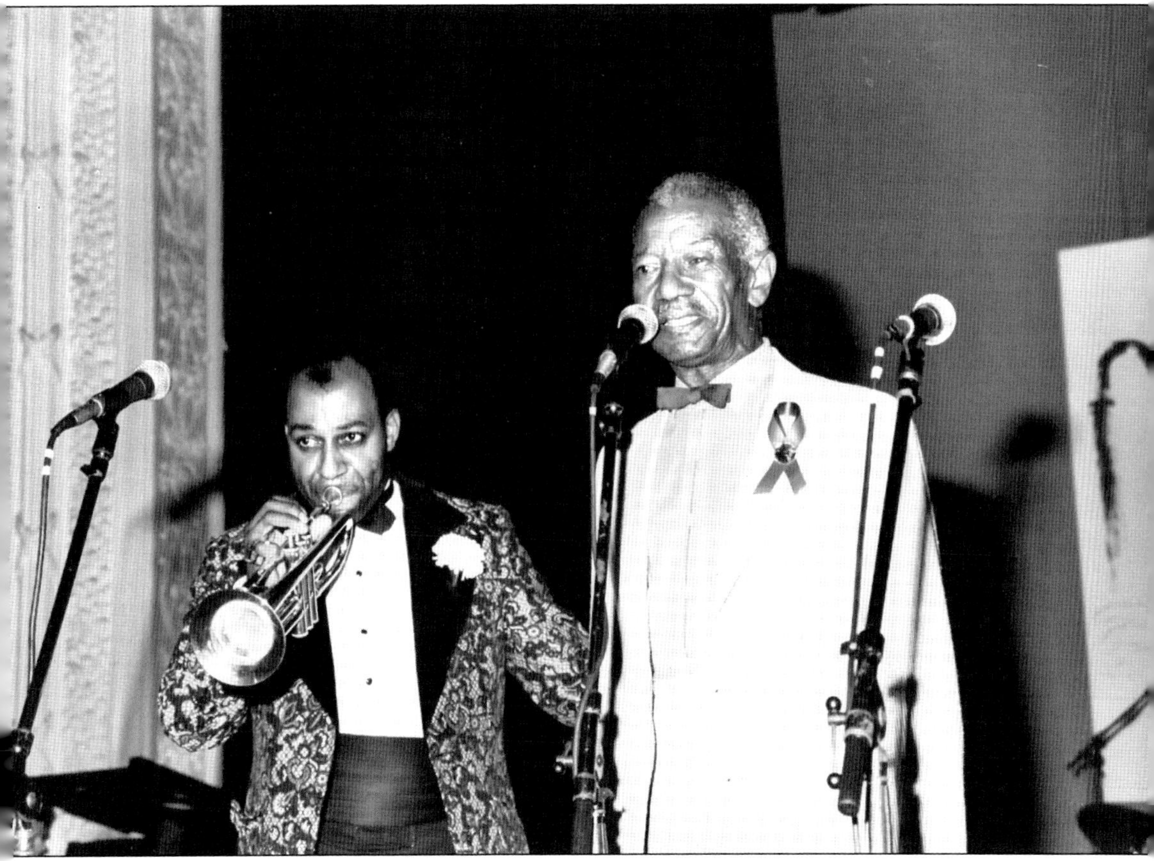

Joey Morant (left) and Jabbo Smith represent the beginning and end of the great trumpet lineage at the Jenkins Orphanage. The two appeared at a 1987 tribute to Smith at the Moja Arts Festival. (Wendell Johnson.)

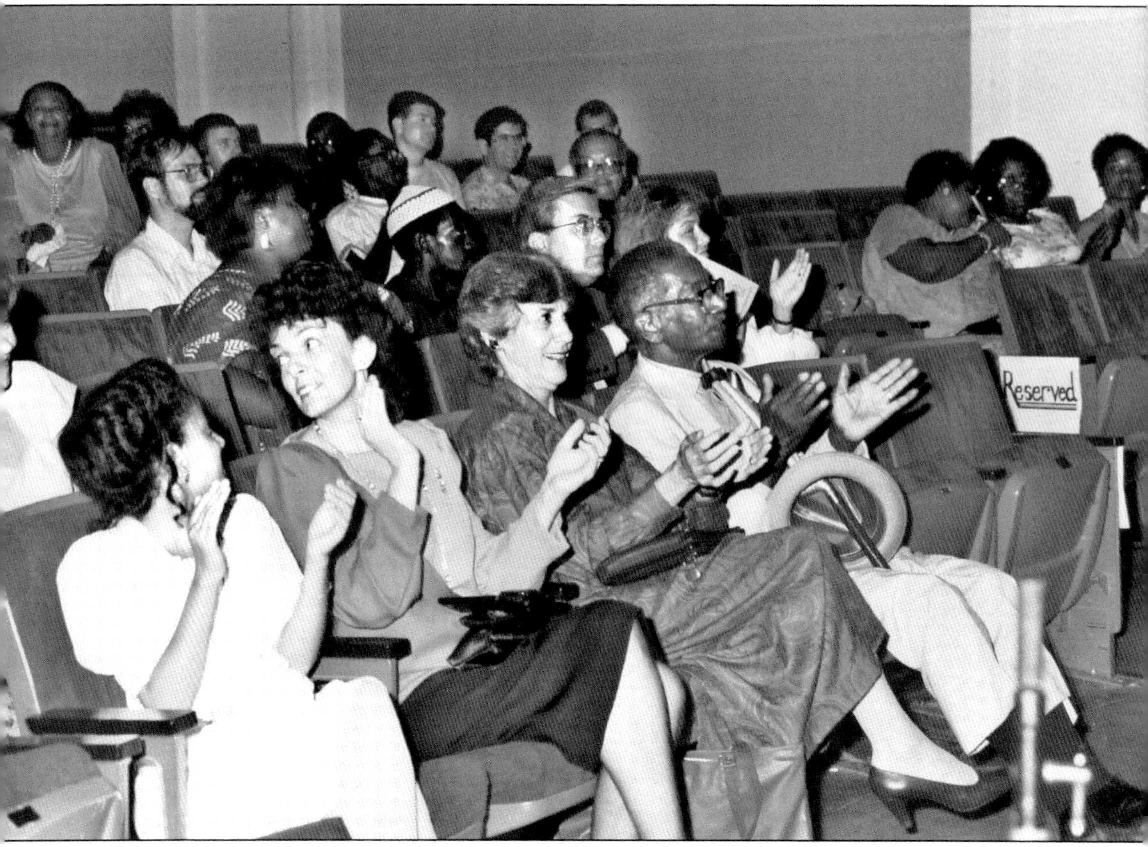

Lorraine Gordon, owner of the famed Village Vanguard jazz club in New York City, accompanied Jabbo Smith to Charleston in 1987 for his tribute at the Moja Arts Festival. Gordon believes Smith is one of the greatest trumpet players ever and that Smith was at the forefront of the American jazz trumpet lineage along with Louis Armstrong, spawning Roy Eldridge, Dizzy Gillespie, Lee Morgan, and Clifford Brown. (Wendell Johnson.)

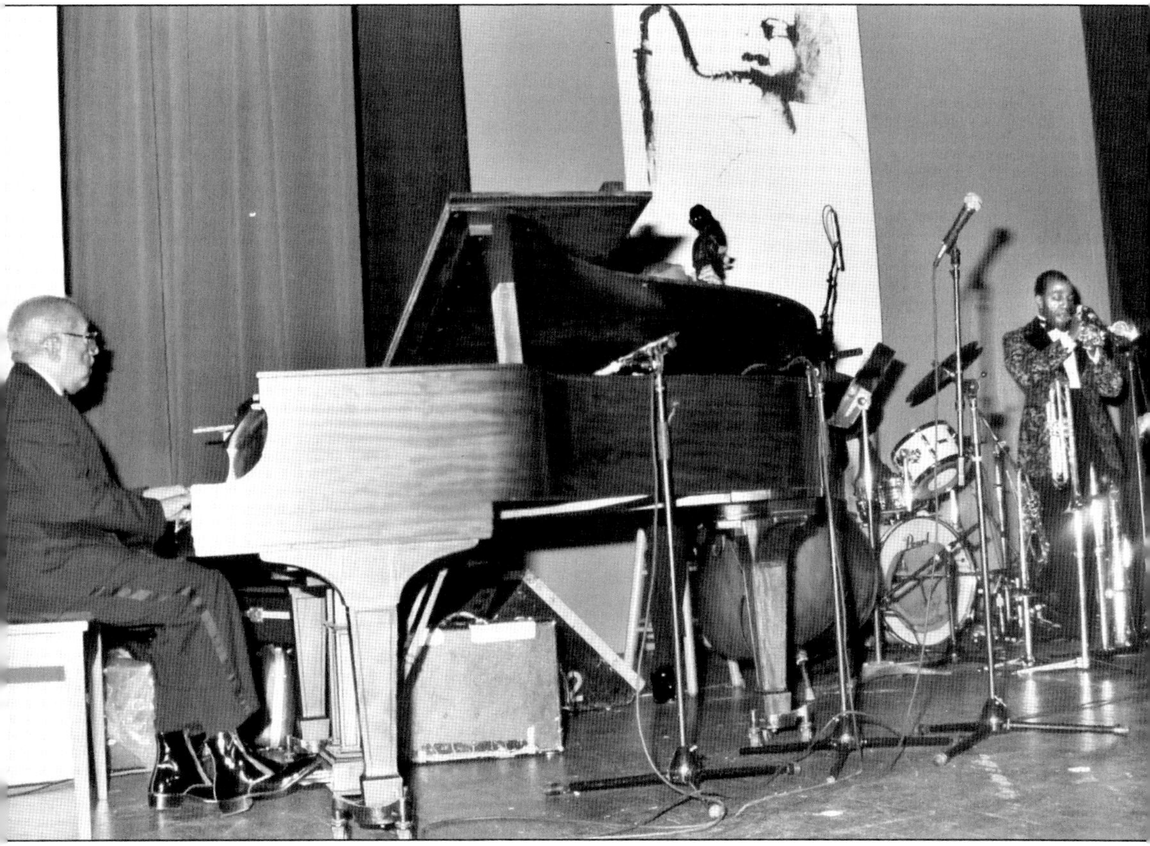

J. Michael Graves, prominent Charleston musician and educator, performs at the Moja Arts Festival at the Garden Theater in 1987. Graves was an Avery Normal Institute graduate and taught at Burke High School for many years. He was especially adept at church music and enjoyed popular music as well. (Wendell Johnson.)

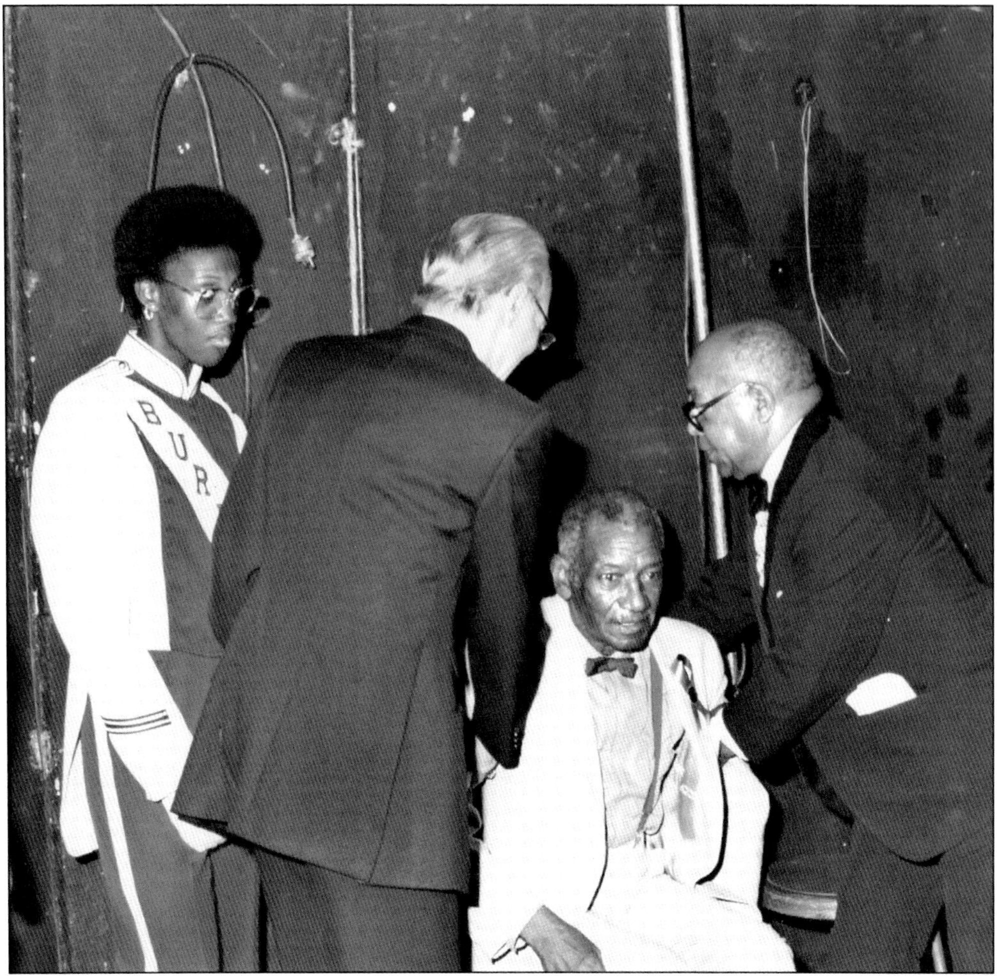

Claddys "Jabbo" Smith (seated), an early Jenkins Orphanage trumpeter who went on to rival Louis Armstrong, is assisted by Eugene Hunt (front) and Jenkins Orphanage official Toby Daniels at the 1987 Moja Arts Festival at the Garden Theater. Smith is a Savannah, Georgia, native who attended Jenkins during his childhood and spent some time at South Carolina State College. (Wendell Johnson.)

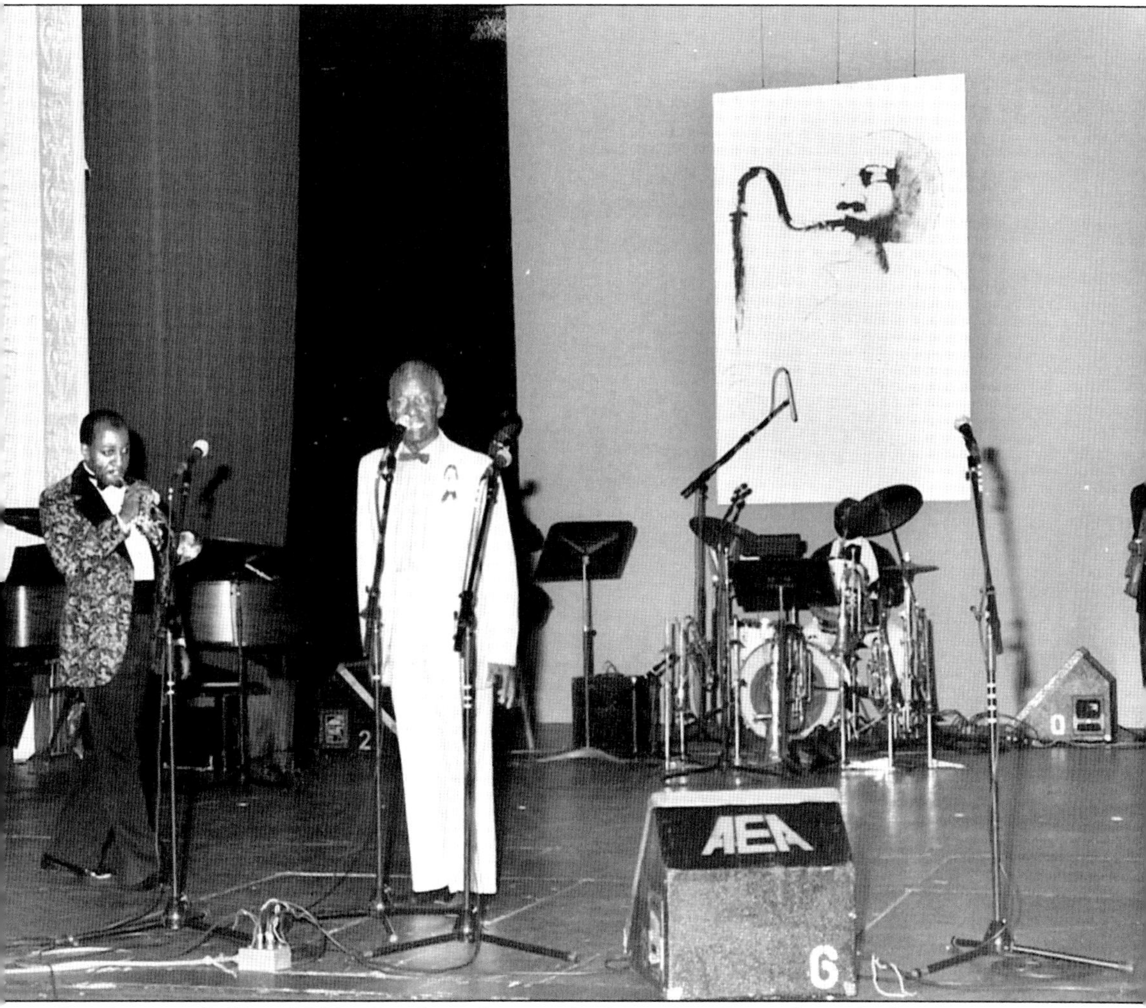

Joey Morant (left) and Jabbo Smith perform at the Moja Arts Festival in Charleston's Garden Theater in 1987. By this time, Smith was unable to play the trumpet but he sang with a sense of swing that enraptured the audience. (Wendell Johnson.)

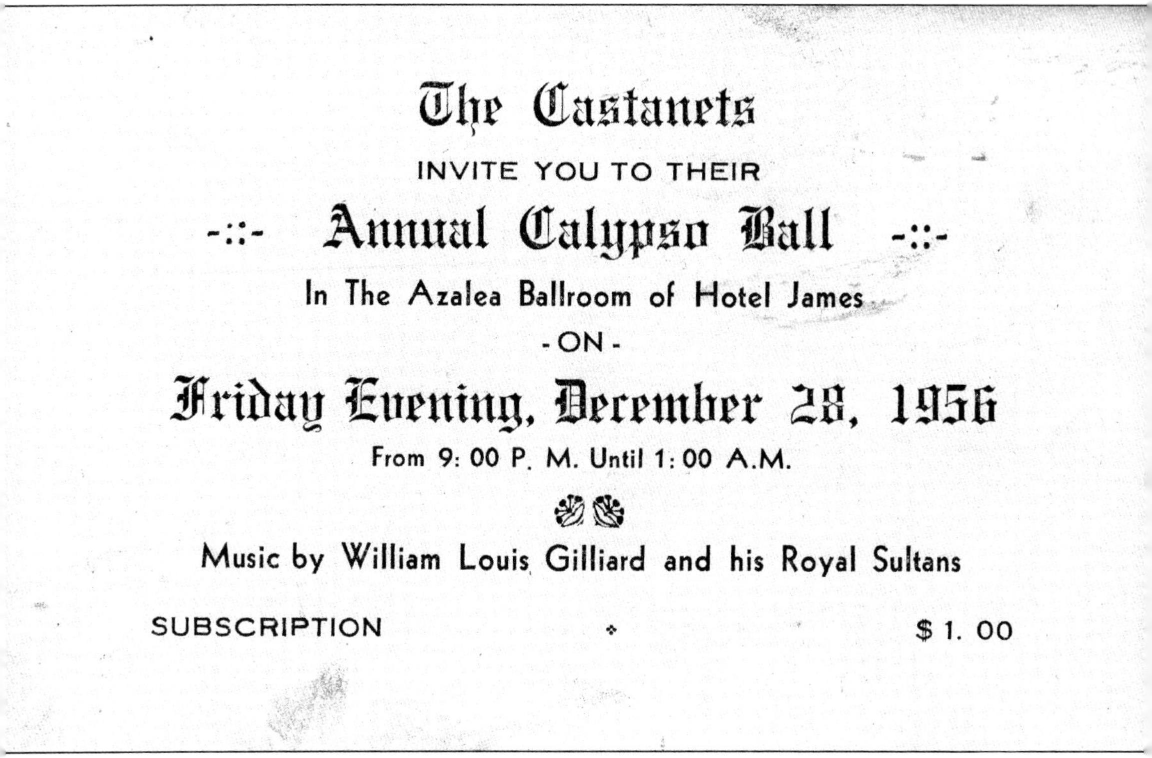

The Castanets

INVITE YOU TO THEIR

-::- Annual Calypso Ball -::-

In The Azalea Ballroom of Hotel James

- ON -

Friday Evening, December 28, 1956

From 9: 00 P. M. Until 1: 00 A.M.

Music by William Louis Gilliard and his Royal Sultans

SUBSCRIPTION $ 1. 00

This event shows the diversity of music enjoyed by Charlestonians in 1956. William Louis Gilliard and his Royal Sultans offered calypso music at Hotel James. (Avery Research Center.)

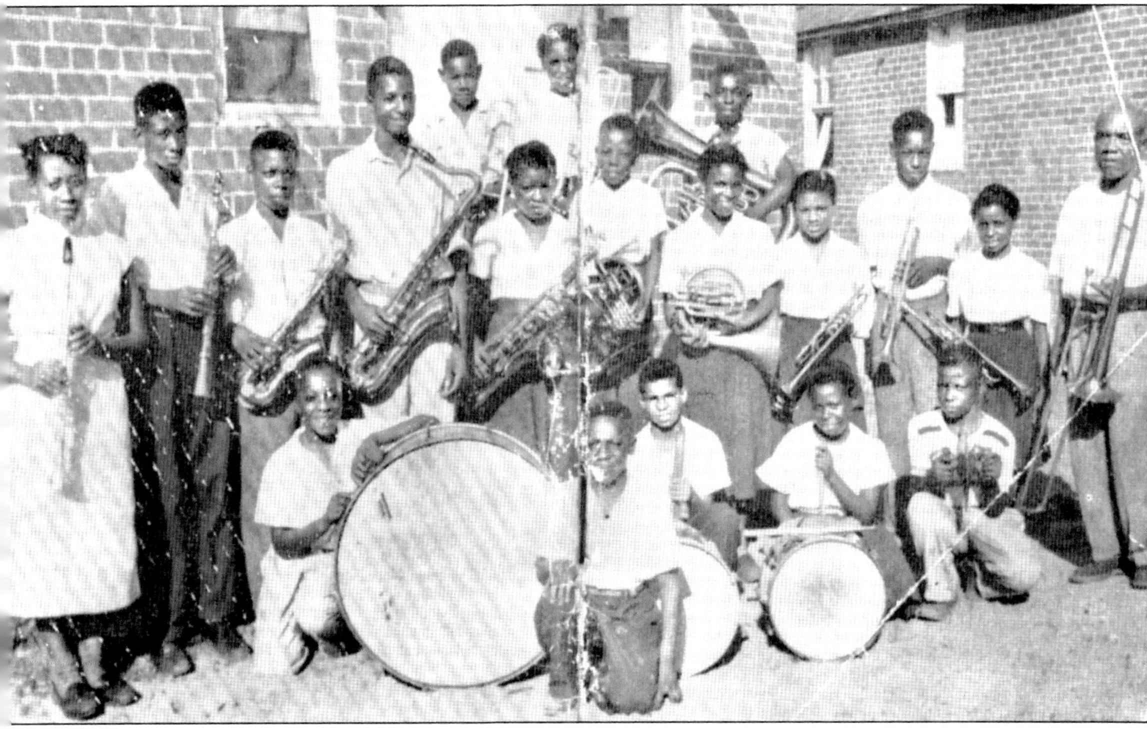

One of the last Jenkins Orphanage bands, under the direction of William Leroy Blake (right), is shown here in 1954 at the orphanage in North Charleston. By this time, many more woodwind instruments—saxophones and clarinets—had been added to the institution's brass band tradition. (Avery Research Center.)

OFFICERS

Mrs. Inez Parker, Pres.
Mrs. Thelma Edwards, V. Pres.
Mrs. E. Seabrook, Fin. Sect.
Mrs. E. B. Furman, Rec. Sect.
Mrs. Lurline Wright, Treas.
Mrs. Alice Brown, Bus. Mgr.

MEMBERS

Mrs. Naomi Corbin
Mrs. Bernice King
Mrs. Fannie Walker
Mrs. Geneva White
Mrs. Annabell Williams

The Semper Idem Social Club
INVITE YOU AND YOURS TO ATTEND THEIR
-: FREE DANCE :-
In The Beautiful Azalea Ballroom of Hotel James
Saturday Evening, April 25, 1959
FROM 9: 00 P. M. UNTIL 1: 00 A. M.

Music by The Metronome All-Stars - Dress Optional

Committee: The Semper Idem Social Club

The Azalea Ballroom in the Hotel James was one of the most popular venues in Charleston, located on Spring Street near the Ashley River. All kinds of event were held there. The entertainment for this dance was provided by the Metronome All-Stars, a very popular 1950s band. (Avery Research Center.)

The Cavaliers
-PRESENT THEIR-
-:- JUNE DANCE -:-
At The D. P. O. Hall, 655 East Bay Street
Friday Evening, June 19, 1959
FROM 10: 00 P. M. UNTIL 2: 00 A. M.

Music by Wm. Louis Gilliard and his Royal Sultans
ADMISSION ◆ $1.00

COMMITTEE: THE CLUB

The D.P.O. Hall on East Bay Street survived until the 1970s as a main social gathering place, especially for dances. It was one of only a few dance halls that far east on peninsular Charleston. (Avery Research Center.)

Five

Post-modern Beat

Nothing can be examined properly in Charleston without taking race into account, including the jazz music scene.

By the 1970s, integration in education and public accommodations had started bringing about a major shift in how music was taught and consumed. Former Jenkins Orphanage students and teachers were now teaching integrated classes in elementary schools, high schools, and newly created middle schools. School marching bands had begun to experiment with popular music, breaking the bounds of traditional John Phillip Sousa–type martial music.

An integrated clientele frequented bars, restaurants, and nightclubs. Very significantly, jazz and pop music bands were becoming integrated, playing in black and white entertainment spots. White musicians who formerly played beach music now played rhythm and blues with black musicians and vice versa. While the big bands were just about gone, the jazz players still played mostly for dancing. The mid-century Charleston jazz masters were as good as anybody else at the high-energy bop sounds, but they incorporated them into dance music, continuing to swing as local bands had since the beginning.

The club scene began to change around this time. George Kenny and others played once-all-white venues after joining integrated bands. At the forefront were the clubs on the navy and air force bases. The presence of sailors and airmen from the bases fertilized the jazz scene in the Charleston area. As a group, military musicians are well trained and proficient, and coming form other parts of the country, they are not as deterred from racial mixing as some from the Old South. Whites started coming around to once-all-black venues such as the Village on Ashley Avenue in downtown Charleston.

The rise of the jazz concert began during this period. The music was beginning to be presented for its own sake. The dances hadn't stopped, but one could now go into a place to sit and just listen.

One such venue was Myskyns on South Market Street. Opened as a private-membership jazz club, it evolved into allowing public access, providing an outlet for national as well as local and regional acts. One very hip feature at Myskyns was a courtyard out back where guests and musicians hung out together between sets and after performances. It was racially integrated, even as a private place. Young and old mixed also at Myskyns. There was even open interracial dating, not yet common in Charleston.

Educator, politician, and jazzman Lonnie Hamilton III opened a jazz nightclub on North Market Street in the 1970s. It became an instant success with his band, the Diplomats, as the house band. The building did not survive the development boom on Market Street, so the club moved down the street to the second floor of the famed Henry's Restaurant. By the 1990s, it was gone.

In the early 1980s, Reno Sweeney's opened on John Street, enjoying a run of only a couple of years. It was devoted to mostly local talent.

The Touch of Class on Meeting Street was run for a few years by Ernest Pinckney, brother-in-law to famous Charleston drummer Alphonse Mouzon. Jack White, an important jazz fan, advocate, and promoter, brought many acts to the club along with Pinckney. It featured mainstay acts such as Red Prysock and Brother Jack McDuff.

In the late 1970s, Spoleto Festival USA showed up in Charleston, bringing a jazz series with it that gave Charlestonians much more access to the national and international modern players. The big bands had always come to Charleston, and smaller hard bop ensembles occasionally came through here, but not much since bebop came to the fore.

In 1980, Charleston's longest-running jazz series, Jazz Afterhours, was one of the first two series in the now famous Piccolo Spoleto Festival, a locally produced program run in conjunction with Spoleto Festival USA. For more than 25 consecutive years, it has been one of the most popular and successful jazz music events in the history of the Southeast. It was independently produced for the festival by the Group for Integrated Studies (GIS) under its banner "Return to the Source," also the name of GIS's house band led by trumpeter and keyboardist Bob Ephiram. Its theme was "360 degrees of Black Music." The series featured hard bop, bebop, gospel, Southern blues fusion (blues-based rock and roll), blues, live jazz cruises along the Cooper River, big band, and the first live reggae ever in Charleston. Much of the standing-room-only series was broadcast live by WSCI-FM Radio, the local station of the South Carolina Educational Radio Network. Lonnie Hamilton and the Diplomats opened the South Market Street series with a tribute to Fletcher Linton and Toby Daniels, two legendary Charleston educators and jazzmen.

The Moja Arts Festival, a black arts festival, appeared in 1984 producing local, regional, and national acts. Just like Spoleto USA and Piccolo Spoleto, Moja continues to this day. The national headliner in its first year was trumpeter Donald Byrd. In 2006, it was Nneenah Freelon. Its first year also saw a tribute to the Jenkins Orphanage bands by a group made up of former Jenkins teachers and players.

As Spoleto and other festivals rose to prominence for live jazz, the local clubs faded. Rock and roll—in all its forms—took over the live music scene. More jazz concerts emerged as independent producers put on shows, and in the 1990s, restaurants began to be the main venues for improvisational music. At the same time, the Charleston Jazz Festival ran for a few years, making a valiant attempt at blending local, regional, and national acts over the course of several days. It did not last.

The 1990s brought to town the Chef and Clef, a three-story Market Street eatery with jazz on the first floor and blues on the third. With live jazz seven nights a week, it became a stop on the east coast tour of jazz musicians, drawing players from around the country. It also served as a venue for up-and-coming locals, including College of Charleston students. The restaurant-club ran for many years, some as home of the Piccolo Spoleto Jazz Afterhours Series.

By this time, the College of Charleston jazz studies program was growing. Bassist Lee Burrows, pianist Tommy Gill, trumpeter Charlton Singleton, guitarists Clay Ross and Jim Bastian, saxophonist Robert Lewis, and multi-instrumentalist Frank Duvall were making their mark on the scene as players and teachers. In the early 1990s, Gill introduced three youngsters professionally at the Charleston Jazz Festival—vocalist Quiana Parler, bassist Kevin Hamilton, and drummer Quentin Baxter. All three have emerged as major players. Baxter and Hamilton have served as adjunct professors at the College of Charleston. Parler is one of the top vocalists in the area and tours with singing sensation Clay Aiken, working Las Vegas, Los Angeles, and national television. Baxter tours the world as first-call percussionist for major-label recording artists.

The three have also contributed mightily to the Latin jazz scene that came about in the 1990s, working a long run with Brazil, the house band at Mitchell's, the successor to Chef and Clef.

Pianist Taras Kovayl led that band. Another important Latin jazz band in Charleston was Para Ti, led by multi-instrumentalist Joe Ambrosia and including drummer Steven Sandifer, bassist Wayne "Nekbone" Mitchum, pianist Gill, and saxophonist John Phillips.

A most interesting group from the 1990s is Baxter's Emanon, a collective of many musicians over the years who played in one configuration or another including saxophonist Kebbi Williams of Atlanta and bassist Delbert Felix of St. Helena, South Carolina. The band, and others, grew out of Clara's, a King Street coffee house in the College of Charleston district that incubates young musicians in the true sense. For years, planned and impromptu live sessions of the highest caliber could be heard there on Sundays under the watchful eye and ear of owners Ron and Nancy Gorlesky.

As development pushed Charleston into the 21st century, the local jazz scene and its players have gone right along with it. The area abounds with great players of all stripes. It's now known around the world, as players come to work restaurants, concerts, and festivals.

A very long and proud tradition continues.

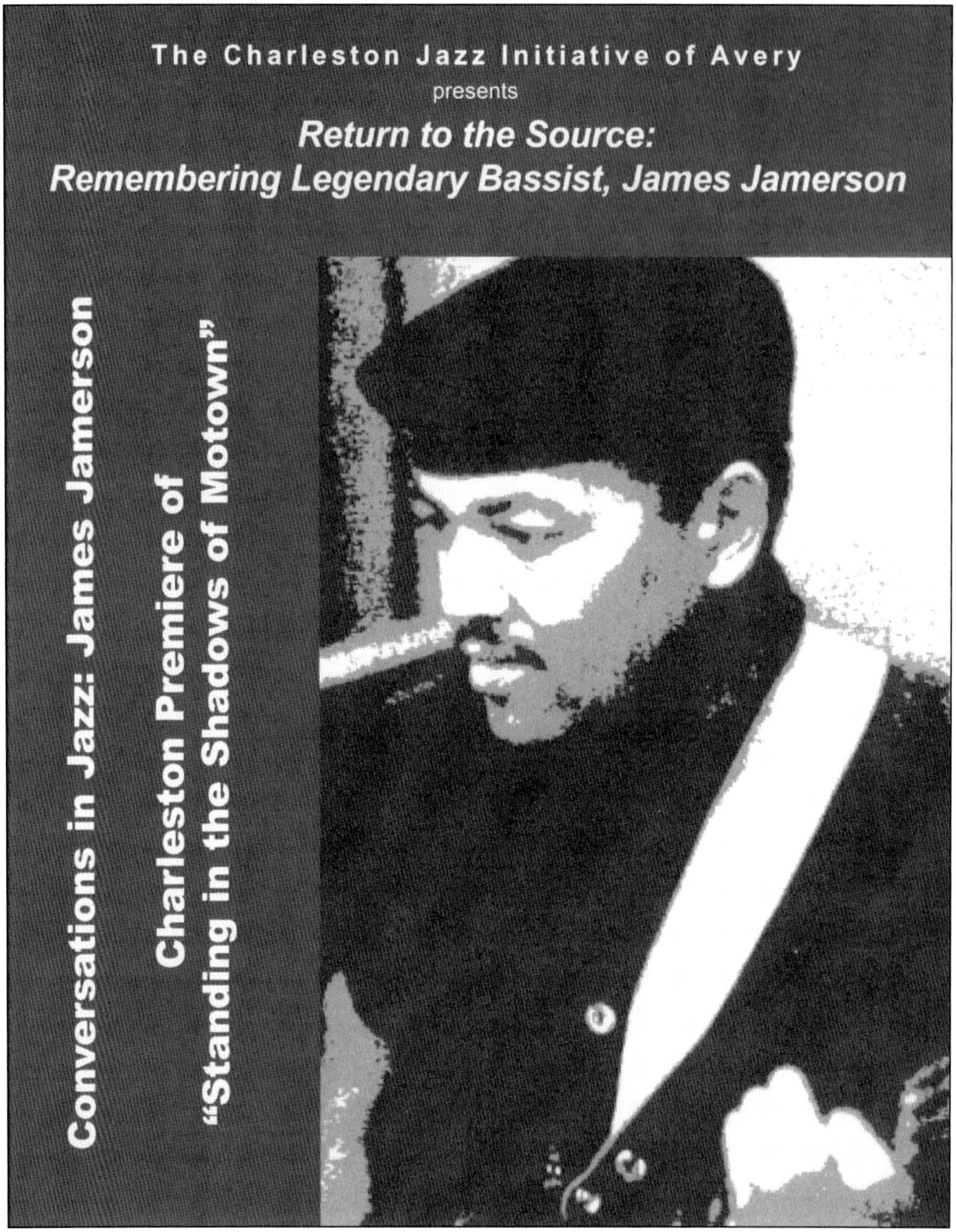

This poster announced the debut of the award-winning documentary *Standing in the Shadows of Motown* in Charleston by the Charleston Jazz Initiative in 2004. It was held at the Sottile Theater. The movie is in large part a biography of bassist James Jamerson, who was born on Edisto Island, where he learned music, and lived on peninsular Charleston before moving to Detroit, Michigan, to join his mother and graduate from high school. (Charleston Jazz Initiative.)

James Jamerson's funeral was held in Los Angeles in 1983. It was attended by many prominent people from the show business world. (Charleston Jazz Initiative.)

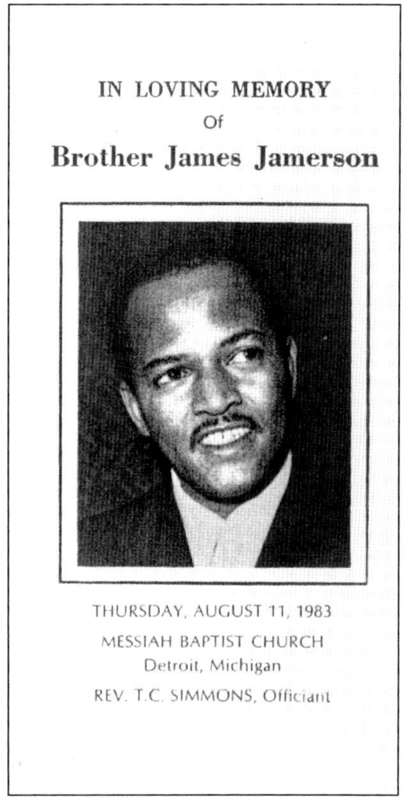
IN LOVING MEMORY
Of
Brother James Jamerson

THURSDAY, AUGUST 11, 1983
MESSIAH BAPTIST CHURCH
Detroit, Michigan
REV. T.C. SIMMONS, Officiant

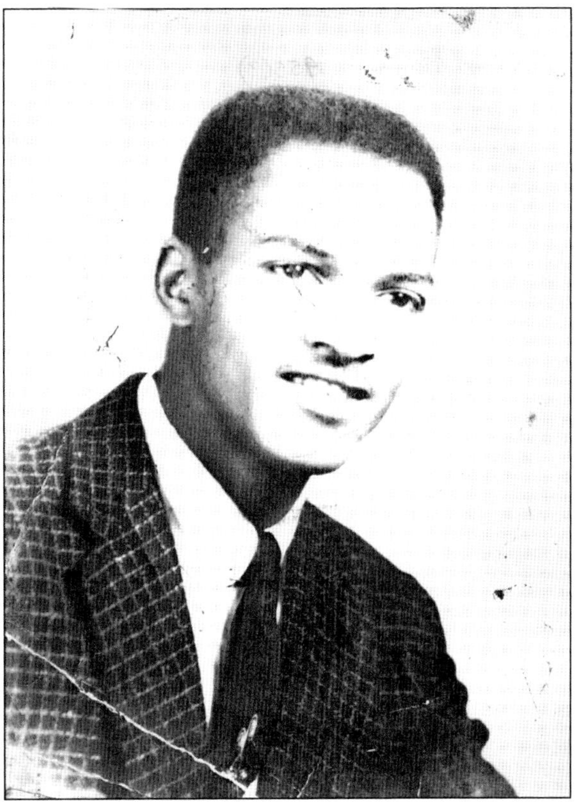

This is legendary Motown bassist James Jamerson's high school graduation picture in Detroit in 1955. (Charleston Jazz Initiative.)

First bass: The man behind the Motown sound

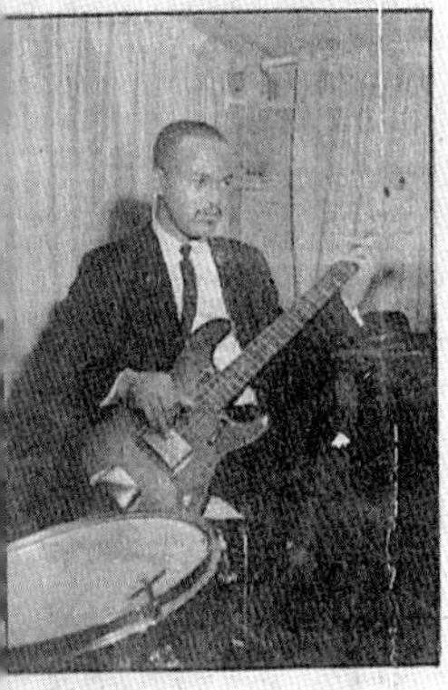

By Susan Whitall
News Music Critic

What made the Motown sound? What is it about Motown recordings that makes them so eminently listenable, whether heard from a tinny dashboard radio in 1966 or from a compact disk player in 1989?

When the question was posed during 1983's Motown 25th Anniversary TV special, Smokey Robinson was the silken voice of reason: "The Motown sound is the bottom, you know. They got the foot working and you can hear the bass real good."

Translation: It's the rhythm section, that fat bass and drum sound that has you pounding the car dashboard.

Who can forget how the bass throbs expectantly in the beginning of the Supremes' *Can't Hurry Love*, just before Diana comes in to coo "I need love, looove ... to ease my mind"? Or how the bass thumps, spooky and dangerous, on the Temptations *Cloud Nine*?

And there are the opening bars to Marvin Gaye's finger-snapping *Ain't That Peculiar*, where the bass takes off like a rocket on a syncopated run that stands the hair up on the back of the neck. The piano comes in to echo the bass line, and so on. But then, on Motown recordings the bass would often take the lead while other instruments would follow or counterpoint it.

These intricate yet funky bass lines intrigued fans all over the world. Paul McCartney and The Who's John Entwistle both were inspired by Motown's bass sound, although they did not know the identity of the mystery bass player.

In Detroit music circles, however, they've always known who it was: James Jamerson, a Northwestern High graduate and impassioned jazz bass player who came to pop music reluctantly, because it paid the bills. Jamerson became so important to Motown's recording sound that one of the eight tracks on every record was devoted to his bass. He died in 1983 when he was only 47.

Now Philadelphia guitarist and technical handbook writer Alan Slutsky, a.k.a. Dr. Licks, has writ-

Please see **Bass/6G**

"James Jamerson's main gripe wasn't money, it was recognition."
Biographer Alan Slutsky

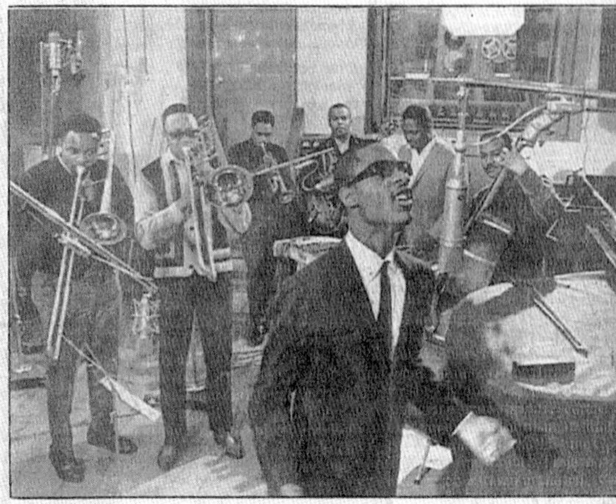

James Jamerson is seen at the extreme right, playing his upright bass, in a typical studio session circa 1966 at Hitsville's Studio A, on West Grand Blvd. The artist is Stevie Wonder.

This is a clip from a publication showing James Jamerson (right) working with Stevie Wonder. All the Motown singers delighted in having Jamerson play on their records and at their performances. There is a story that Smokey Robinson did not want to record without Jamerson in the band behind him. (Charleston Jazz Initiative.)

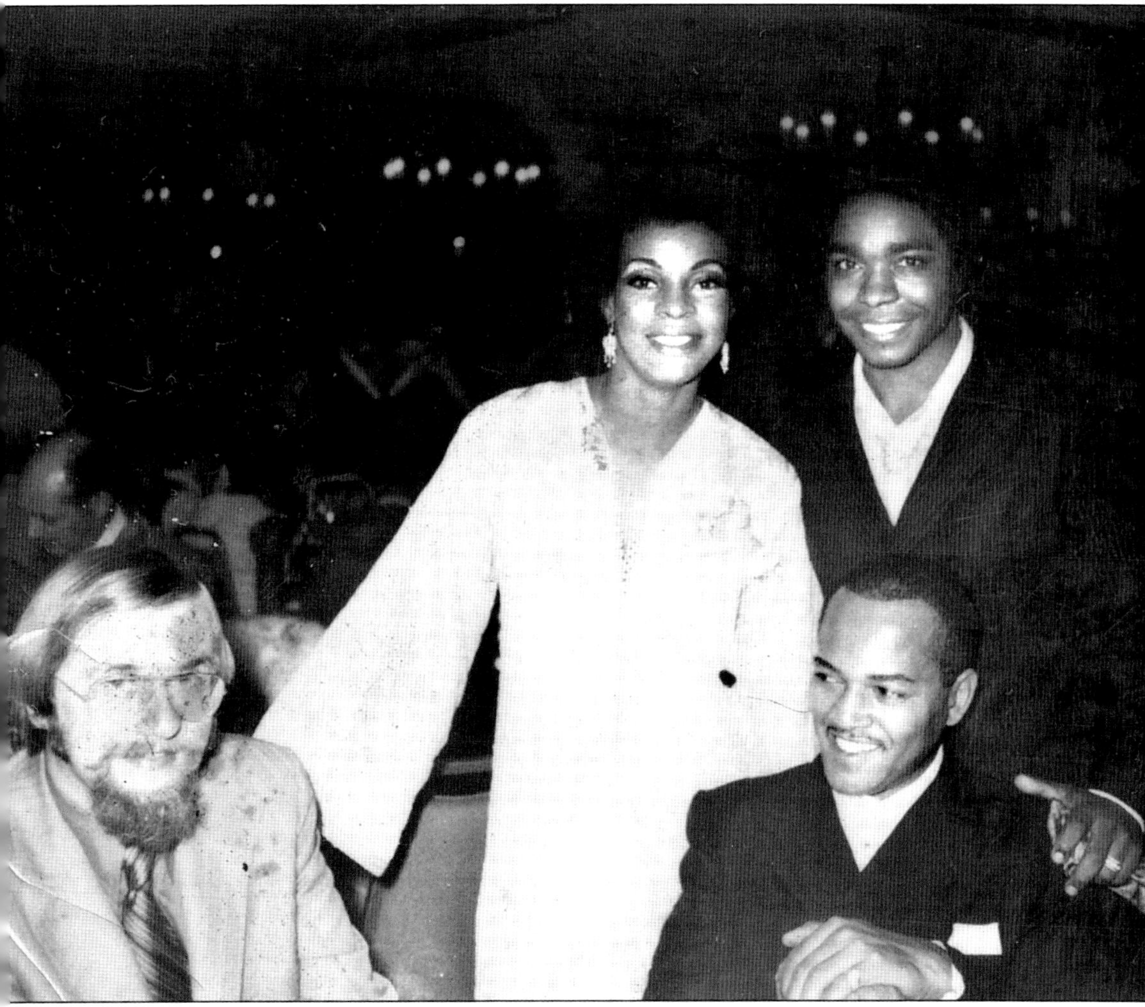

James Jamerson is shown here at a nightclub in Detroit with Martha Reeves of Martha and the Vandellas in the 1960s. Jamerson was a big part of the nightlife scene in Detroit in those days. (Charleston Jazz Initiative.)

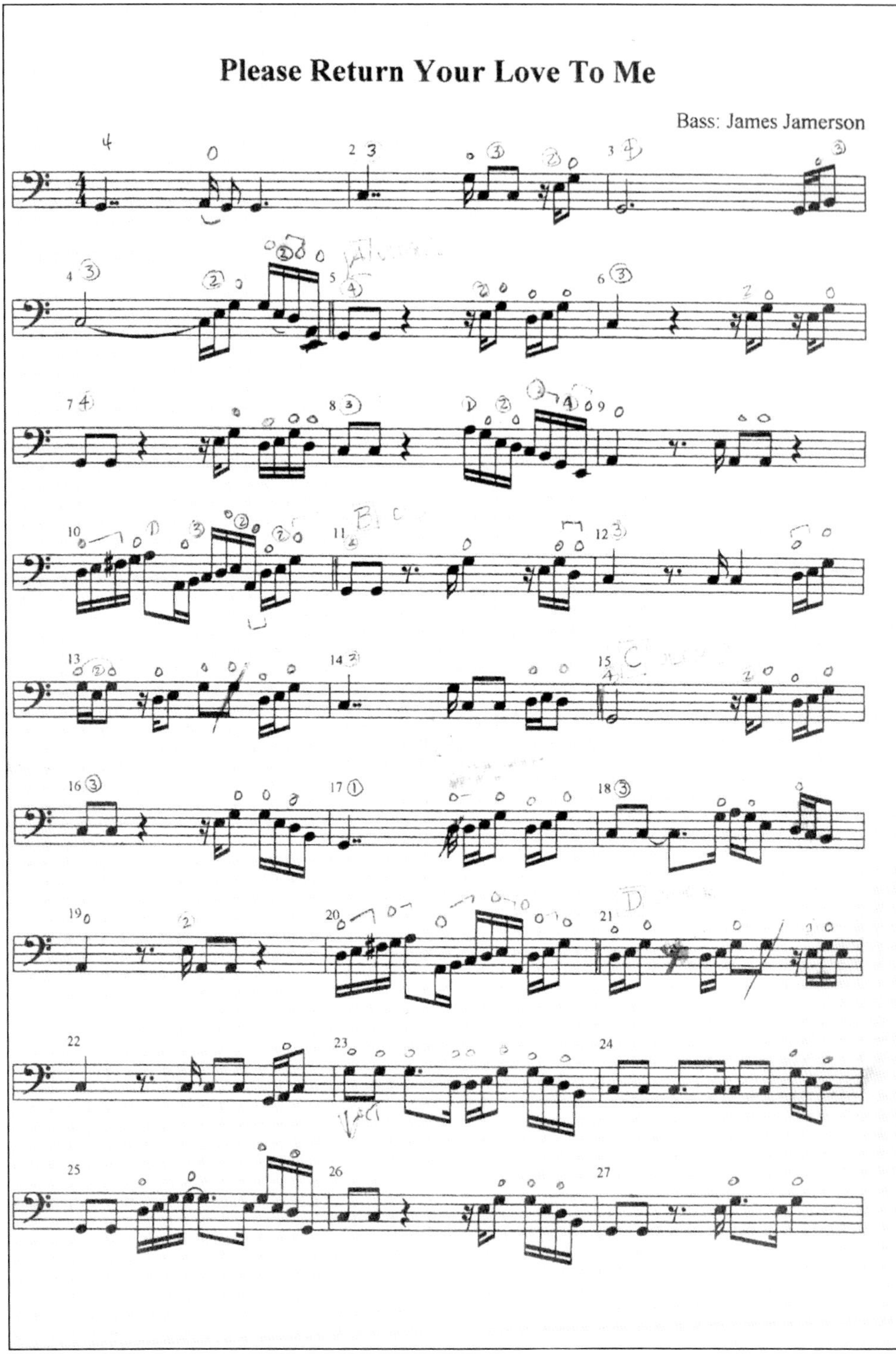

This is the bass line for Motown Records' "Please Return Your Love to Me," as played by Charleston native James Jamerson, an original member of the Funk Brothers, the house band that played behind all the Motown stars during the record label's heyday. (Charleston Jazz Initiative.)

This magazine cover announces the film Standing in the *Shadows of Motown*, featuring James Jamerson. The film was based on a book written by Alan "Dr. Licks" Slutsky, a Philadelphia-based radio disc jockey. Slutsky also produced the film. (Charleston Jazz Initiative.)

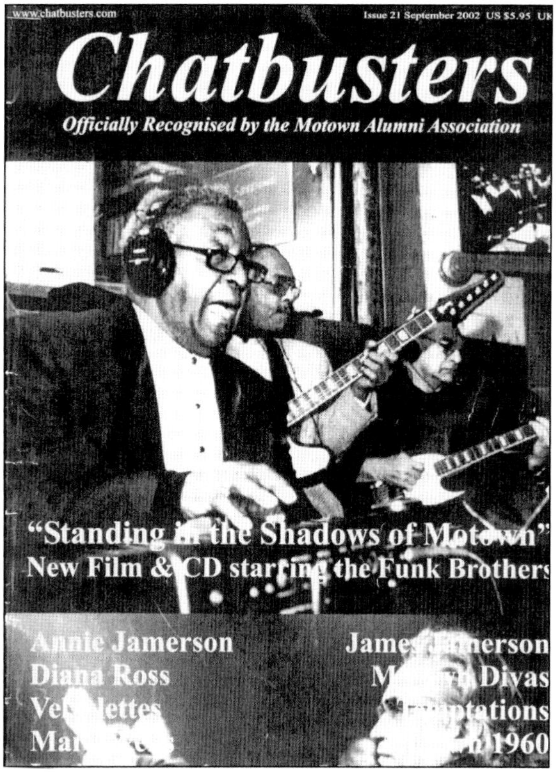

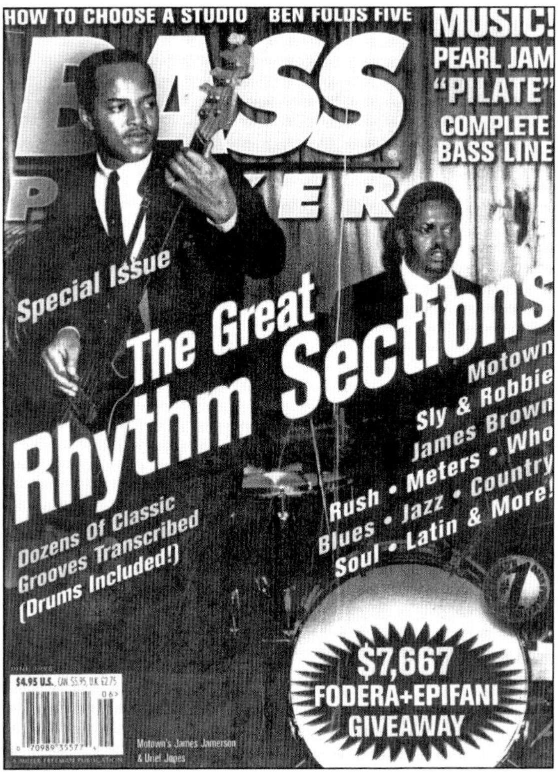

Bass Player magazine featured James Jamerson on a cover. Jamerson is revered by bassists from all over. Alan Slutsky's Standing in the *Shadows of Motown* is full of tributes to Jamerson from the likes of Paul McCartney, Phil Chen, John Patitucci, and Allen McGrier. (Charleston Jazz Initiative.)

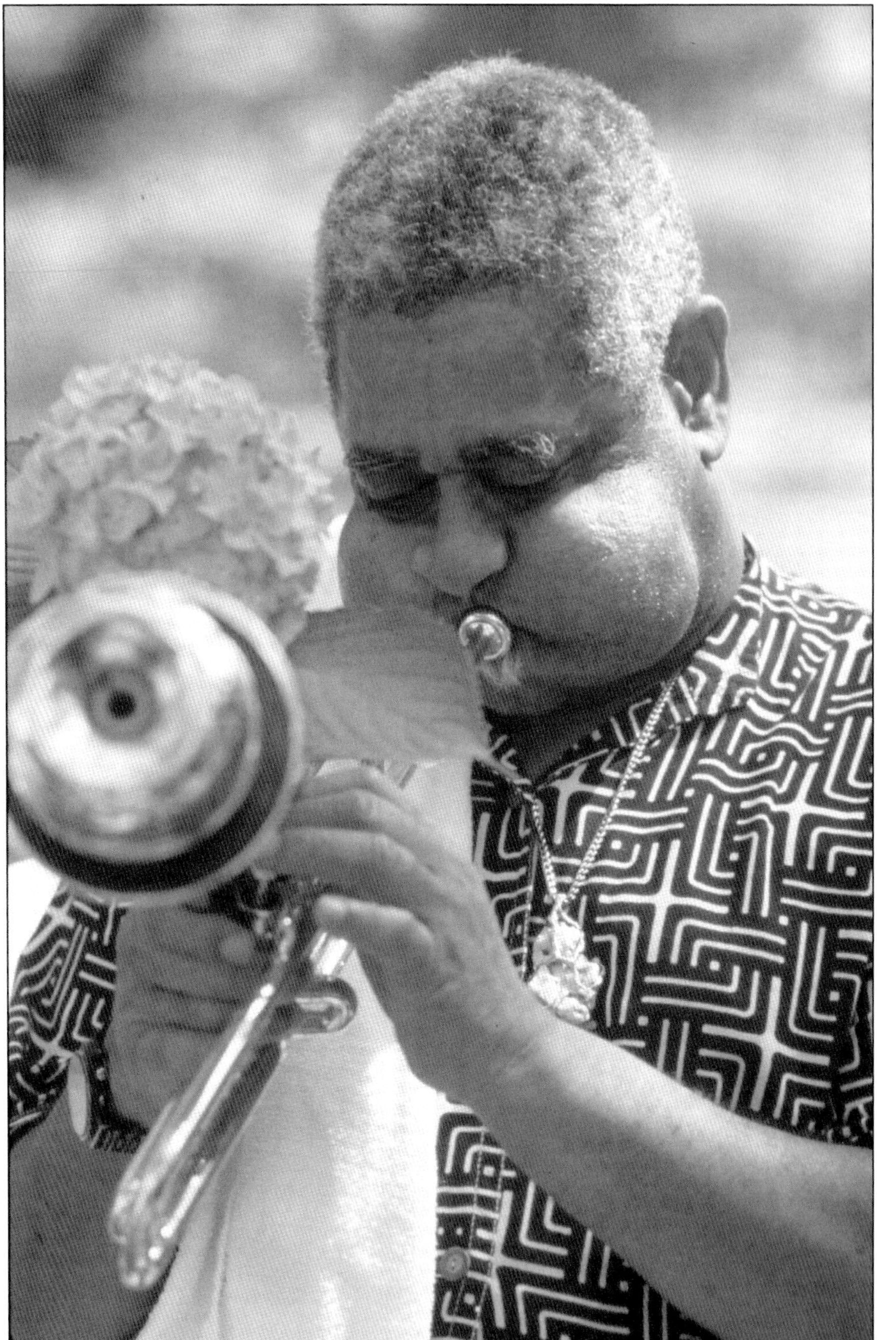

World-renowned trumpeter Dizzy Gillespie played the Spoleto Festival in Charleston at Magnolia Gardens in the 1980s. Gillespie told of the great Charleston and South Carolina musical tradition around the world. He was known to open all his live performances with noting that he was from South Carolina. At a concert in the 1970s at Gaillard Municipal Auditorium in Charleston, Gillespie spoke of the great jazz tradition from Charleston but couldn't help but poke a little fun at the city for the high regard in which it holds itself. (*Post and Courier.*)

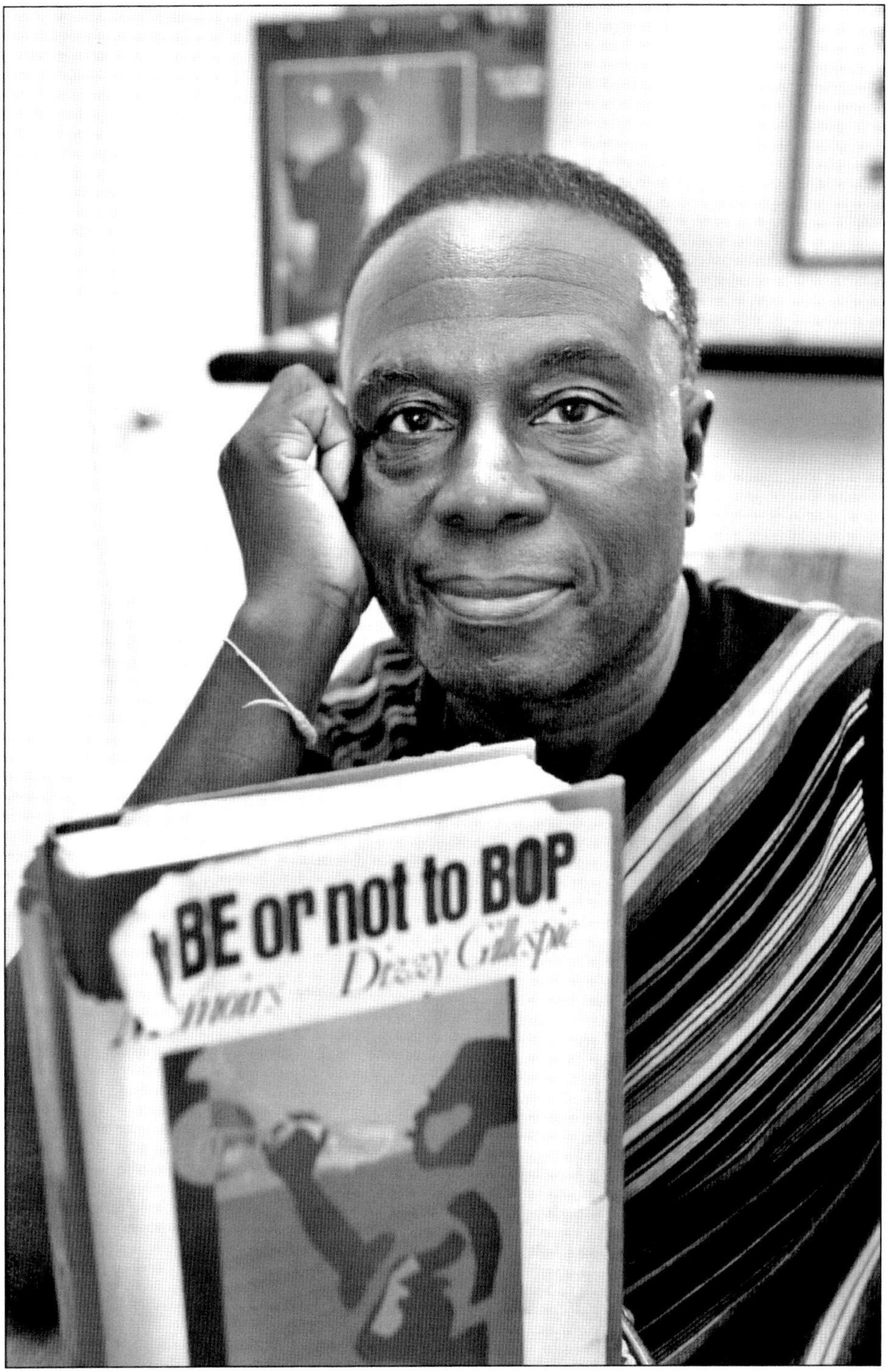

Dr. Al Fraser of Charleston wrote the highly acclaimed *To Be or Not to Bop* with Dizzy Gillespie. Fraser knew Gillespie well over the years and befriended him. They were summertime neighbors in Queens, New York, when Fraser was a young man visiting relatives there. Fraser's book is one of the highest-respected jazz books in the world. (*Post and Courier.*)

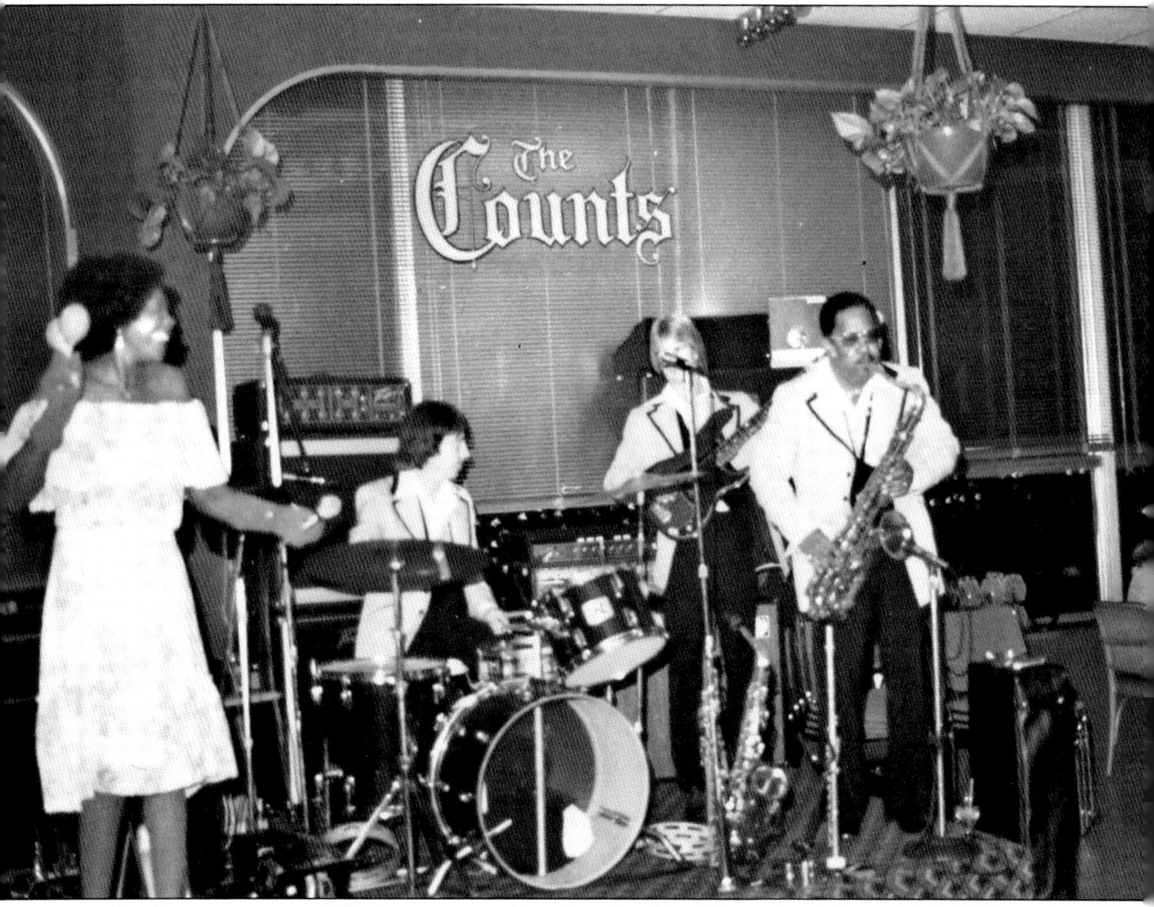

The Counts were one of the first integrated bands in the Charleston area. George Kenny was a moving force in the band, which played in all sorts of venues to all sorts of crowds. (George Kenny.)

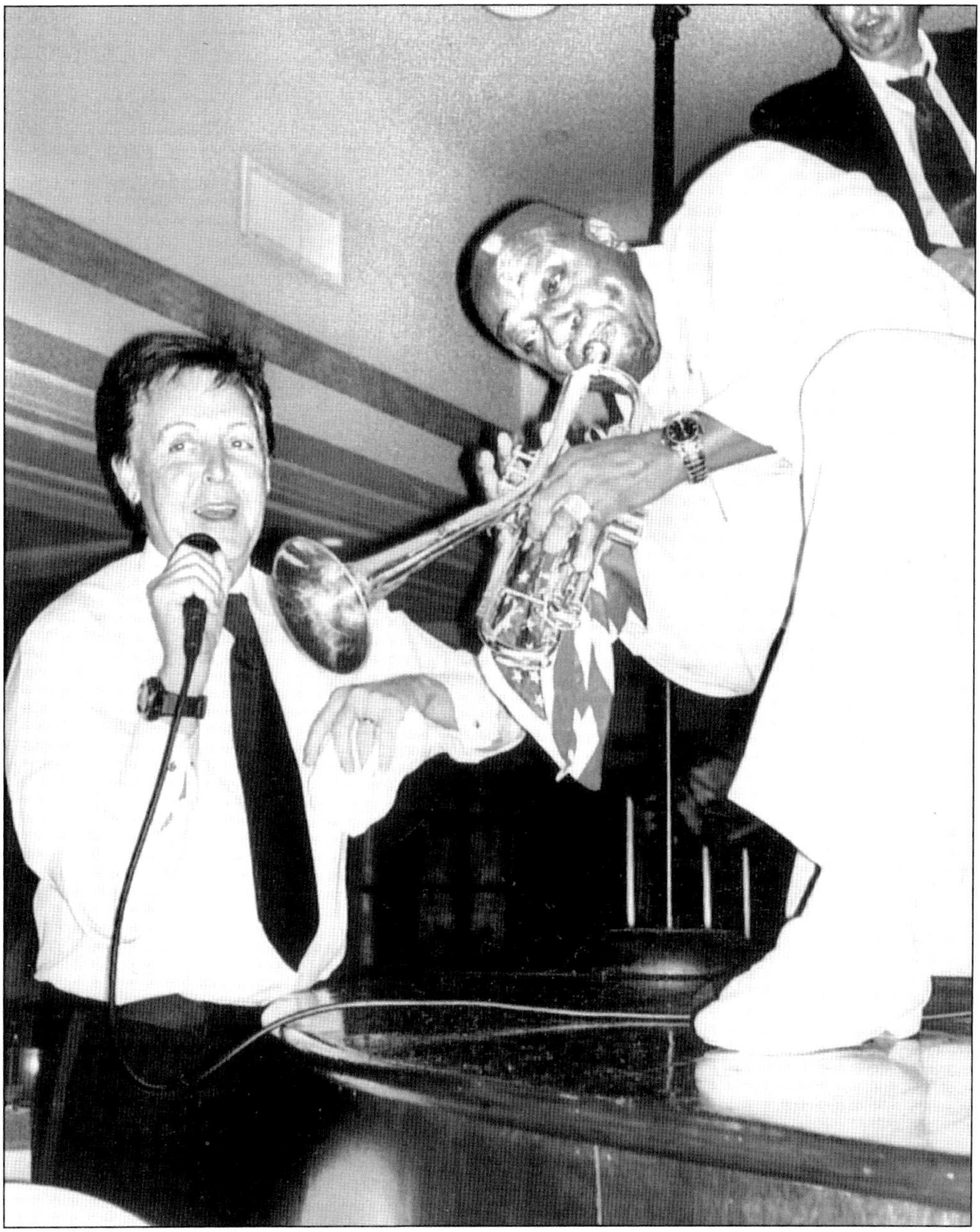

Charleston trumpet player Joey Morant once jammed with Paul McCartney. Morant is an excellent example of the versatility of musicians from Charleston. (Charleston Jazz Initiative.)

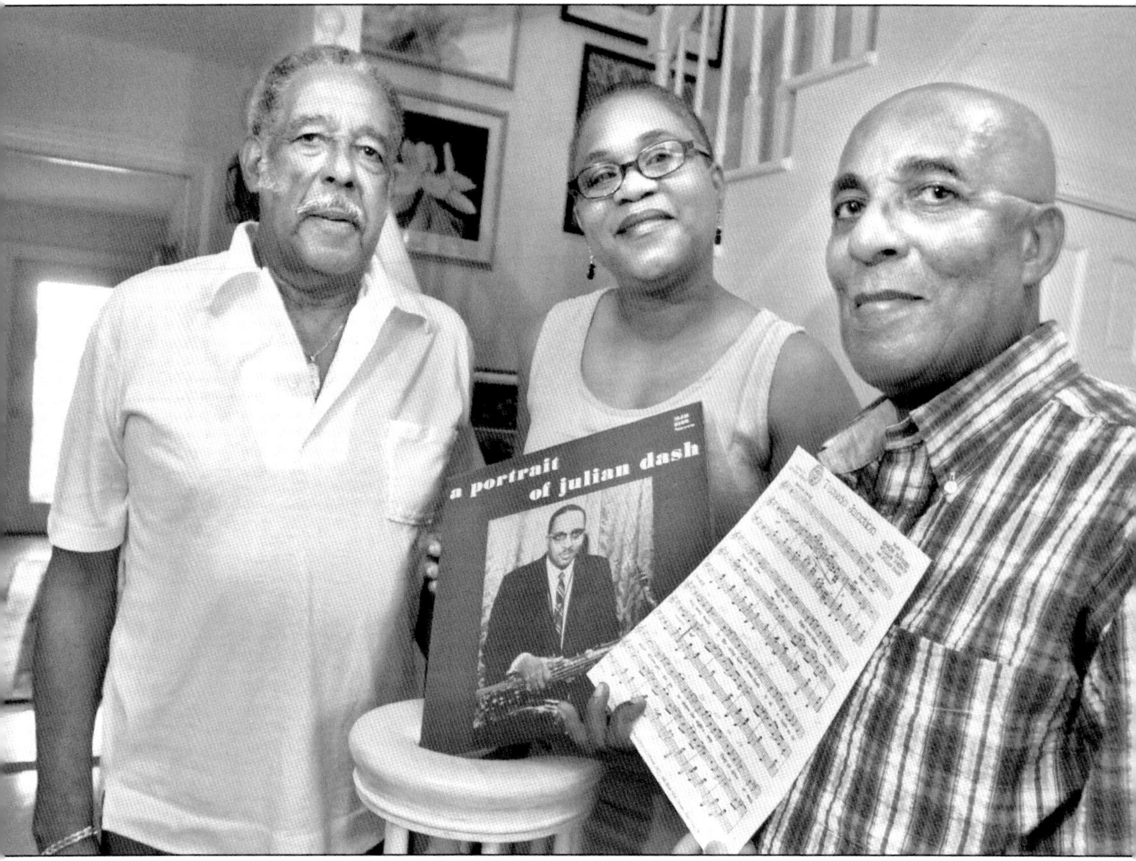

Roger Dash (left), Dr. Karen A. Chandler of the Charleston Jazz Initiative, and John Dash prepare for the initiative's tribute to St. Julian Dash in 2005. The family and the research project paid homage to Dash for his role in jazz music. (*Post and Courier.*)

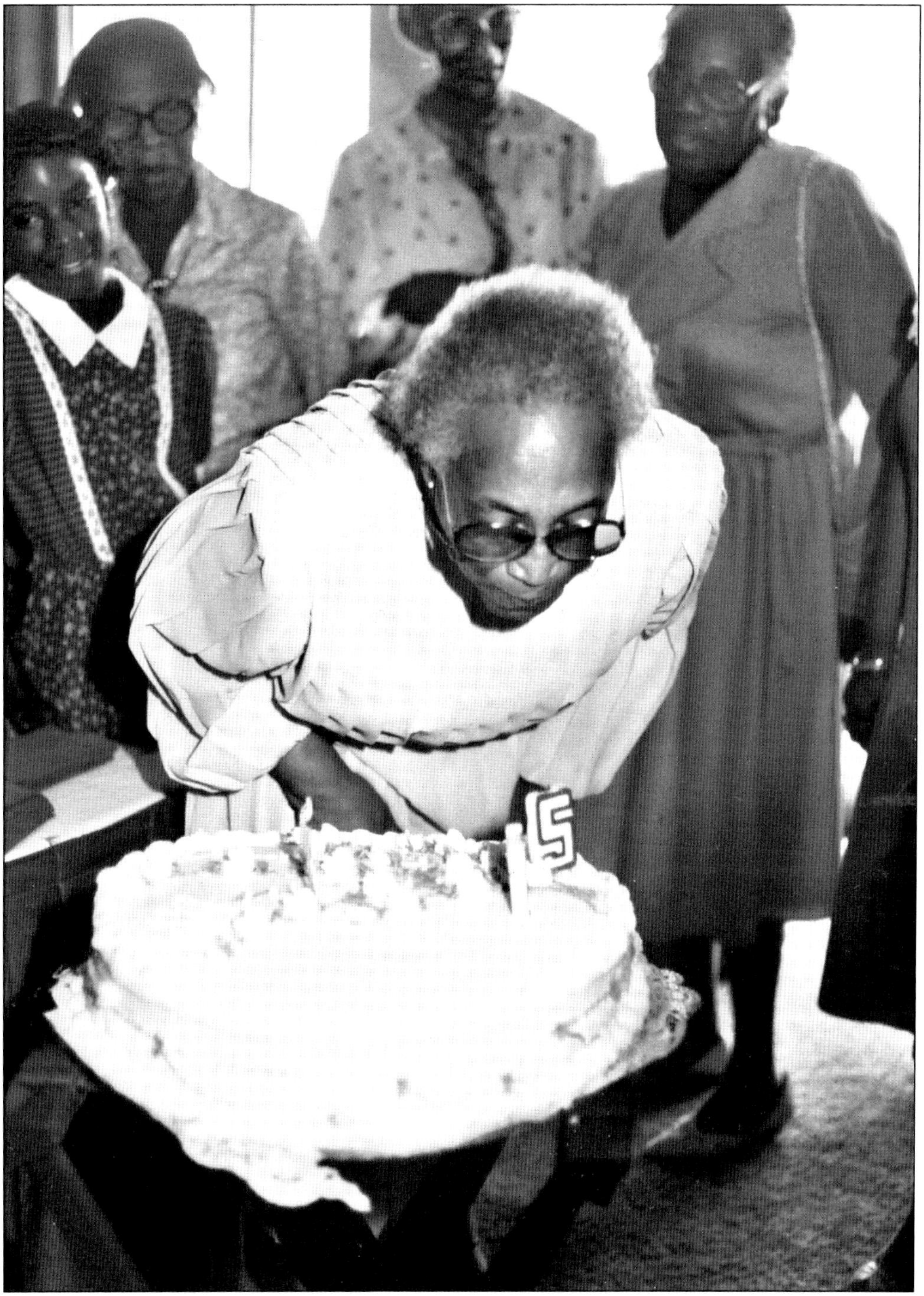

Sarah Dowling, longtime administrator at Jenkins Orphanage, celebrates her birthday. Dowling and her husband, the Reverend John Dowling, were a large part of the evolution of Jenkins Orphanage over the decades, having held many posts at the institution and giving much of their lives to it. Both are deceased. A street in North Charleston near today's Jenkins Institute for Children, the new name for Jenkins Orphanage, is named after them. (Wendell Johnson.)

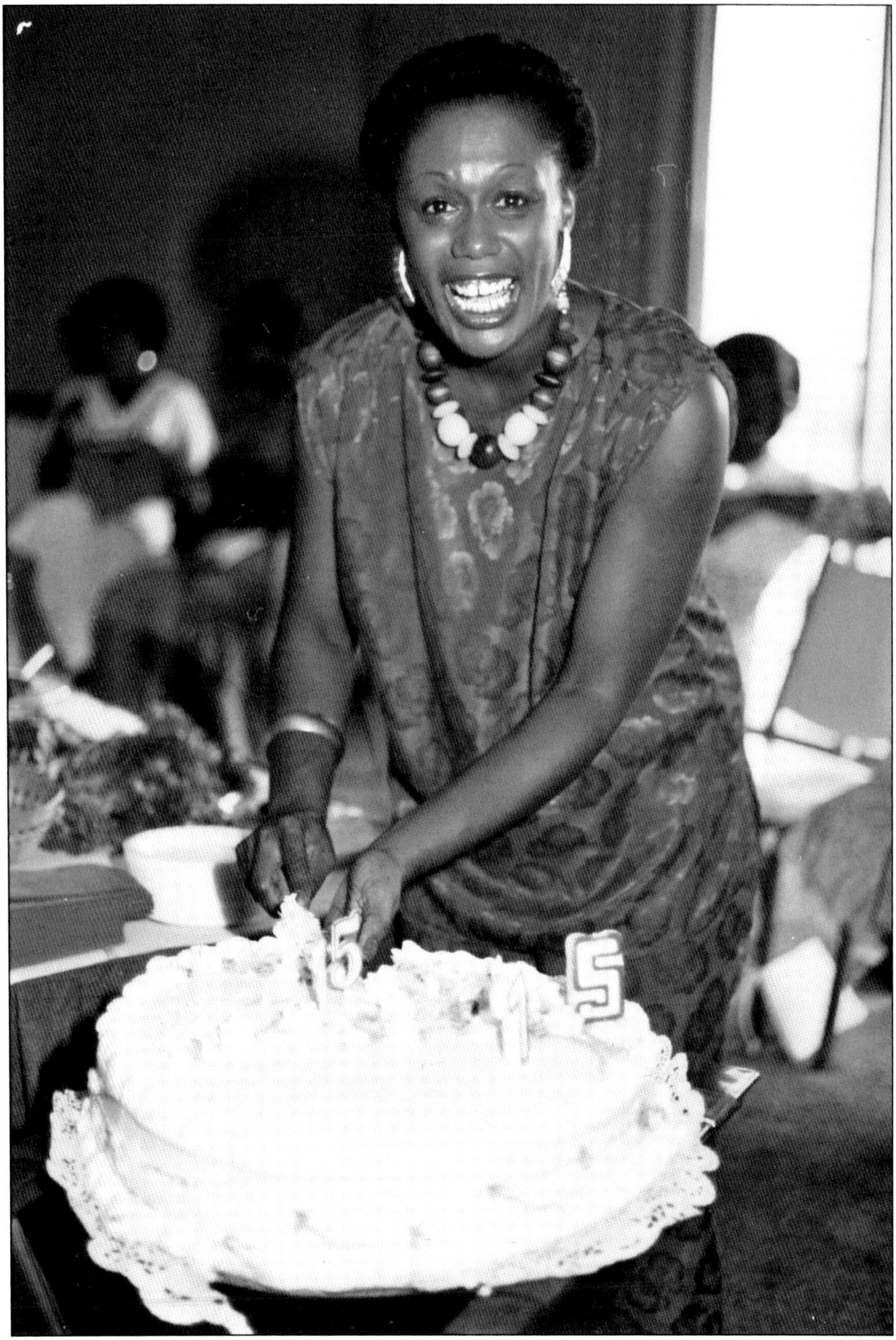

Rachel Dowling, daughter of John and Sarah Dowling and a member of the last Jenkins Orphanage Band, celebrates her mother's 75th birthday. (Wendell Johnson.)

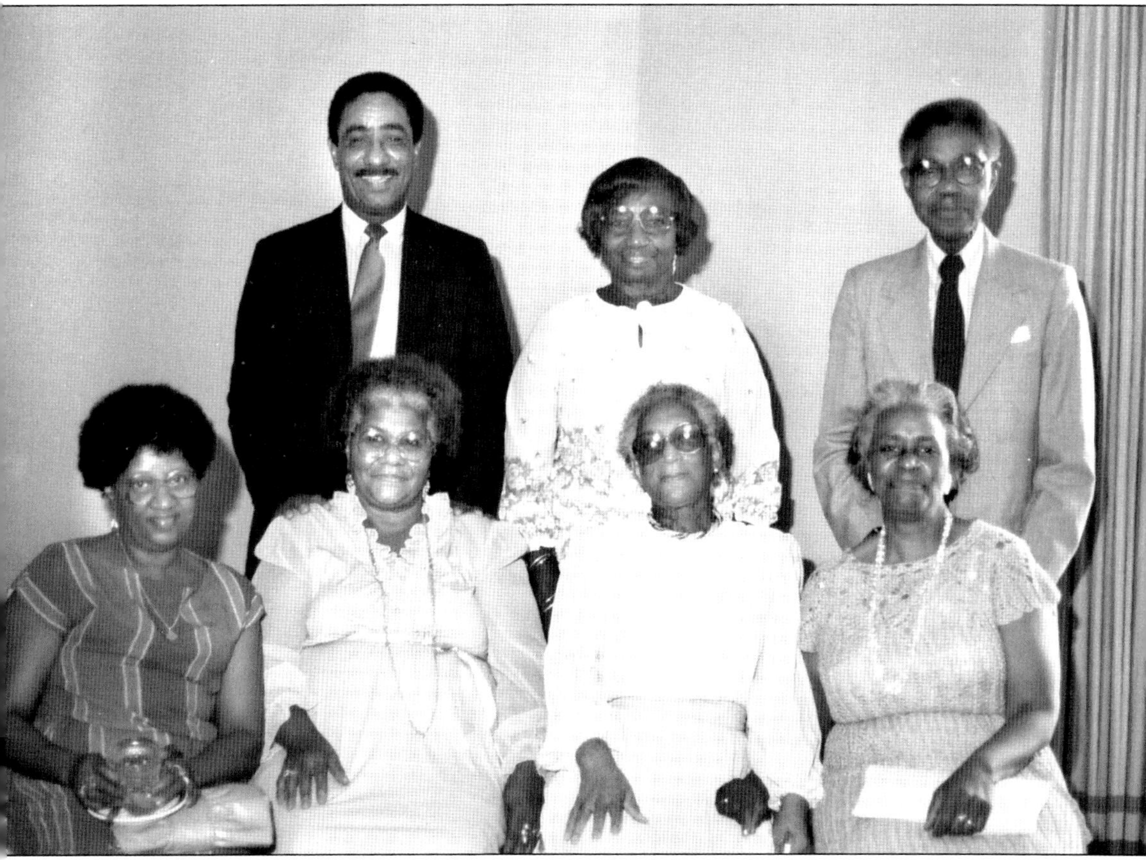

The Reverend A. R. Blake (top left) and Louis Gilliard (top right) were among the guests at the 75th birthday party in the 1980s for Sarah Dowling, longtime administrator at the Jenkins Orphanage. (Wendell Johnson.)

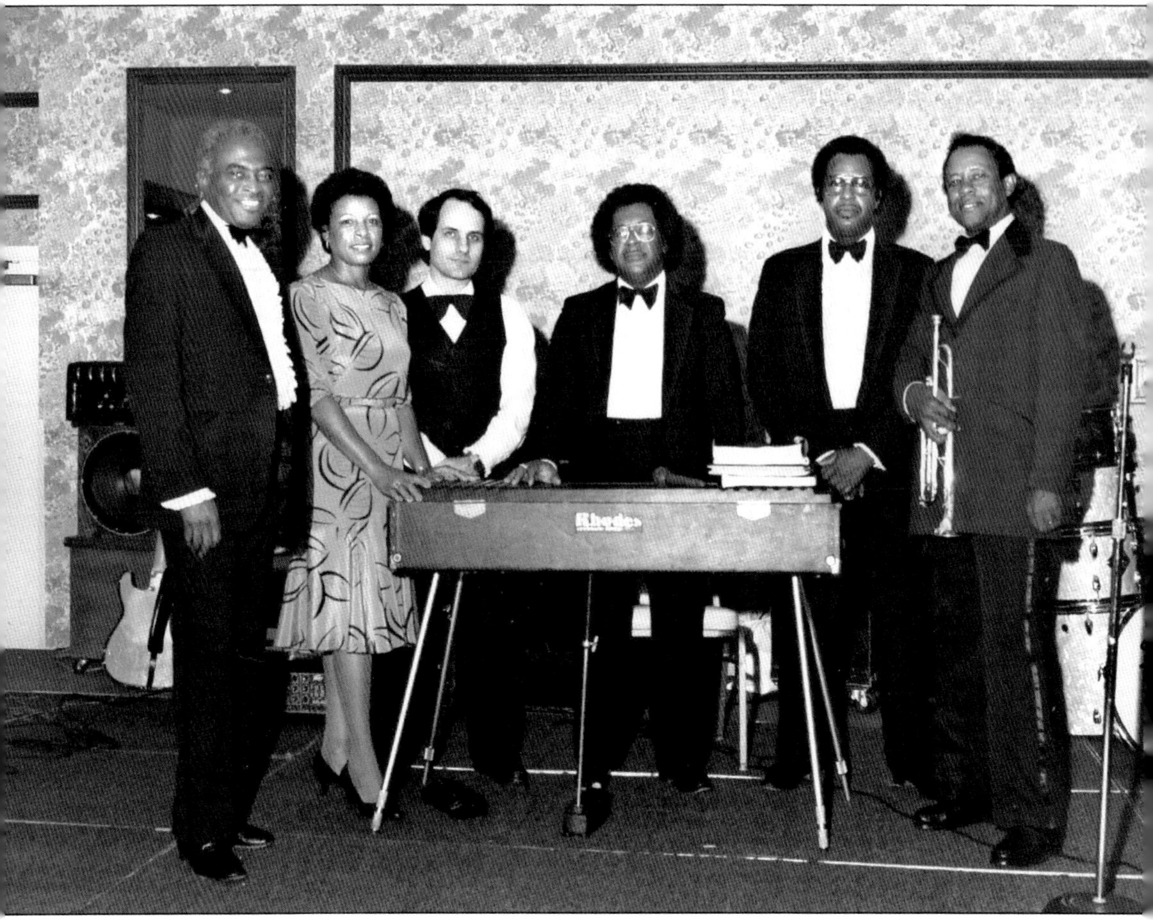

Lonnie Hamilton (left) and the Diplomats played around Charleston for decades. The band became the signature Charleston jazz band for a time, working nightclubs, receptions, restaurants, and all kinds of venues. (Lonnie Hamilton.)

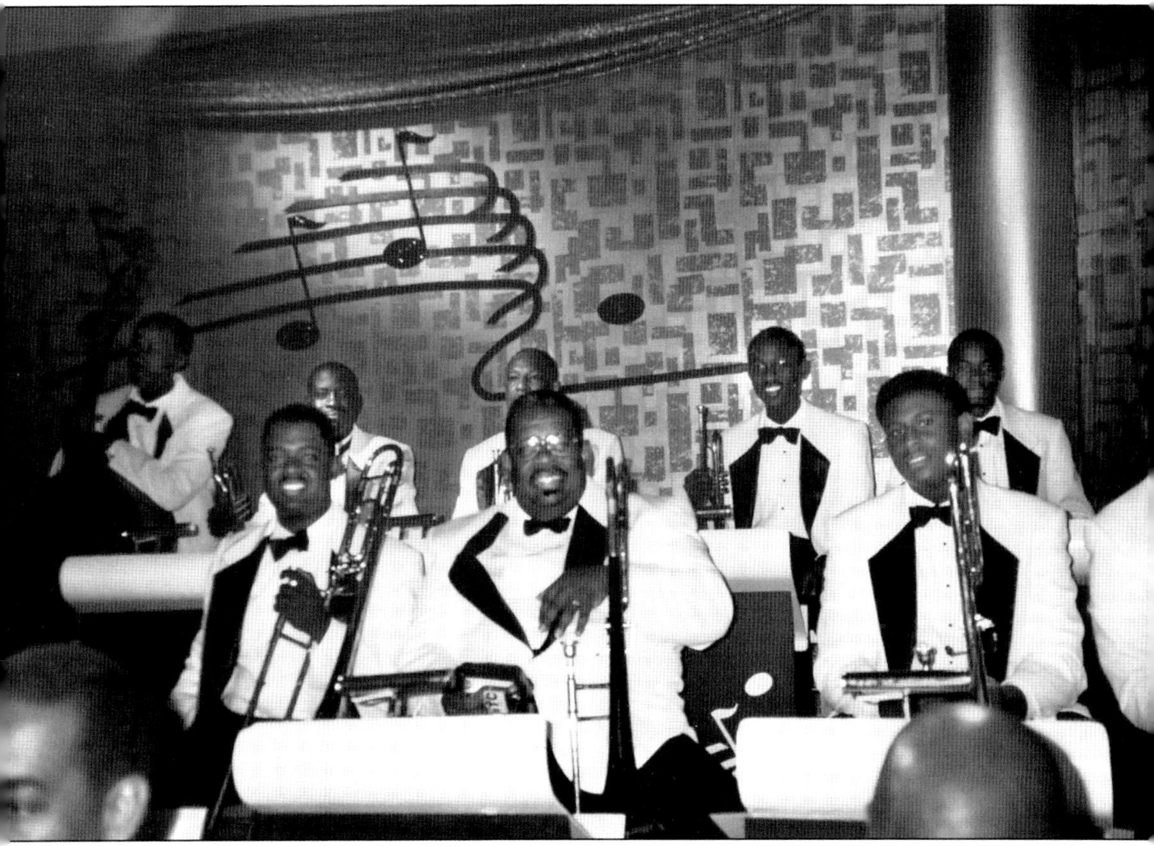

T. J. Robinson (front right) was a cast jazz band member in *The Notebook*, a 2004 feature movie shot in Charleston. Fred Wesley (front center), of Fred Wesley and the JB's fame, was also in the movie. Wesley lives in Manning, South Carolina, and often plays in Charleston. He said he loves to play here because the musicians in Charleston challenge him with their abilities and their approach to music. Wesley grew up in Mobile, Alabama, loving jazz and learning from his father before joining Brown on the road to play rhythm and blues. (George Kenny.)

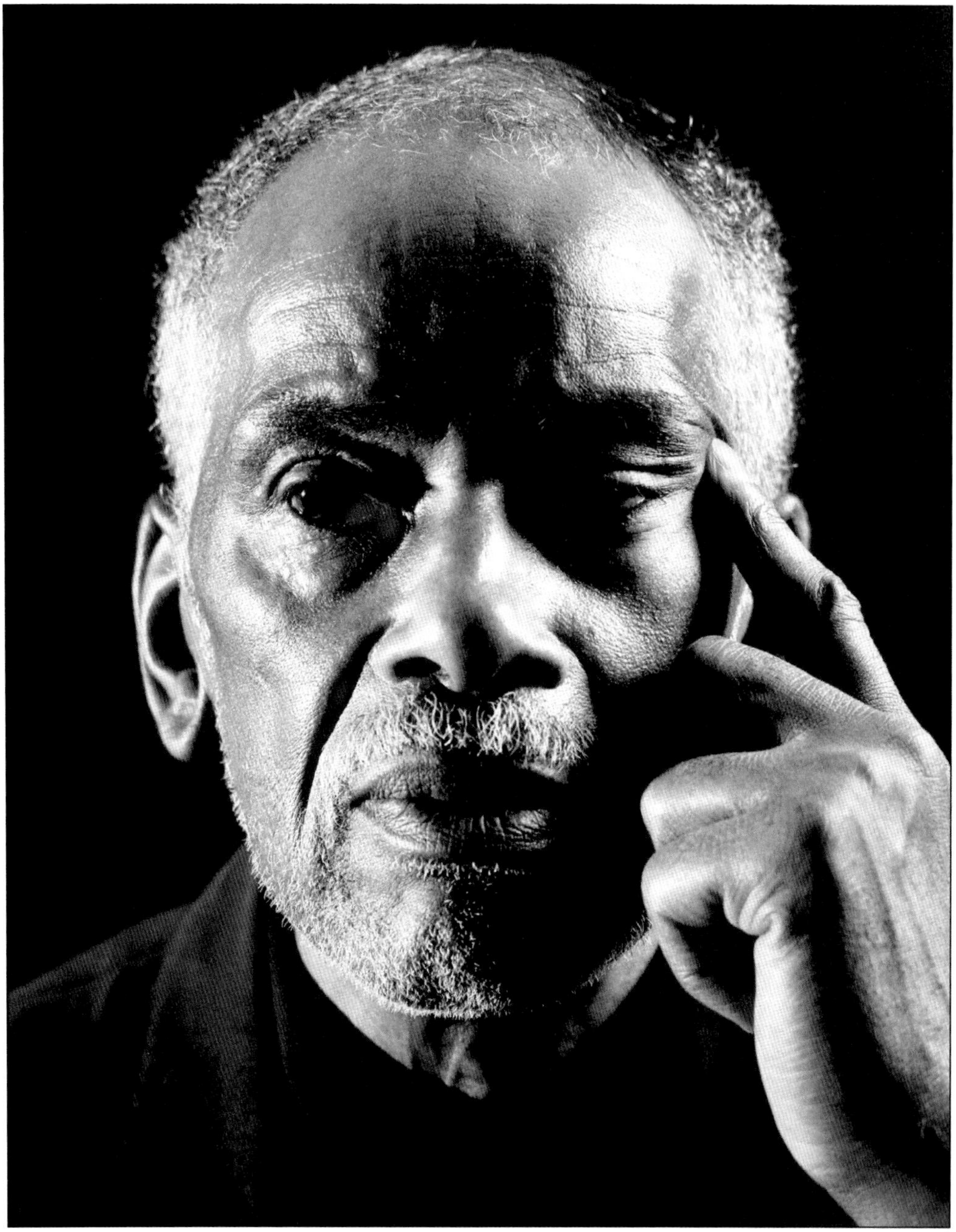

Emmanuel Abdul Rahim is a Charleston percussionist, educator, and composer who returned from Copenhagen, Denmark, in 2005. He was very instrumental in furthering the introduction of the Latin sound to American jazz in 1960. Abdul Rahim worked with many jazz greats, including Duke Ellington and John Coltrane. True to the Charleston jazz education tradition, he has taught at universities and conservatories all over Europe. (Charleston Jazz Initiative.)

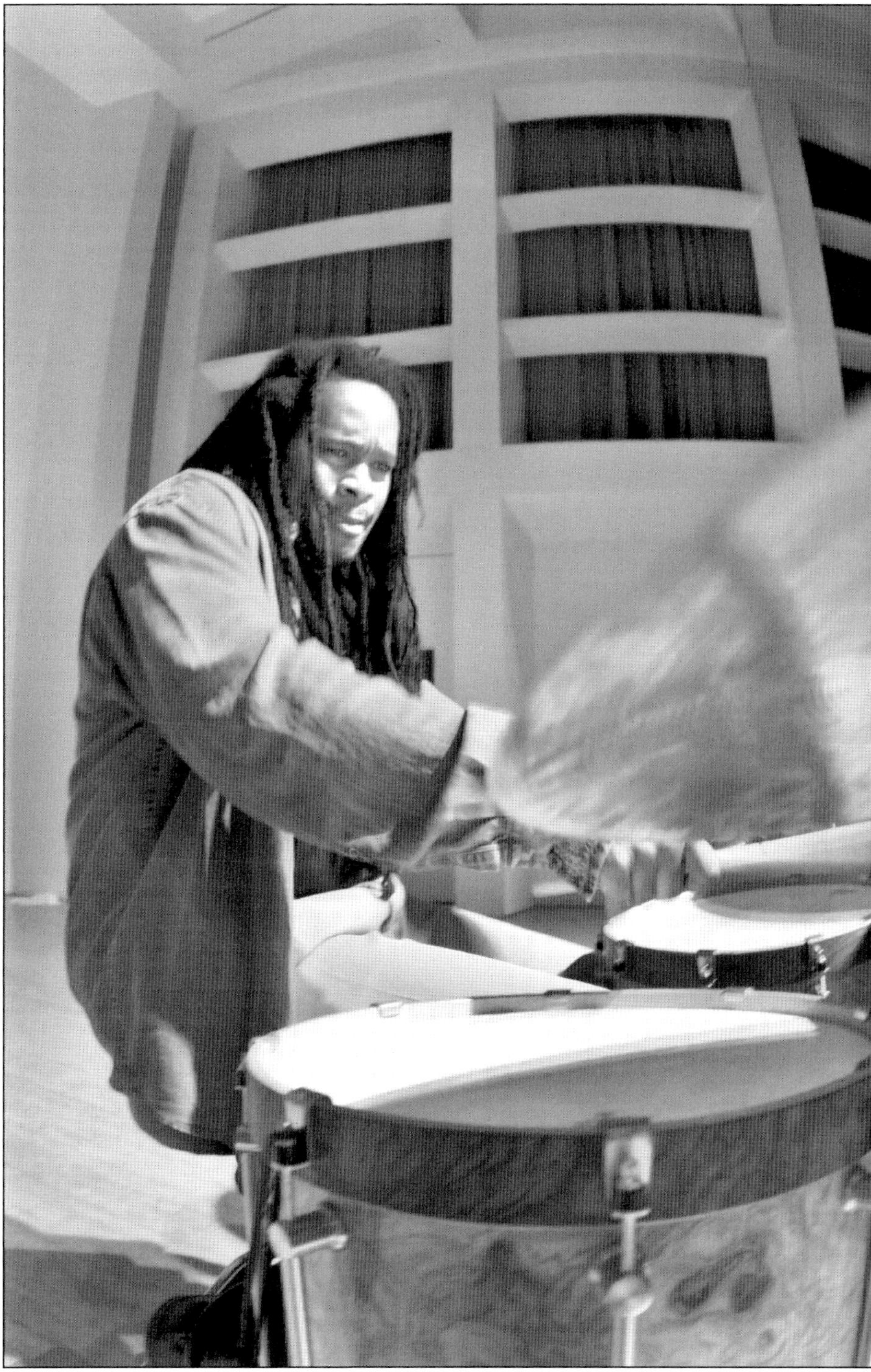

Quentin Baxter, percussionist, composer, and educator, is a highly acclaimed drummer who tours the world. He has formed many bands around Charleston, teaches at the College of Charleston, and is first-call drummer for many top-notch performers. He has played on the continents of North America, Europe, South America, Africa, and Asia, as well as in the Caribbean. (Tony Bell.)

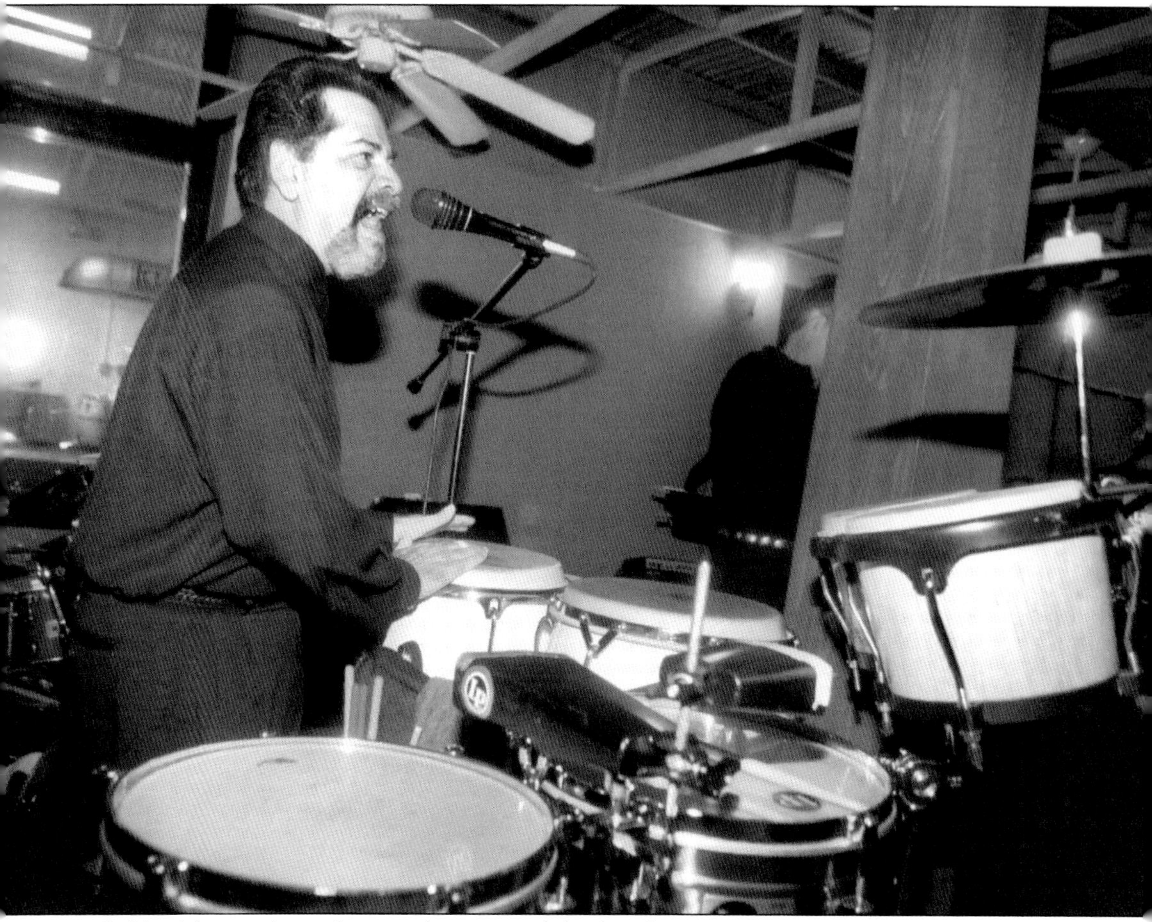

Bobby Alvarez, shown here performing with his band Para Ti, is a big contributor the Latin jazz scene in Charleston. Like New Orleans, the Latin tinge is important to the Charleston sound, given its historical ties to the Caribbean. Charlestonians also love to dance, and Latin music lends itself to that. Along with others, Alvarez has been on the cusp of the popularity of this music in Charleston, working the restaurants, nightclubs, and dance clubs. (*Post and Courier.*)

EPILOGUE

Charleston has a pretty swinging jazz scene in the 21st century. The history of jazz here is a long and storied one, having ups and downs but swinging all the way. It has and continues to produce great players who draw on a very important tradition that dates back to the 19th century. The people out of here are complete musicians. They not only swing; they are technically proficient as a result of excellent education and nurturing by teachers and mentors who love the music and want to see their students reach their full potential.

All along the way, Charleston players have made significant contributions to American swing, from the minstrelsy of Jim Crow days to the avant-garde in the 21st century. It seems not as many native Charlestonians are coming out of here as once before, but the influences of the area and its legacy are still strong, putting out great music and showmanship, also an aspect of Lowcountry performance.

Research has entered into the mix.

In 2003, the author cofounded the Charleston Jazz Initiative, a multi-year project exploring the history of jazz in Charleston, with Dr. Karen A. Chandler, professor of arts management at the College of Charleston. It is slowly but steadily growing, with support from the grassroots of Charleston to international jazz personalities, including critics, authors, and historians.

Along with the music, Charleston Jazz Initiative (www.charlestonjazz.net) and now Arcadia Publishing are putting out to the world the sound of Charleston.

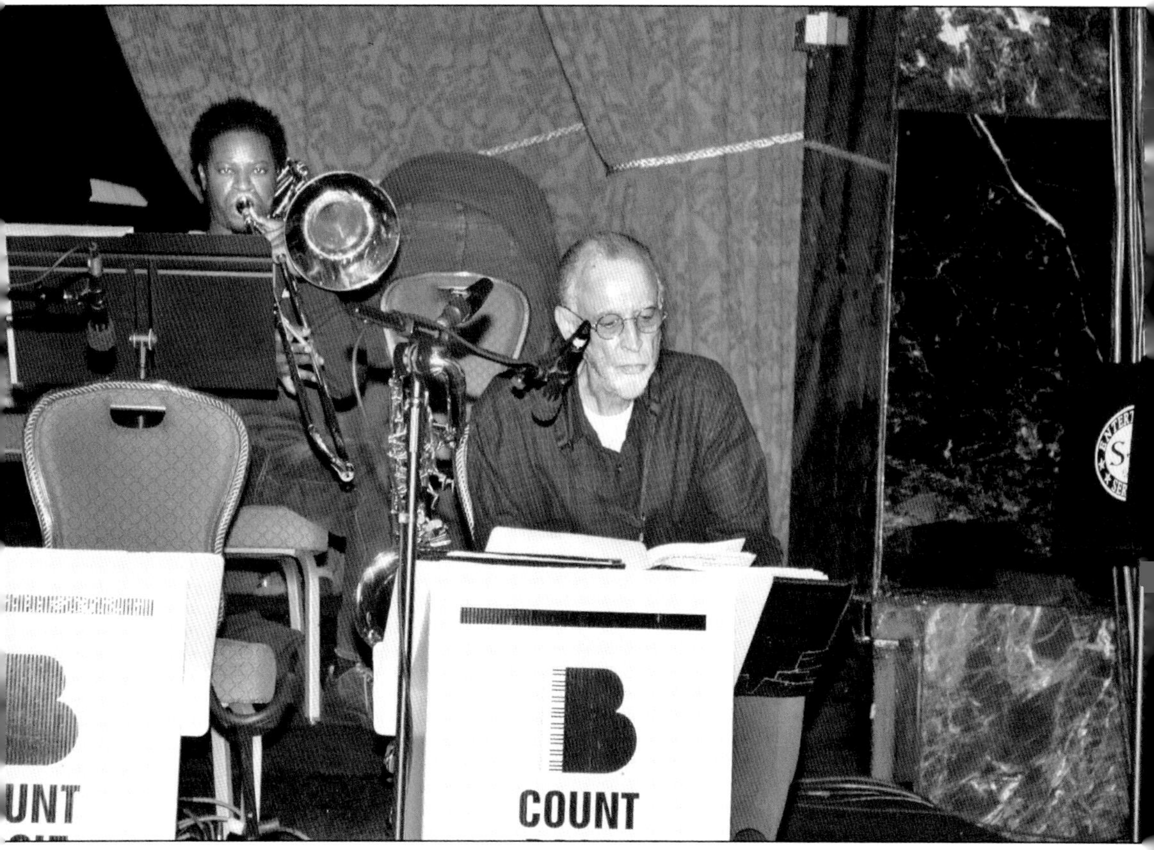

Baritone saxophonist John Williams plays at a sound check for the Count Basie Orchestra in January 2006 at the International Association for Jazz Education conference in New York City. Williams, one of only a handful of remaining band members hired by Basie himself, is a big advocate of Charleston jazz musicians with whom he has played over the years. Williams attended South Carolina State College in the 1950s with George Kenny, Bob Ephiram, Lonnie Hamilton, Aaron Harvey, and other Charleston jazz musicians. Williams has said some of the best musicians he has heard came out of Charleston. (Tony Bell.)

Vocalist LaToya Smith is a student of the Charleston jazz tradition who graduated from the Charleston County School of the Arts in 2006. She has performed with the Franklin Street Five and other Charleston jazz bands. (Tony Bell.)

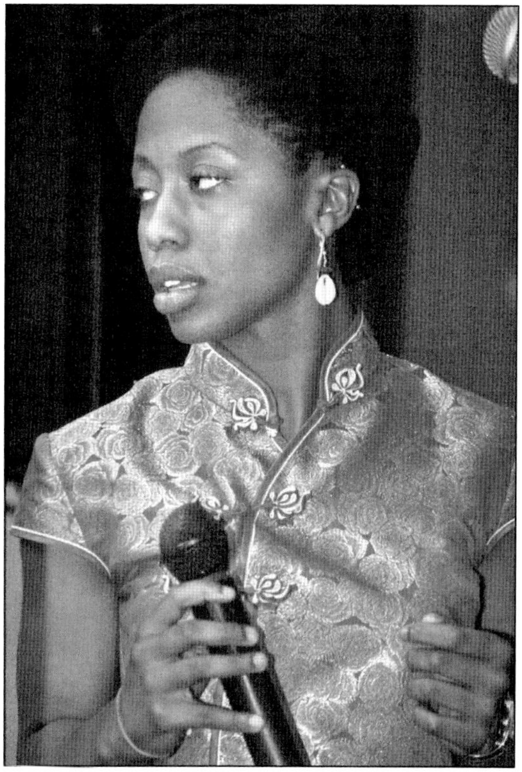

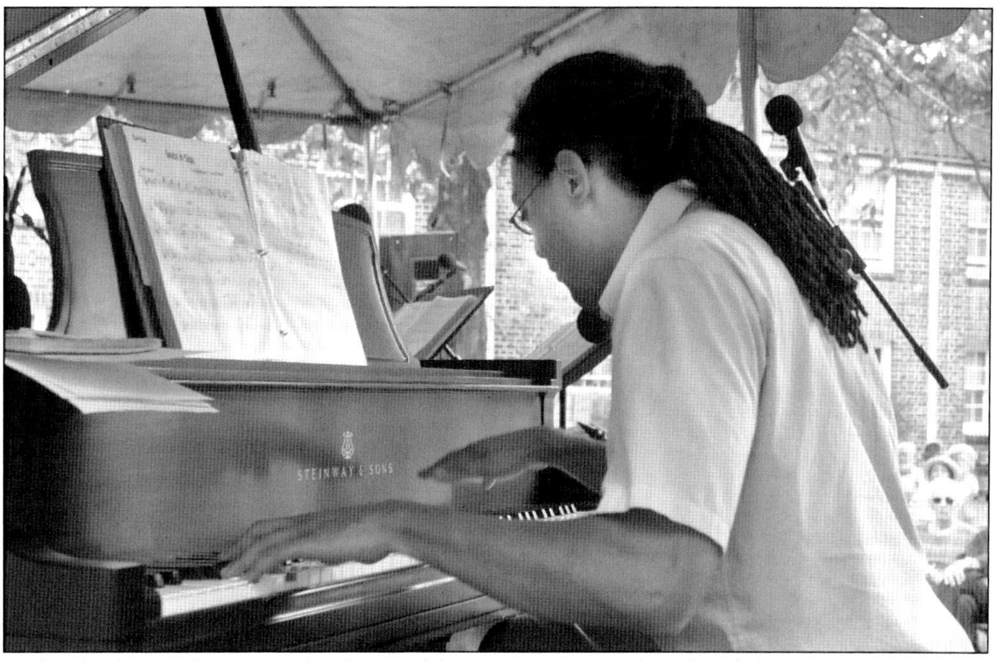

Richard White is the pianist for the Franklin Street Five, a tribute band that pays homage to the Jenkins Orphanage Band tradition. The band debuted at the Jazz Picnic at Robert Mills Manor in June 2005. White found himself in Charleston after growing up in St. Louis. He is very versatile and is especially known for his skills at accompanying singers. (Charleston Jazz Initiative.)

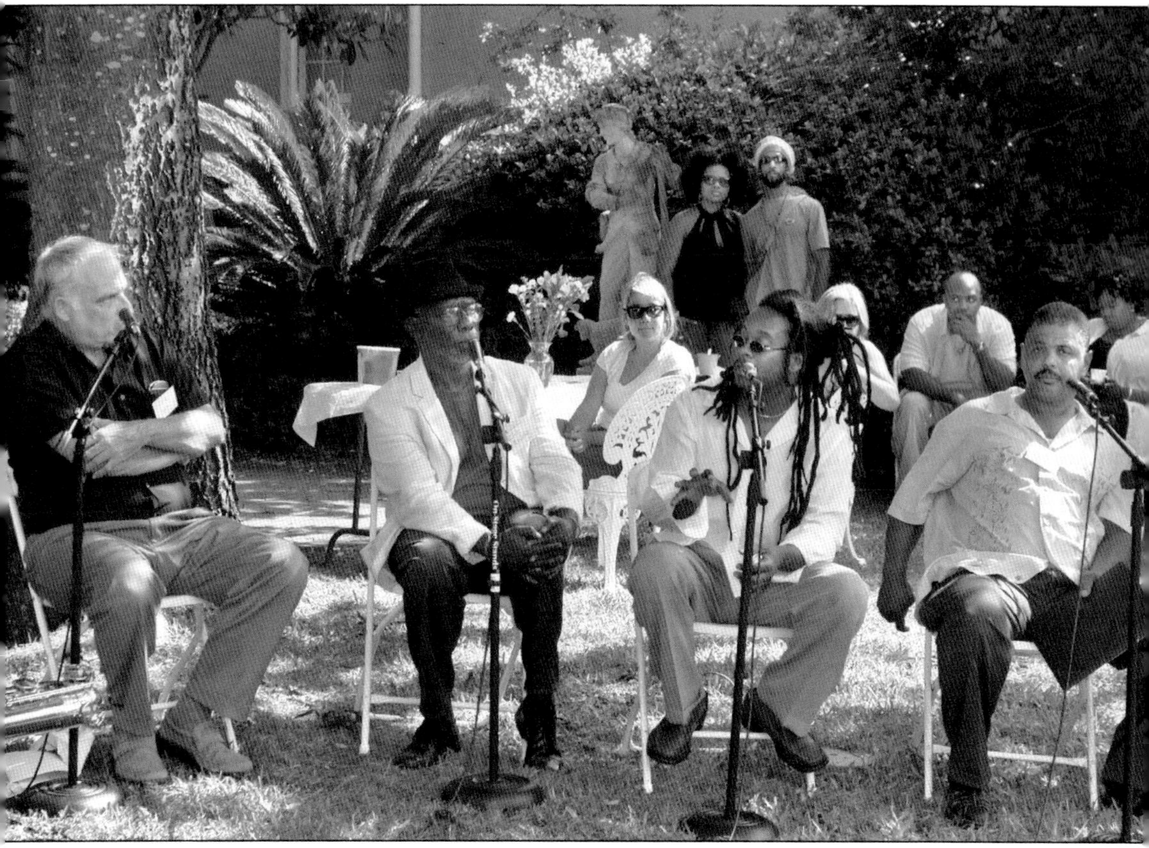

From left to right, Jeffrey Green, Jack McCray, Quentin Baxter, and Jonathan Bloom were on a panel at the Charleston Jazz Initiative's 2006 conference at the College of Charleston's Blacklock House. The theme was Sister City Jazz, a collaboration of Charleston and New Orleans jazz history and legacy. The event drew locals and tourists in town for the Piccolo Spoleto Festival. Charleston has a lot in common with New Orleans culturally, especially in music and cuisine. (Charleston Jazz Initiative.)

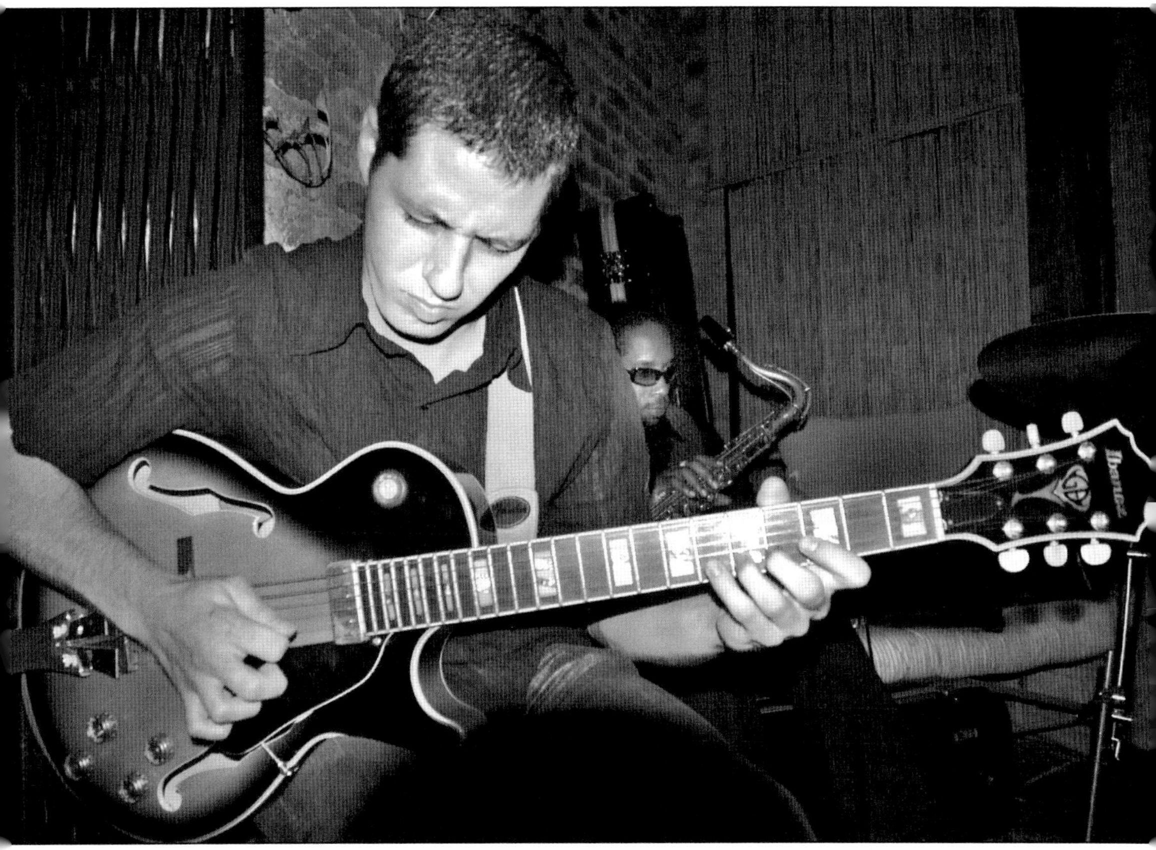

Charlestonian Lee Barbour performed at the jam session at Coast Bar and Grill during the Charleston Jazz Initiative's 2005 conference. Nationally renowned guitarist Joe Beck has said he thought Barbour is the best young jazz guitarist in the country. (Charleston Jazz Initiative.)

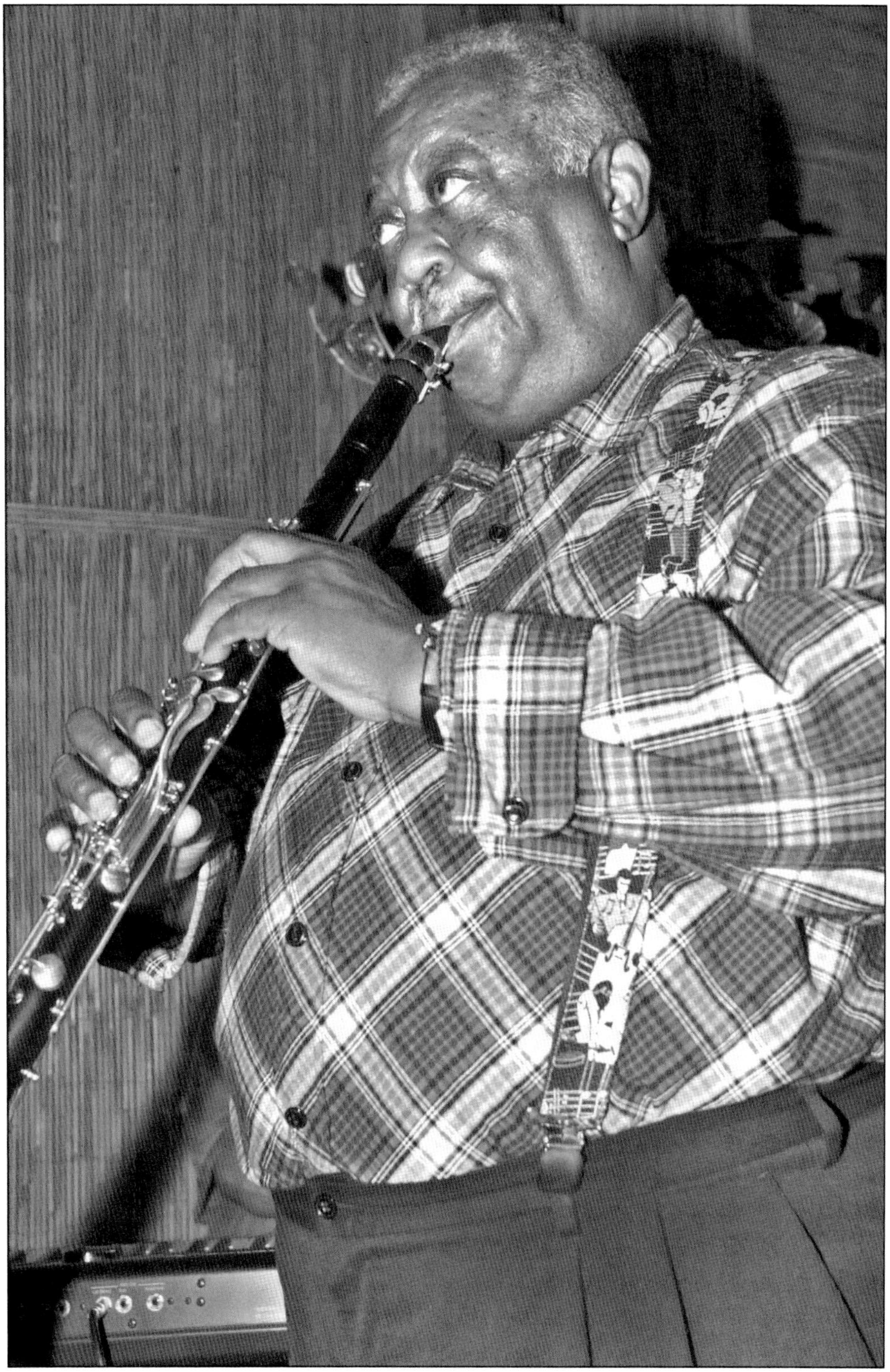

New Orleans performer, composer, and educator Alvin Batiste, National Endowment for the Arts jazz master and advisor to the Charleston Jazz Initiative, sat in at a jam session at Coast Bar and Grill in 2005. Batiste said it is time for Charleston and New Orleans to get together to explore what they have in common and how the both of them can best retain the cultures that have contributed so mightily to American culture. (Charleston Jazz Initiative.)

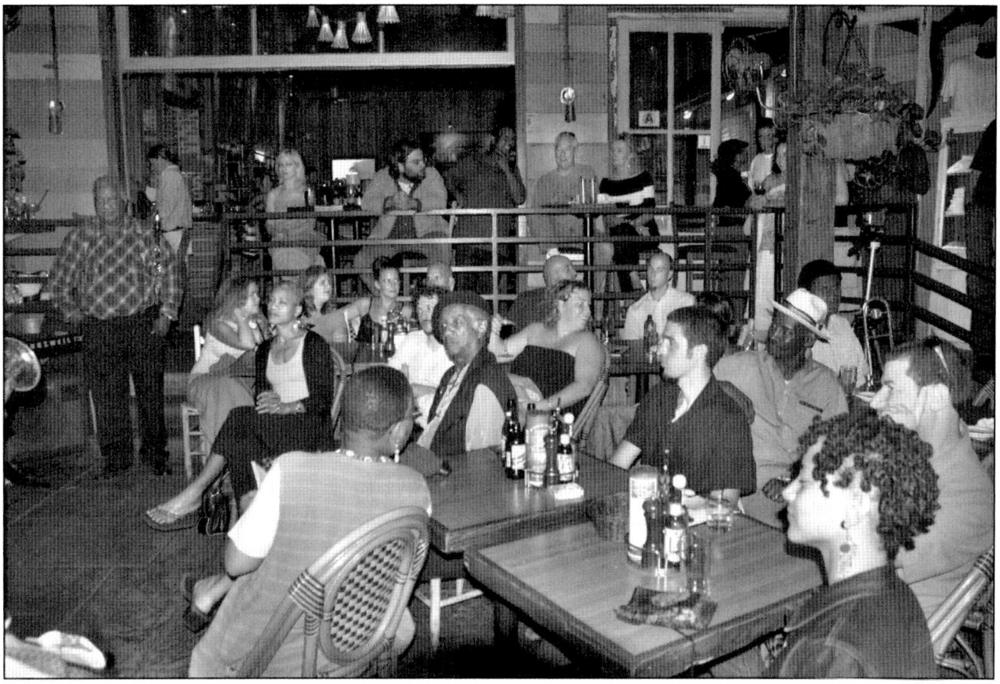

The crowd checks out a jam session at Coast Bar and Grill in 2005. (Charleston Jazz Initiative.)

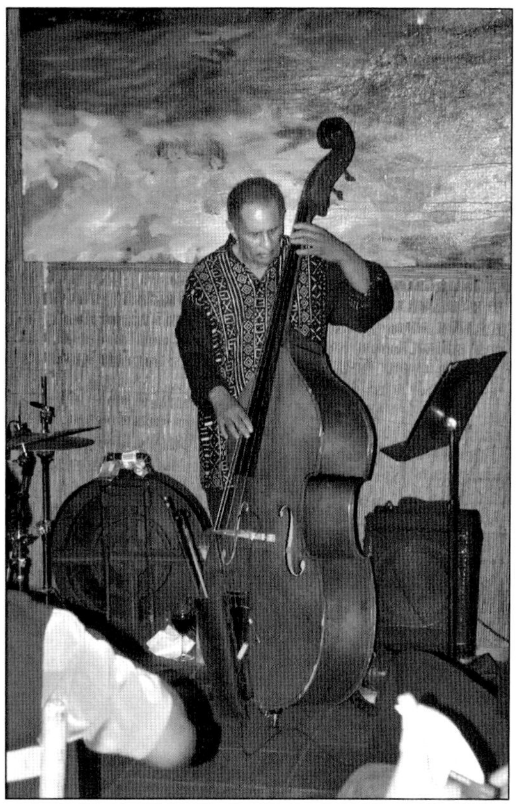

National jazz bassist, educator, and administrator Larry Ridley sits in at Charleston's Coast Bar and Grill in June 2005 at a jam session during the Charleston Jazz Initiative conference. (Charleston Jazz Initiative.)

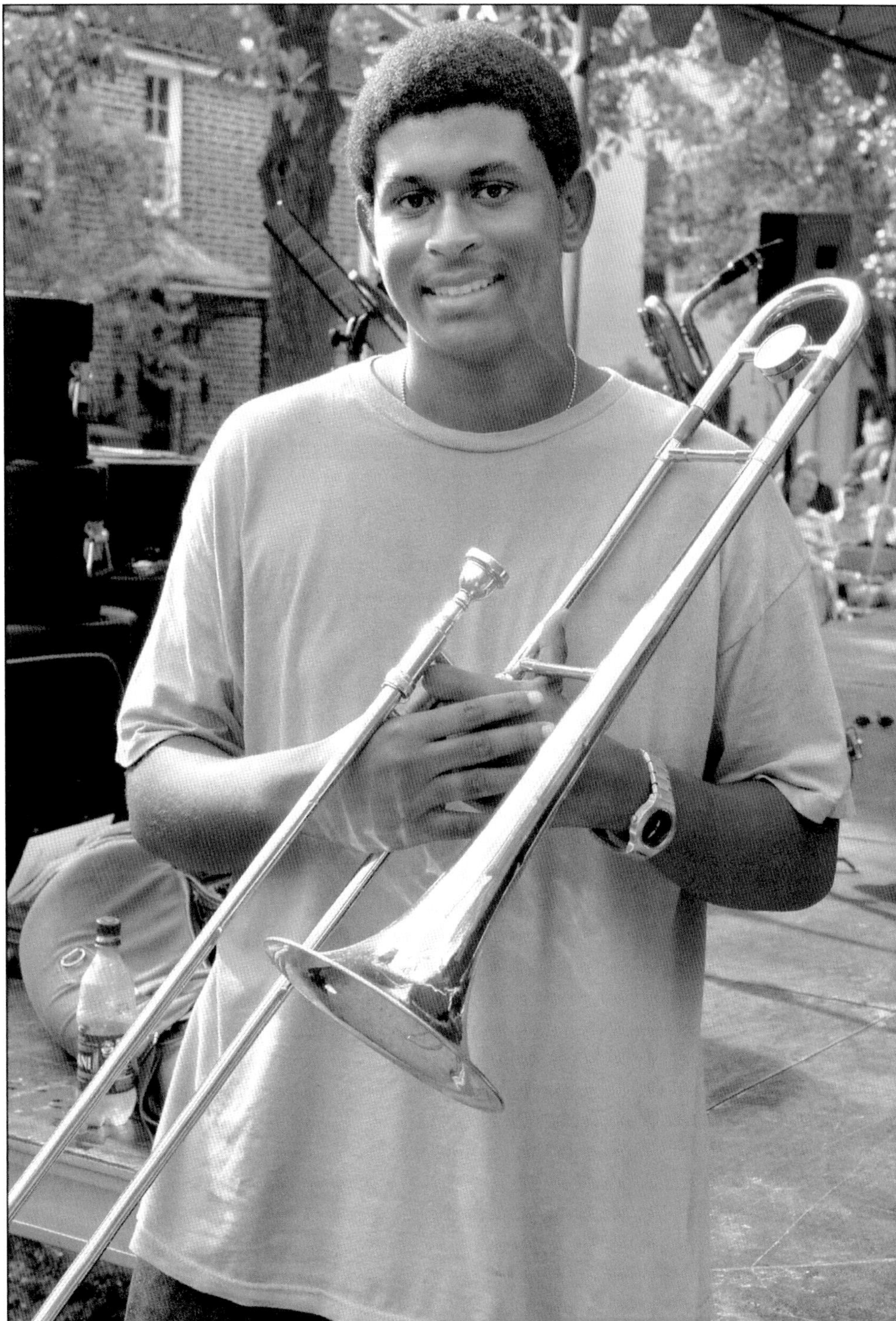

T. J. Robinson sits in with the Franklin Street Five at the Jazz Picnic sponsored by the Jake McGuire Savage Foundation, the City of Charleston Housing Authority, the Charleston Jazz Initiative, and Piccolo Spoleto Festival in June 2005. (Charleston Jazz Initiative.)

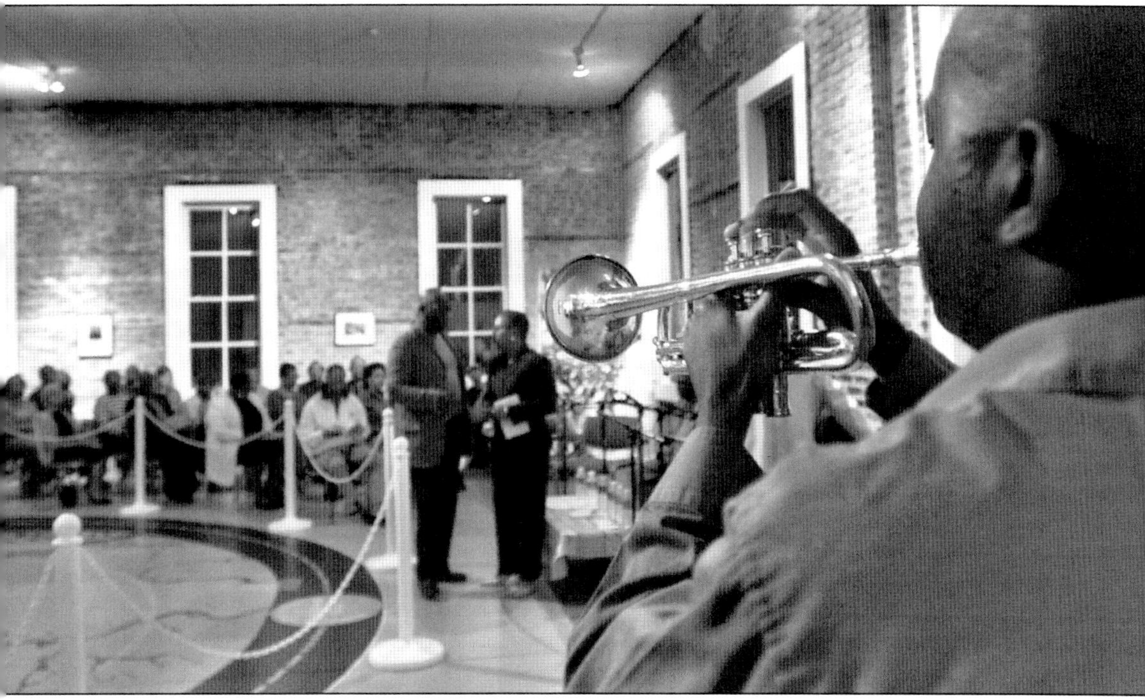

Charlton Singleton performed at the first official public event of the Charleston Jazz Initiative in 2003 at the Avery Research Center for African American History and Culture. The program brought together Charleston musicians who over the years had been associated with the music program at the Jenkins Orphanage. Singleton is a vibrant member of today's Charleston jazz tradition. He is also an extension of the South Carolina State College tradition, where he also went to school. He is an educator as well, giving private lessons and teaching in Charleston public schools. (Charleston Jazz Initiative.)

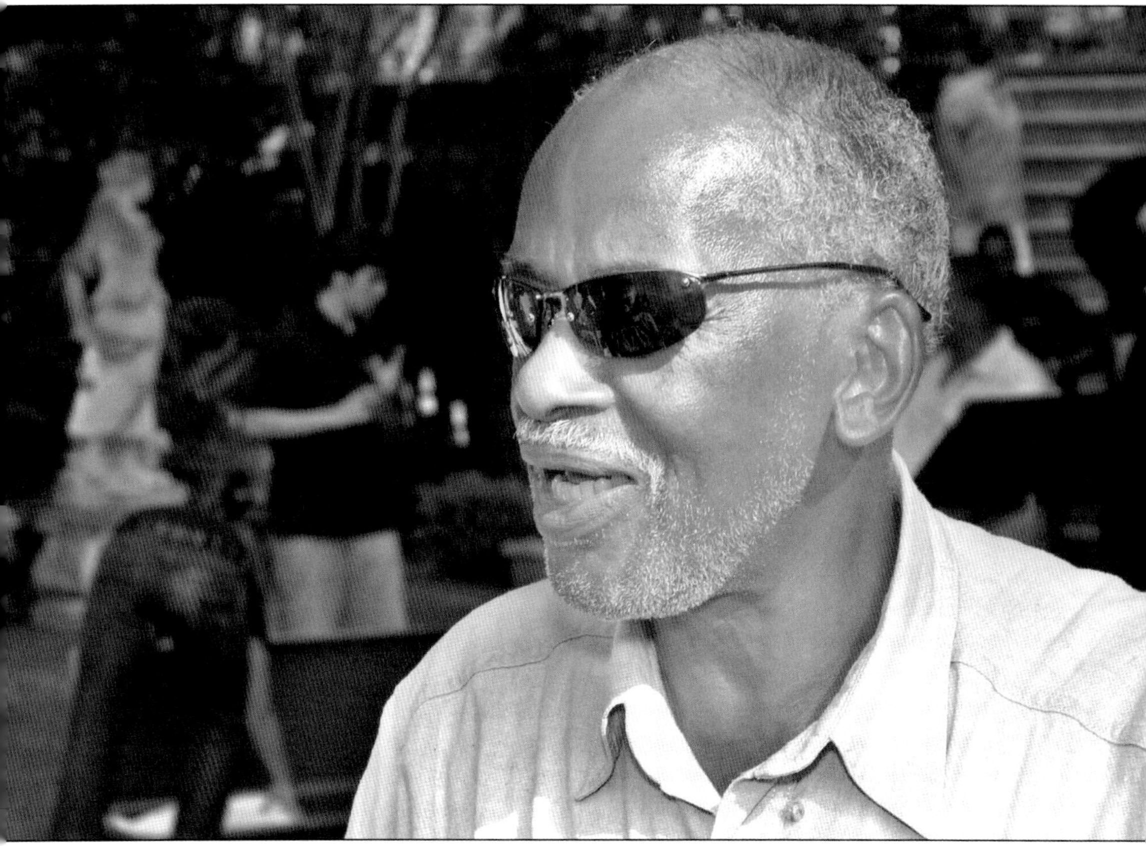

Emmanuel Abdul Rahim was a prominent figure at the annual conference of the Charleston Jazz Initiative at the College of Charleston's Blacklock House in May 2006. He said he has plans to build a recording studio here for musicians from around the world. (Charleston Jazz Initiative.)

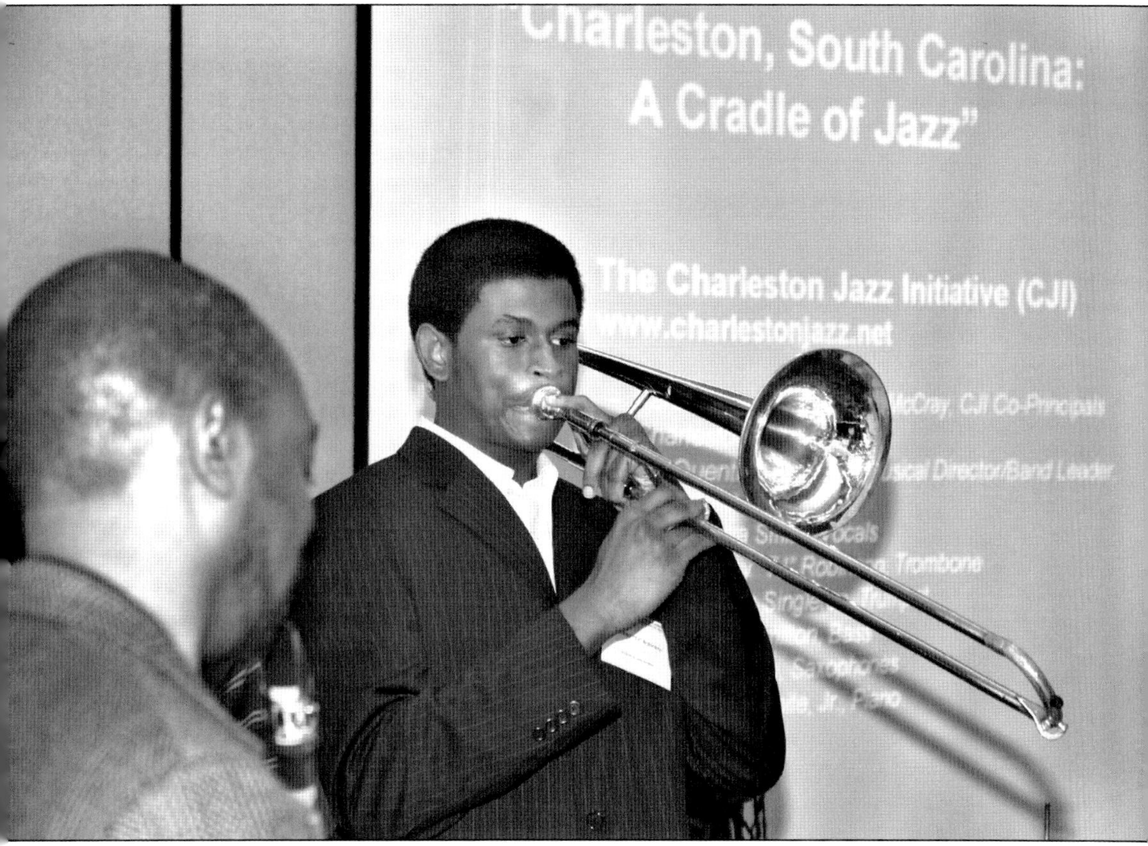

T. J. Robinson, a graduate of the Charleston County School of the Arts, plays with the Franklin Street Five from Charleston at the annual conference of the International Association for Jazz Education in New York City in January 2006. (Charleston Jazz Initiative.)

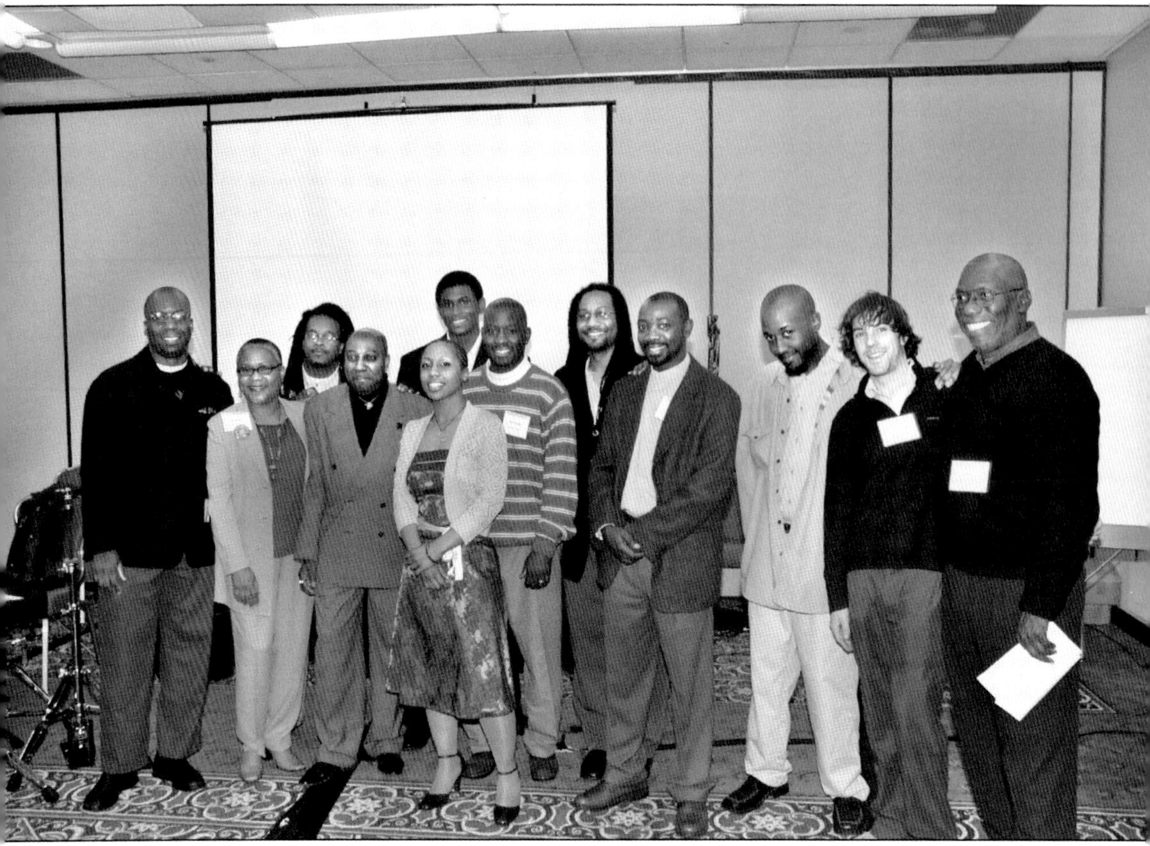

The Charleston Jazz Initiative contingent at the International Association for Jazz Education in New York City in January 2006 takes time for a photograph after a very successful performance workshop at the meeting that attracts 8,000 people from around the world. (Charleston Jazz Initiative.)

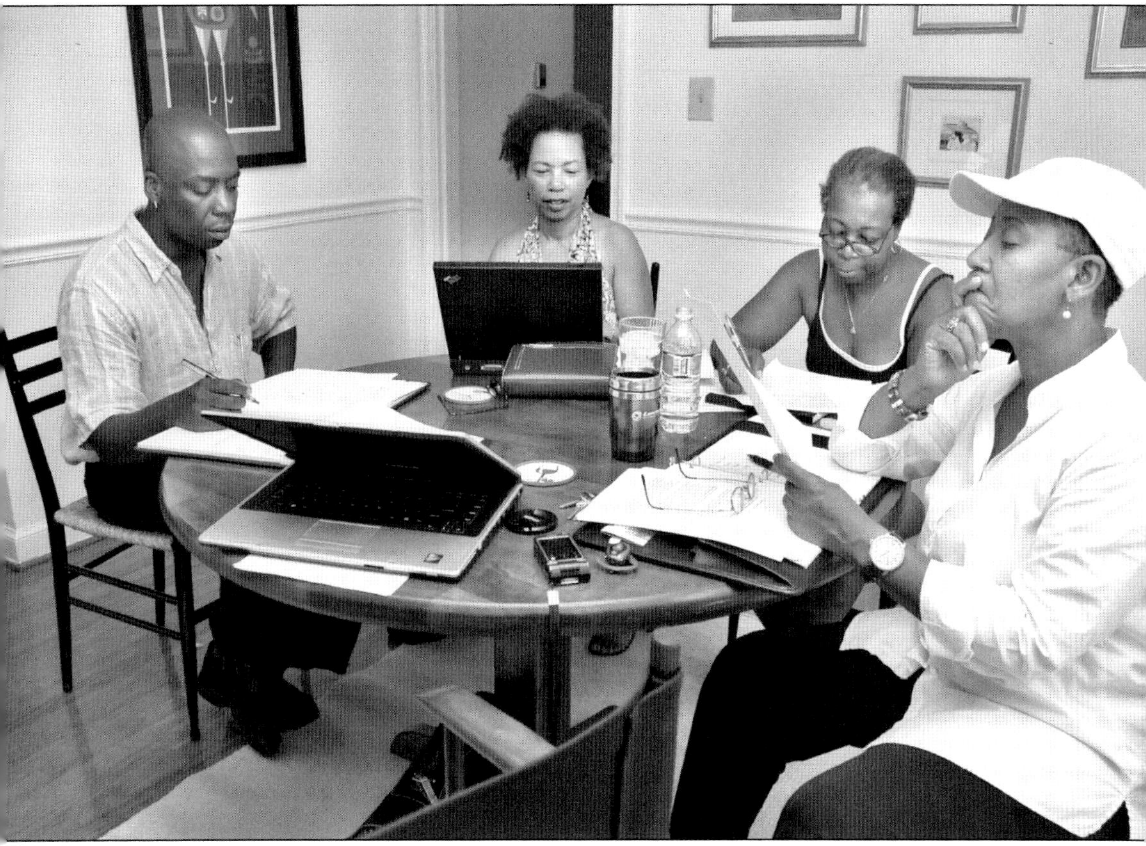

From left to right, Tony Bell, Dena Davis, Barbara Blackwell, and Ann Caldwell were among the founding board members of the Charleston Jazz Society in 2006. This group is dedicated to the performance of jazz music in Charleston, putting onto the stage local, regional, and national acts. (*Post and Courier.*)

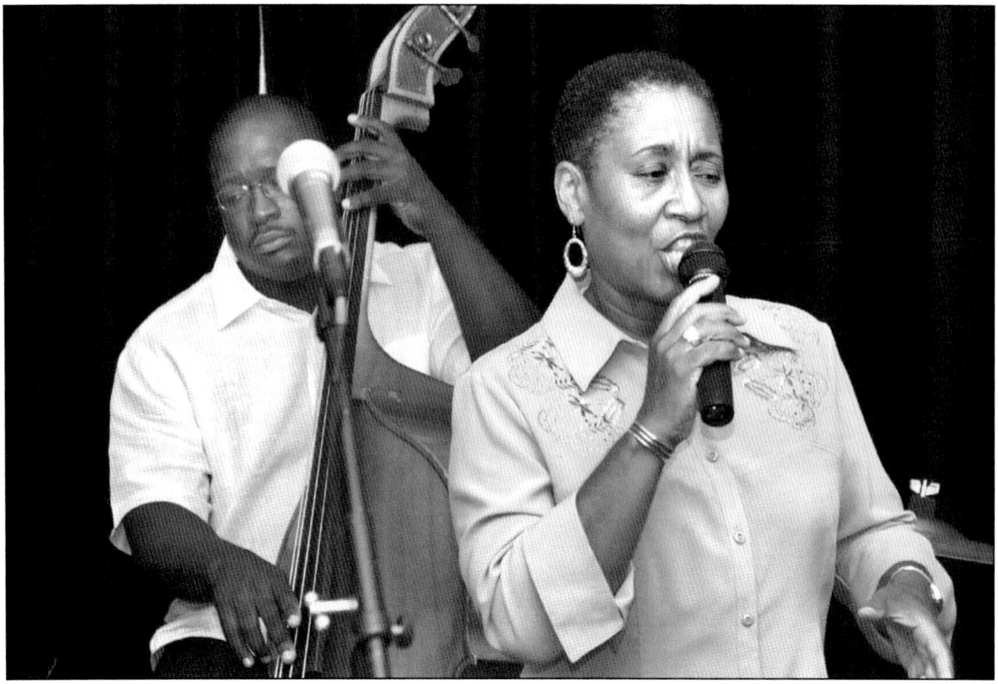

Ann Caldwell and her band, Loose Fit, opened the monthly series sponsored by the Charleston Jazz Society in July 2006 at the Renaissance Charleston Hotel. The society has found its legs and is going strong. (Tony Bell.)

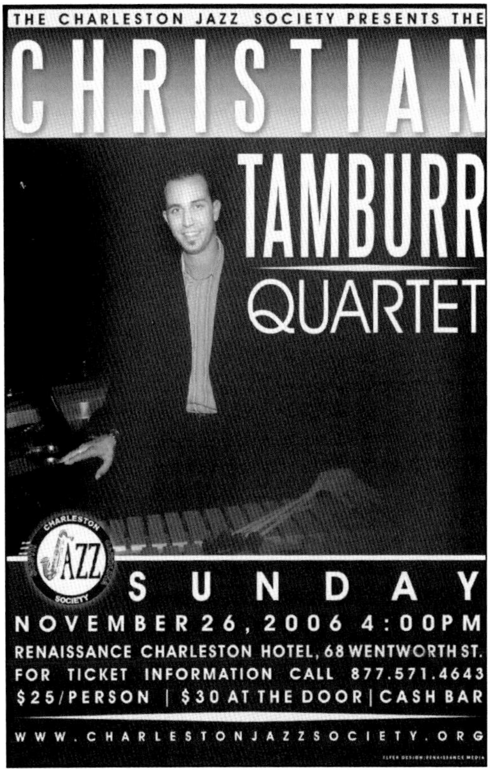

The Christian Tamburr Quartet was the November 2006 event for the Charleston Jazz Society's series. Tamburr hails from North Florida and performs in Charleston a couple of times a year. (Tony Bell.)

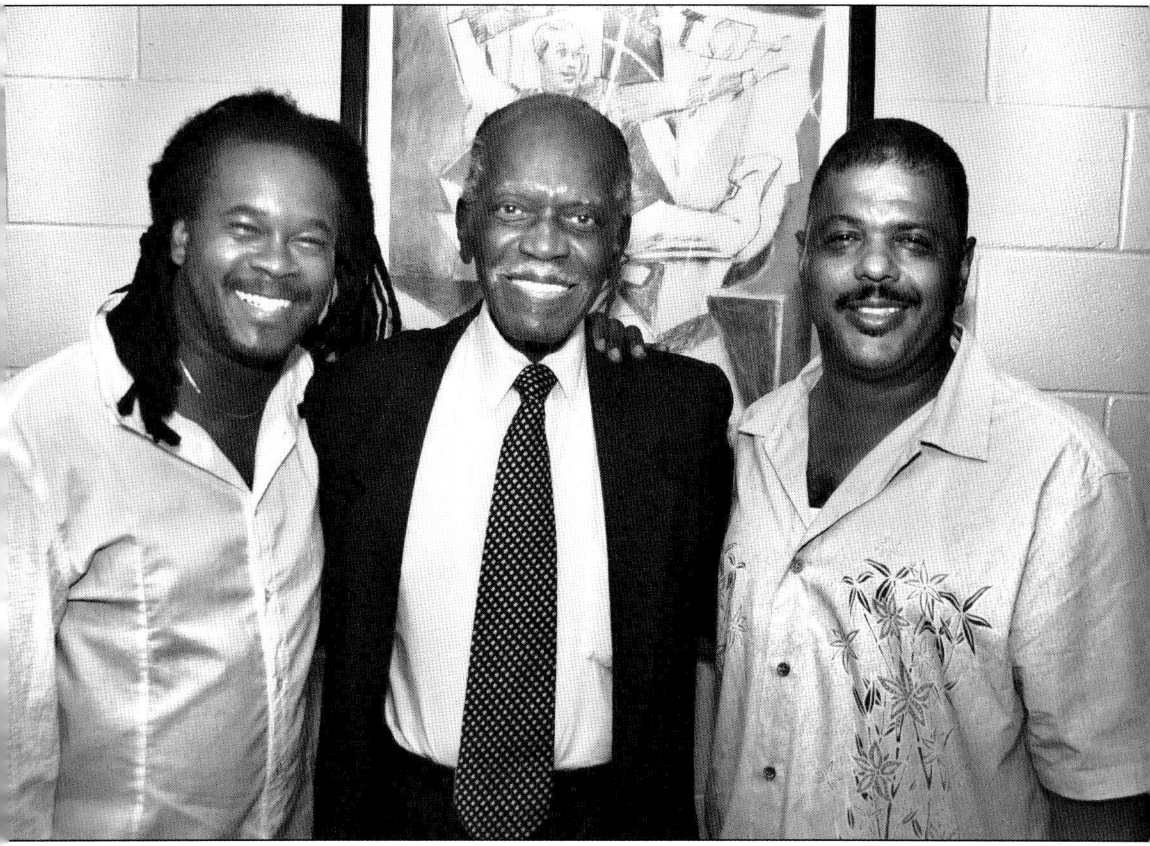

From left to right, Quentin Baxter, Hank Jones, and Jonathan Bloom pause for a photograph after Jones's trio perform at the Spoleto Festival USA in Charleston. Jones is considered by many the greatest living jazz pianist. His longtime wife is a native of Lincolnville, in the Charleston area. (Charleston Jazz Initiative.)